Ten Software Patterns Every Student Should Know

Michael Kilian

Ten Software Patterns Every Student Should Know

Michael Kilian
Harvard, MA, USA

ISBN 978-981-92-0259-1 ISBN 978-981-92-0260-7 (eBook)
https://doi.org/10.1007/978-981-92-0260-7

This Springer imprint is published by the registered company Springer Nature Singapore Pte Ltd.
The registered company address is: 152 Beach Road, #21-01/04 Gateway East, Singapore 189721, Singapore

Foreword

While working at Ab Initio (a company that builds very high-performance software primarily for commercial data processing), I had the good fortune to interview rising seniors for summer internships and new graduates, usually with a bachelor's degree in computer science, for full-time positions. These were invariably very bright students. Some had significant real-world experience in jobs from programming hearing aids to predicting dairy herd production. Yet despite attending some of the best schools in the United States, I often found gaps in their understanding of basic algorithms and programming concepts.

I decided to make a list of algorithms and programming techniques (collectively called *software patterns* in this book) that I felt every student should know about at least cursorily.

There are lots of reasons for a student to be unfamiliar with some of the basic software patterns discussed in this book. Computer Science (which encompasses software engineering) is a very broad field. It includes concepts such as web programming, artificial intelligence techniques (like neural networks), programming graphics cards, highly distributed systems, database systems, and computational complexity. Quantum computing is an emerging topic. The list goes on and on. A certain degree of specialization is required for a student to complete a degree in four years.

Nevertheless, there are algorithms and programming models that are at the root of an awful lot of software. There are also approaches to problems that are elegant but not necessarily obvious (finding palindromes using polynomial arithmetic is one example). Just as every English major should be familiar with a variety of literary forms, a computer focused major (such as software engineering or theoretical computer science) should be acquainted with a suite of fundamental software patterns.

This book is not comprehensive by any means. There are many more algorithms than can be covered in any single book. Even Donald Knuth's amazing volumes on algorithms can't cover everything. Some algorithms are specialized, designed for more esoteric purposes. There are also more clever and more powerful algorithms for some of the tasks presented that are not included in this book, mostly because they exceed the scope of what an undergraduate student can understand in a compressed amount of time. I've chosen a set of algorithms and program designs that I have personally encountered multiple times in a nearly 40-year career as a software engineer that I think should be in any canon of algorithms.

The goal of each software pattern presentation is to be complete and clear enough that a student could implement the pattern. This book does not include an in-depth analysis of the algorithms presented. For example, the pattern on hash tables does not discuss how to evaluate the efficacy of a hash function. We will touch on the complexity of each algorithm (i.e., how fast the algorithm performs, how much space it will use up). More detailed complexity analyses are left to books focused on that topic. Occasionally more subtle performance implications will be explored, especially when one implementation approach may be more efficient than another in a non-intuitive way.

Like reading classic literary works, understanding classic algorithms, even if not used day-to-day, provides a foundation for a deeper understanding of how software is built and optimized. One of the goals of this book is that it could serve as the basis of a college semester class. Each Pattern represents about five hours of lecture with recommended exercises. The goal would be that a student would learn about a topic and program the previous week's topic's exercise concurrently. Some topics (such as concurrency control and socket programming) are broader topics that require more than one week to address. By the end of the course a student will have added some new tricks to her programming portfolio and perhaps a greater appreciation for the underpinnings of the more elaborate software such as databases and web application frameworks.

The patterns presented here assume that the student will have a non-trivial knowledge of fundamental data structures such as linked lists and queues. This book is not an introduction to data structures. We will present the software patterns using C. The choice of C is because it is relatively simple and low level enough that CPU specific aspects of an algorithm can be expressed. A basic familiarity with the C programming language and how to express elementary data structures (arrays, linked lists) in C is assumed.

As mentioned above, I've been a software engineer for a long time. I have encountered finite state machines and parsing (see Pattern 2) building an incremental compiler for the Trellis object-oriented language (Schaffert et al., 1986) at Digital Equipment Corporation. While completing my Ph.D. at Harvard (my thesis was *Parallel Sets: An Object-Oriented Methodology for Massively Parallel Programming*. (Kilian, 1992)) I had the good fortune to meet Michael Rabin and new ways of using algebra to solve non-numeric problems (see Pattern 4). I applied some of my thesis ideas at Kendall Square Research (CBR Staff Writer, 1993) where we built a parallel high-performance object-oriented database and computation model that was used for modeling passenger load for all the flights for a specific airline (see Pattern 7)

After Kendall Square Research I built an interpreter for C++ leveraging sophisticated finite state machines and a unique P-code structure used to execute the programs that also leveraged new memory management (Pattern 9). Following this, I helped develop the Centera platform at EMC (eG Innovations, 1993) which featured a new way of accessing content with cryptographically strong hashing (see Pattern 6). At a startup, I worked on a distributed web platform for content management (which became the basis of the Unified Delivery Network for Ericsson) (CIO Applications,2023) again leveraging some of the finite state machine technology described in Pattern 2, the hash tables from Pattern 1 and much of the lessons from Patterns 4 and 5. That was followed by building a large scale, high bandwidth, low latency distributed, highly available, in-memory object repository and compute platform at Ab Initio. Much of the discussions on extensible hash tables (Pattern 1) and message-based concurrency (Pattern 8) derive from my experiences at Ab Initio.

Most of the products that I've referenced have faded into the technological sunset. The underlying algorithms have not, and the lessons learned from building these systems retain their value. Over the course of nearly 40 years, computers have not changed fundamentally (with the exception of quantum computing). The greatest changes are in the proliferation of multicore processors, a more dramatic shift in-memory hierarchies, and a huge increase in speed and capacity. Until quantum computing becomes mainstream, the software patterns presented in this book should apply to computer architectures for many years to come.

Harvard, MA, USA Michael Kilian

Acknowledgments Many people have helped with this book, and I would like to call out a few. First is my wife Valerie who copy-edited the book. She has been responsible for straightening out much of my tortuous prose. I would also like to thank my brother Joe who went over the text with a fine-tooth comb and challenged some of the reasoning, especially in the cryptographic discussions. Jan van Riel, a colleague from my days at EMC and a truly forward-thinking engineer, pointed out numerous details that needed correction as well as substantial gaps in explanations. Finally, I would like to acknowledge the many coworkers I've had the pleasure of learning from over the past 40 years.

Competing Interests The author has no competing interests to declare that are relevant to the content of this manuscript.

Notation Used in the Book

Using C to Express Algorithms

The algorithms in this book will be presented in the C programming language (and if you need to brush up on C, then (Kernighan et al., 1988) will suffice). Why base it on C? The main reasons are:

1. It is a fairly simple model of computation. We will not consider object-oriented paradigms in this book though almost all of the algorithms can (and probably should) be implemented with some sort of object-oriented interface.
2. Many aspects of the algorithms are concerned with efficiency, especially with respect to common processor architectures (e.g., caching of memory in the CPU). The notation needs to be low level enough that it allows explicit notions of addressing memory and control of threads.
3. Most of the algorithms presented are relatively short that become components of more elaborate systems.

This is not a tutorial on how to program in the C language. The reader is expected to understand the basic structure of C including defining data structures, functions, variable types, and pointers.

The examples will use the types declared in the stdint and stdbool model for C representing integer and real numbers, boolean values, and non-specific values. There are four types of signed integers: int8_t, int16_t, int32_t, and int64_t, where the digits represent how many bits in the integer. In C, int is a synonym for int32_t though we will always use the version with the number of bits specified. There are also unsigned versions of these: uint8_t, uint16_t, uint32_t, and uint64_t. The type char is equivalent to int8. The type char is used primarily when we know we are manipulating (ASCII) characters. Note that in today's highly interconnected and international world, strings almost always should be represented in unicode, and frequently UTF8 which is quite similar to ASCII but not identical and can represent characters like 'é' and 'ñ'. Most of the algorithms we present are largely string representation neutral and features that are not will be called out.

Real numbers also have variants. A single precision real number is float and takes 4 bytes, and a double precision real number is double and requires 8 bytes.

The type void simply denotes no value is expected. It is primarily used in two cases: When a function doesn't return a value, and when we don't know what a pointer is referencing.

A basic understanding of variable scoping and function invocation is also assumed, in particular, the use of recursive functions will be used in some patterns.

A couple of points here. malloc returns a void *, i.e., an untyped block of memory of the size given by the parameter. A cast (for example (struct Point *)) indicates that the pointer should be treated as a pointer to a Point structure. In many of the algorithms below, we will assume a function exists that performs the allocation, initializes the structure and returns a pointer to the initialized memory. For example, we might assume a function to allocate a Cartesian point:

```
struct Point *make_Point(float x_coor, float y_coor)...
```

The details of make_Point will not be elaborated; it will be assumed to dynamically allocate a Point structure with the Point's x and y coordinates initialized to the values passed in as the parameters.

Complexity

This book will not provide an exhaustive discussion of computational complexity of the patterns presented. There are many references for that (for example (Sipser, 2023)). Instead, two broad categories of complexity of an algorithm will be touched on. The first is how fast an algorithm will run based on some measure such as the number of items in a set, or the numbers of nodes in a graph. The second category is how much space will be used by the algorithm. This does not include the actual data in the space complexity. If we are measuring the space complexity of sorting n items, we don't include n in the measure. Instead, the space the algorithm requires above and beyond the input is measured. Often space complexity is related to recursion depth of recursive algorithms (where the accumulated space is from the stack frames for each nested call).

The complexity of the algorithms will be presented in big-O notation, e.g., $O(n)$, $O(\log n)$. An algorithm that touches every item in a list once is $O(n)$ where n is the number of items in the list. Searching an ordered list using binary search is $O(\log n)$ and you may find innumerable discussions of this (see (Sipser, 2023) for just one example). Most of the algorithms here are straightforward in their complexity and we will often focus on tuning the algorithm to achieve the best implementation with a given big-O complexity.

For O(*log n*), the base of the logarithm is not terribly important when deriving the big-O analysis of an algorithm. That being said, using 2 as the base of the logarithm will typically be more "natural" to the algorithm. For example, when analyzing binary search we successively halve the search space. The number of halves is given by $\log_2 N$ where N is the number of items in the search space. Complexity analysis doesn't substantially differentiate between $\log_2 N$ and $\log_{10} N$.

Our analysis will usually be straightforward and well documented by many other sources. There will be situations where an O(n) algorithm will actually be better than an O(log n) algorithm. This can happen when n is small and on certain processor architectures (i.e., certain memory cache architectures). Discussions will follow when these cases apply.

Use of "We" in Algorithms

Occasionally the algorithm will be explained using "we do something." For example, "We scan the list for an item matching a key." The "we" in this case is the computer executing the algorithm. Sometimes it is simply easier to speak of the execution of an algorithm from the viewpoint of the processor executing the program. It may also provide a more intuitive feel to the algorithm if it is somewhat personalized.

Contents

Chapter 1
Hash Tables

One of the most common tasks in software is to look something up based on some piece of information. In everyday life, we consult a building directory to find the floor and office number for a given tenant's name. For those of us of a certain age, there were phone books that organized every resident in a city by name and associated with that name their phone number and address. In the online world, finding one thing from another is ubiquitous.

Most of these associations can be viewed as a table, with one column containing a string identifying the item (called the *key*), and one or more other columns containing the data associated with the key. The key may be anything that uniquely identifies the item: A Social Security number, a phone number, the name and address of a person, or any sequence of bytes that identifies the object (and only that object).

Here is an example where a Social Security number identifies a person[1]

Social Security number	Individual
123-45-6789	Leonardo da Vinci
888-12-9999	Leonardo DiCaprio

In this example, we want to efficiently find the individual with a given Social Security number (we'll call this *SSN*). The simplest approach is to start with the first row, compare *SSN* with the Social Security number in that row and if it matches, declare victory and return the Individual. If it does not match, advance to the next row and try again. If all the rows are visited without finding a matching Social Security number, declare failure and signal such (e.g., by returning a void pointer or throwing

[1] The table can also be thought of as a function: *F(key) → object. For example, F("123-45-6789") → "Leonardo da Vinci".*

Supplementary Information The online version contains supplementary material available at https://doi.org/10.1007/978-981-92-0260-7_1.

M. Kilian, *Ten Software Patterns Every Student Should Know*,
https://doi.org/10.1007/978-981-92-0260-7_1

an exception). Various approaches to handling failure conditions are discussed in Chap. 10.

The number of comparisons made to the key in this simple approach depends on the size of the table. On average, half of the records must be compared to find a matching record. The number of comparisons is therefore O(n), where n is the size of the table.

The average number of comparisons is half of the number of records. Assuming no misses, half the time the object will be found in the first half of the table, and half the time it will be found in the second half of the table. This averages out to half the table size. Note that if the object can't be found a large number of times, the average will skew greater than a half of the number of records. In big-O notation the fact that the average is $n/2$ is still equivalent to O(n) (i.e., constant multipliers are not explicit in big-O notation).

This is one of the most inefficient ways of looking up records. A much quicker way of finding a record is to sort the records in the table by their key. In this case, we assume that all the SSNs have the format nnn-nn-nnnn (a string of 11 characters including hyphens). One SSN is less than another if it is lexically (i.e., alphabetically) less than the other. 012-34-5678 is lexically less than 123-45-6789 since the character value for "0" is less than "1" (at least in the character set we are using to represent the SSN).

Once the list of records is ordered by SSN, a record can be found much more quickly using *binary search* (Knuth, Vol. 3, 1998). Let's say there are 101 records. We compare *SSN* with the middle (51st) record. If it matches, we're done. If *SSN* is less than the key of this record, we can retry with records 1–50 (i.e., treat records 1–50 as a new table and search that starting with record 25). If SSN is greater than the item at record 25, we repeat the process with the records in rows 26–50. With each iteration, the number of items to search through is halved until either the item is found or there are no more items in the table to compare (and the record is not found). Since the number of records that need to be searched after each comparison is half of the previous total, the number of searches is O(log n).[2] O(log n) is much faster than O(n)!

There is a cost to this approach. In the first case, searching for an item is O(n), but the cost for adding an item is very cheap: simply add the item to the end of the table. Assuming we don't have to find the end of the table, this is O(1), i.e., it takes the same amount of time no matter how many rows are in the table. In the sorted approach, adding an item is more expensive. The position of the element has to be found and that is as expensive as a search: O(log n). Adding a billion items will require a search to find the correct position for each item, which is O(log n). Since $log_2(1,000,000,000)$ is roughly 30, it requires approximately 30 times as much computation to insert 1,000,000,000 items for the sorted case as the serial case. However, the moment we access more than around 30 items in our 1,000,000,000 rows, the sorted case will be

[2] log(n) is the number of times you can divide n by 2 before you get to less than or equal to 1. For big-O notation we typically don't worry about the base of the logarithm though 2 is often the best choice for an accurate bound on the complexity.

much more efficient than the serial case, even with the additional cost to insert new items.

Can we do better than using a sorted table? The answer is: Of course. We can organize the records so that an estimate of where the item is will quickly narrow our search to the precise item. We can determine if the item is not there just as quickly, and inserting an item is likewise very fast. Consider a table of 1000 items containing a Social Security number and personal information. We can create 100 buckets, labeled 0–99. We take the first three digits of the Social Security number as an integer and calculate this number modulo 100.[3] All the records with a Social Security number with the first three digits modulo 100 equal to 0 will be placed in the first bucket. Likewise, Social Security numbers that result in a remainder of 1, 2, etc., will be placed in their corresponding buckets. To look up an item, we calculate the modulo of the first three digits of the Social Security number with 100. This identifies the bucket in O(1) time. Then we search through the items in the bucket. Assuming Social Security numbers are evenly distributed over the 1000 keys in the table, then each bucket will have about 10 items in it. Searching through a given bucket will be O(1) time so finding the item is overall O(1) time: O(1) to find the bucket, and O(1) to search the bucket.

We call the estimate of where the item is the *hash* of the item, and a table organized to facilitate this style of lookup is a *hash table*. The way we estimate the item index is using a *hash function*. In our previous example, the set of buckets is the hash table, and the hash function was the modulo of the first three digits by 100.

Hash tables can "find" an object in the same amount of time regardless of the number of entries in the table (i.e., constant time or O(1)). The hash function maps the key we are looking for to the index of the item having that key. Inserting is similar: Hash the key to where the record needs to go and insert the record there.

A picture of mapping a Social Security number to a table location using a hash function F is shown in Fig. 1.1.

In this example, the hash function F maps the key to the index of the item belonging to that key. In a perfect world, all keys would be mapped directly to their entry in the table and a lookup would be as fast as the function F takes to calculate the index. Of course the world is not perfect. It is not often that a hash function will be a one-to-one mapping between keys and the precise slot in the table corresponding to the key. It is also usually the case that a table is not a fixed size. Entries will be added and sometimes removed. The goal is to allow such a dynamic table to be still accessed in O(1) time.

The next section introduces some hash functions that can be used in a hash table. That will be followed by techniques for organizing a hash table that can grow while maintaining an O(1) access time.

[3] Modulo is the remainder after we divide one number by another. For example 8 modulo 5 is 3 since $8/5 = 1$ with a remainder of 3.

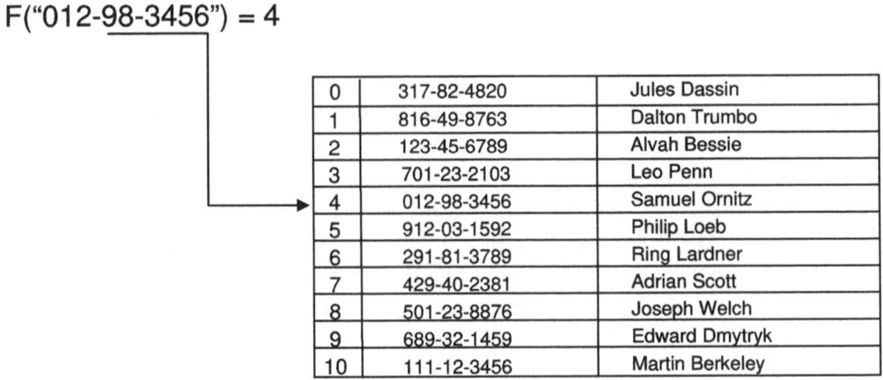

0	317-82-4820	Jules Dassin
1	816-49-8763	Dalton Trumbo
2	123-45-6789	Alvah Bessie
3	701-23-2103	Leo Penn
4	012-98-3456	Samuel Ornitz
5	912-03-1592	Philip Loeb
6	291-81-3789	Ring Lardner
7	429-40-2381	Adrian Scott
8	501-23-8876	Joseph Welch
9	689-32-1459	Edward Dmytryk
10	111-12-3456	Martin Berkeley

Fig. 1.1 Social Security numbers are hashed to indices in a table

Hash Functions

Unfortunately, the world is not so generous as to provide a hash function that can map an arbitrary input to a precise index—at least not with a reasonable amount of space. For example, the hash function F used above could simply return the integral value of the Social Security number (a number between 0 and 1 billion). That would require the table to have a billion rows even if only a handful of the rows were occupied. Furthermore, such a hash function would typically not be useful if the key were anything besides the Social Security number (like a name).

Much work has been done to come up with more or less general hash functions. While it is not inconceivable to have a different hash function for each hash table (e.g., one for Social Security numbers, one for names, etc.), functions have been developed that map an arbitrary string of bytes to an integer (of various sizes). A good hash function can take an arbitrary string of bytes and generate a value such that:

1. The values generated are well distributed throughout the hash functions output range.
2. Two different inputs are unlikely to hash to the same output (this is called a *collision*).

For example, the *MurmurHash* (API Park Blog 2024) is in wide use and basically treats byte strings as unsigned integers and applies various mathematical operations to obtain values that are well distributed across a range of inputs. Other commonly used hash functions are Cyclic Redundancy Codes (Peterson et al. 1961) and Knuth's Multiplicative Hash (Knuth, Vol. 3, 1998). Knuth's multiplicative hash is extremely simple, especially if we are creating 32-bit hashes:

```
1    uint32_t hash(uint32_t input) {
2      uint64_t product = (uint64_t) input * 2654435761;
3      return (uint32_t) (product > > 32);
4    }
```

The value 2654435761 in line 2 is a value that spreads the hash results out (particularly the high-level bits) even if the input values only differ a little.[4] For example, hash("aardvark") results in a value of 155533359, while hash("aardvarq") is 217746697. We will discuss how we convert the string "aardvark" to a 32-bit unsigned integer below. To get the right row in the table, we take the result of the hash function modulo the size of the table (there are 11 rows in the example above so the modulus would be 11).

The choice of the "magic" multiplier and the choice of bits is important. You might try the following as a hash function:

```
1    uint32_t hash(uint32_t input) {
2      uint64_t product = (uint64_t) input * 2654435762;
3      return (uint32_t) (product);
4    }
```

If we used hash(x) modulo 11 to get an index in the table in Fig. 1.1, we would soon see that only even rows would be populated, since multiplying an input by an even number (in this case 2654435762 on line 2) will always give you an even number. After taking the modulo of the table size, only even-numbered rows will be selected!

In general, use of a "canned" hash function such as MurmurHash is good enough except when every last CPU cycle is necessary and a hash with fewer operations (like the multiplicative hash above) might be required.

There are also *cryptographic hashes* (Merkle 1990) used to create a hash that hides all structure of the input (hence it is impossible to guess the input to the hash function from the hash value). These are used when it is critical to prevent someone "guessing" the input given a particular hash. Secure transmission of information on the internet relies on cryptographically strong hashing. Cryptographically strong hashes include SHA-1 (and follow-ons SHA-2 and SHA-3), and MD5 (though it has been found that collisions for MD5 can be manufactured too easily to ensure true safety in a security-sensitive application). These will generate a minimum of 128-bit outputs though most security-intensive applications now require at least 256 bits (such as SHA-2 which can output between 256- and 512-bit hashes). As you can imagine, cryptographic hashes are computationally more expensive than hashes such as MurmurHash and the multiplicative hash and are not necessary for everyday hash tables.

[4] It is related to Fibonacci hashing. See the Knuth reference.

Folding Strings

Hash algorithms such as MurmurHash and SHA-x take a pointer to a string of bytes and return the hash. In the case of Knuth's hash, the string has already been boiled down to a 32-bit integer. You might think that this integer would be a suitable hash in of itself but for a variety of reasons it is not, and the extra multiplication greatly enhances the pseudo-randomness of the hash.

A popular way of converting a string of N bytes to a 32-bit number is to *exclusive-or* the bits of consecutive 4-byte chunks of the string (Knuth, Vol. 3). The exclusive-or of two bits is 1 when the bits are different and 0 when they are the same.

XOR	0	1
0	0	1
1	1	0

The string "quickfox" would be represented in ASCII as two 32-bit integers with lower-indexed characters as low-order bits:

`q`	`u`	`i`	`c`	`k`	`f`	`o`	`x`	string
`71`	`75`	`69`	`63`	`6b`	`66`	`6f`	`78`	ASCII values (hex)
`71756963`				`6b666f78`				32-bit integers (hex)

`71756963 XOR 6b666f78 = 1b06131a (hex)`

Note that if the strings being hashed are already largely random, then it is possible to simply pick a deterministic substring (e.g., the middle 4 bytes) and consider that as the input to the hash function though this is not much simpler than the exclusive-or algorithm and less reliable.

Table Structure

Getting a good hash function is only part of the solution to building an efficient hash table. We need to organize our items in the table to use as little space as possible yet still ensure constant time lookup. The way this is typically done is to arrange the table into buckets. Each bucket contains 0 or more items whose key hashes to the bucket. For example, let's take the table of Social Security numbers mapping to names from Fig. 1.1 and put them into a table with 8 buckets. The index is calculated by first hashing the Social Security number (as a sequence of bytes using the multiplicative hash function) and then returning the hash value modulo 8 (Fig. 1.2).

In this case, the Social Security number 429-40-2381 folds into the value 0x162f5a33, which hashes to 0xdb60863, a value which is 3 when we take the

Fig. 1.2 Reducing hashes to indices of a table of size 8

317-82-4820	→	2
816-49-8763	→	0
123-45-6789	→	4
701-23-2103	→	4
012-98-3456	→	0
912-03-1592	→	3
291-81-3789	→	6
429-40-2381	→	3
501-23-8876	→	0
689-32-1459	→	7
111-12-3456	→	3

remainder after dividing by 8. This is the index of the bucket. Note that three Social Security numbers map to bucket 0, two map to bucket 4, three map to bucket 3, and none map to buckets 1 or 5. When two entries map to the same bucket we say they *collide*. We need to sort through the conflicting items to find the entry (if any) corresponding to the original key we are searching for.

Our hash table would look something like this (Fig. 1.3).

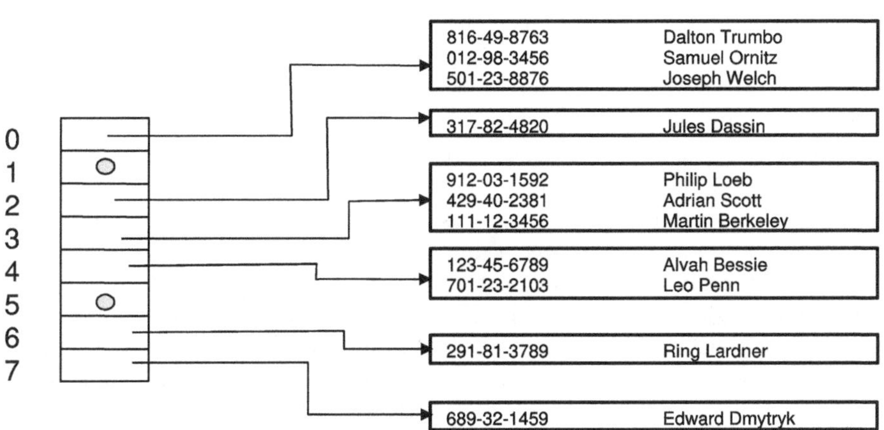

Fig. 1.3 Bucket structure of the hash table

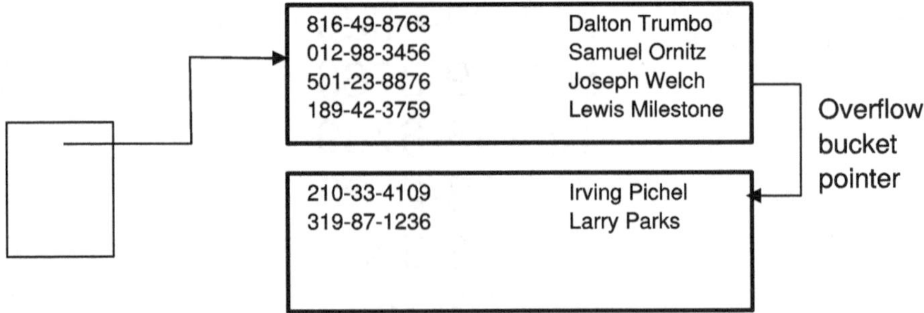

Fig. 1.4 Bucket structure of the hash table with overflow

Index 0 has a bucket with three items in it. In this case, the keys 816-49-8763, 012-98-3456, and 501-23-8876 would collide in bucket 0, and we would need to look at each entry in the bucket to see which entry was actually being requested.

Retrieving the item matching a particular Social Security number takes three steps:

1. Hash the Social Security number to an index. Since the table is 8 items long (a power of 2), we can simply take the last three bits of the hash as the index to the bucket.
2. If no bucket exists at this index, then we report "Not found."
3. Otherwise, linearly search the bucket referenced at this index for the Social Security number we are interested in. If the item is found, then return the information associated with it (in this case, the name associated with the Social Security number). If no item matches in this bucket, then report "Not found."

If more entries are hashed to a bucket than can fit, the bucket can be expanded in a number of ways. One way is to reallocate a new, larger bucket and copy the entries into it. More typically, a new bucket is allocated and linked to the existing bucket. Searches for items now may need to iterate over each bucket in a linked list (Fig. 1.4).

As long as a fixed number of entries are added to the table, then the search time is constant: a constant time to calculate the index of the bucket and a constant time to search through the fixed number of entries in the bucket (assuming a reasonable distribution of the entries over the buckets).

Having a constant time to search the bucket is only true if we cap the number of entries in the table. If we know that we will never have more than a dozen items stored in the hash table, then a table size of 8 buckets should disperse the items to roughly 2 per bucket, and we can find an item most of the time in one hash and a single comparison of the keys. This is not a guarantee, however. A pathologically bad case would be that all the items hash to the same bucket, in which case finding an item would be O(n), not O(1).

If the maximum number of entries is known, then an appropriate hash table size can be used and except in very rare cases, the access time will be O(1).

What happens when we need to store an unbounded number of entries in a hash table? That is where we need an *extensible* hash table.

Resizing a Hash Table

Suppose we don't know how many items are going to be inserted into the hash table. If we just keep adding entries to a fixed number of buckets, we end up being O(n) in access time. As an absurd example, suppose we add 100 million entries to our 8-bucket table above. All the table is doing is reducing the number of items that need to be linearly searched through to 1/8 of the total number—we search through 12.5 million entries, a far cry from a handful of accesses we expect from an O(1) algorithm.

One way of avoiding this problem is to have the table grow as the number of entries increases. Let's suppose we start with a table of 8 buckets with five items per bucket. A completely full table would have 40 items (8×5). Let's set a goal of only allowing the table to reach 85% of capacity, i.e., 34 items.

Before we add an item to the table, we check to see how many items are in the table. If we are at the capacity goal (34 items in this initial table), we decide to increase the size of the table before adding the new item. One way is to double the table size. We then have to "rehash" the entries into the new table.

Let's say the table has 2^k buckets and we are going to grow to 2^{k+1} buckets. An entry will either hash to the same bucket index (say b) or a bucket that is 2^k buckets away ($b + 2^k$). If the $k + 1$st bit of the item's hash is 0, it will remain in the current bucket; otherwise, it goes to the new bucket. If we double the example table, it would grow to be shown in Fig. 1.5.

The table does not need to double in size each time we grow it. We could create a brand new table and rehash all the entries from the old one to the new one. The new one could be 20% greater rather than $2\times$ bigger. The disadvantage of not doubling the size of the table is that, unless you are very clever, you must allocate and populate an entirely new table since virtually every item will have a new bucket index. The old table is thrown away (in memory allocation terms, it is *freed*). All of this is extra work and can lead to *memory fragmentation* (see the section on Memory Fragmentation below).

If the table is doubled, then we can retain the existing buckets and simply add new buckets. Roughly half of the entries will be moved from one bucket to another. Notice that in the previous example (Fig. 1.5) that buckets 0–7 are the same buckets that existed in the previous table with some of their entries relocated to the new buckets. Bucket 2 was emptied (its sole entry was rehashed to bucket 10). We only need to reallocate the bucket index (growing that from 8 to 16 entries), allocate new buckets as necessary for the new section of the table, and optionally delete the buckets that have been emptied.

Deleting empty buckets is usually unnecessary. If more items are going to be later added to this table, it is likely the bucket will be needed for a new item so

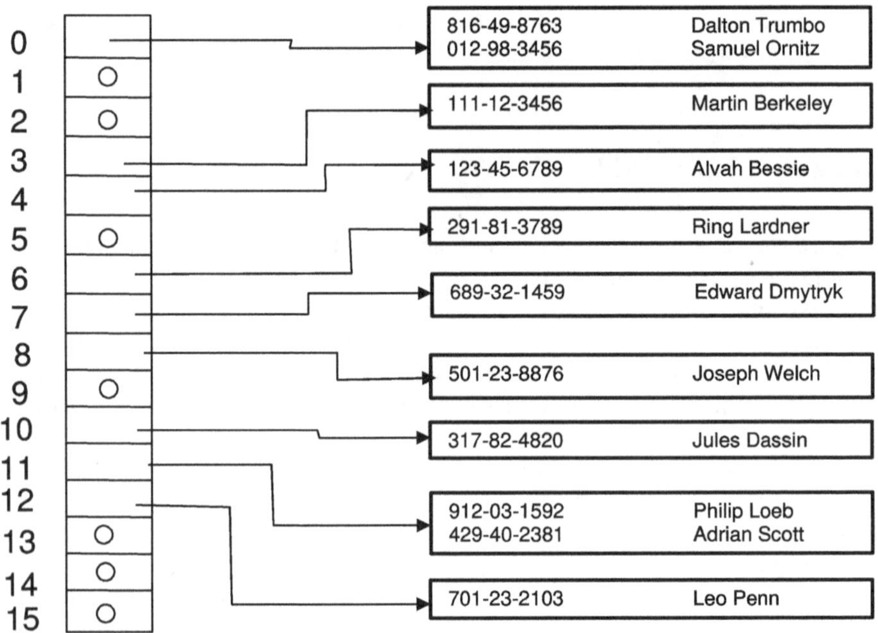

Fig. 1.5 Resizing the 8-bucket table to 16 buckets

deallocating and then later allocating the bucket not only require processing time but can also contribute to memory fragmentation.

Including the hash of the key with the item in the bucket accelerates both lookup and the rehashing process. Suppose we are looking for Social Security number 012-98-3456. The hash of this is 312215072 which resolves to bucket 0 in our example. Including the hash in the bucket means we can now do a 4-byte integer comparison to exclude items that don't match which resolve to the same bucket. In our example above, our bucket would become (Fig. 1.6).

As we iterate through the contents of the bucket, rather than doing a string comparison of 11 characters on each item to see if it matches, we compare the hashes (a faster 32-bit integer comparison). If the hashes do not match, we know that the item's key will not match and we can skip that item immediately. If the hashes do match, then we must compare the keys completely since it is possible (though unlikely) that two different keys could hash to the same value.

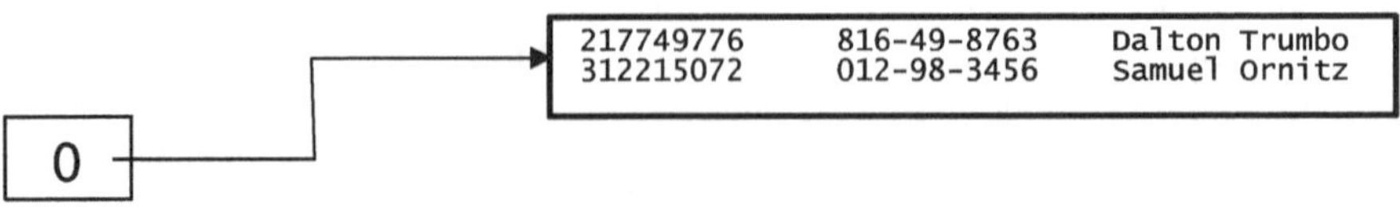

Fig. 1.6 Including the hash in the bucket

Including the hash in the entry not only allows faster search, but can be used to better utilize a processor's *cache line*. This will be discussed below.

Storing the hash with the item in the bucket improves rehashing the items into the new table structure. Instead of running the hash function on each item's key to determine the new placement, the hash stored in the bucket can be directly accessed. If we are rehashing bucket 0 above, then we need only look at the bits of 217749776 and 312215072 to determine where to place those two entries. For more complex key structures and more sophisticated hash algorithms, this can save significant processing time.

Of course, growing a hash table by rehashing every item is very expensive (imagine growing a table with 100,000,000 entries). An appropriate policy for when to expand the table and by how much can be tricky unless there is significant knowledge about how the hash table will be used. Predicting the use pattern may not be practical when building a general-purpose hash table. We will discuss ways to avoid rehashing the entire table when expanding the table in the section Litwin's Linear Hashing below.

Memory Fragmentation

Some languages such as C and C++ feature explicit dynamic memory allocation. A program that wants memory that is available outside of a given scope (e.g., a function call) must be explicitly allocated. In C, the *malloc* library function is used, and in C++ the *new* operator is used. When the memory is no longer needed, the *free* function is used in C, and *delete* is used in C++.

When memory is allocated, various system functions are used under the covers to carve up the virtual memory assigned to the program. The system functions (like *sbrk*) will assign a chunk of memory to your program. This chunk will not only have memory to satisfy the request but also bookkeeping information. For example, if you say *malloc(10)* to allocate 10 bytes, the system does not just hand out 10 bytes. It needs to "remember" this piece of memory so that it doesn't try to allocate it while it is in use, and when it is not in use, it can recycle it for other allocations. There are all sorts of optimizations that memory allocators do to make allocating memory efficient that are outside of the discussion of this book.[5]

To better understand memory fragmentation, consider this memory layout after allocating several items. Here is a memory layout of objects A, B, C, D, E, and F. Each piece is contiguous to the next (Fig. 1.7).

The overall memory consumed is growing with the new item G because G cannot fit in either the B or E slots. For now, those slots are "wasted." Eventually those slots will be reused but you can imagine a set of pathological allocations and deallocations that can cause the amount of memory required to hold some number of items to be

[5] Many man-years of effort have gone into the allocators provided in the run-time packages of the systems we use every day. Many a man-month has been wasted by programmers trying to build a "better malloc." We will discuss specialized cases below that can "beat" malloc.

Fig. 1.7 Memory fragmentation due to deallocation and new allocations

A
B
C
D
E
F

Now let's delete B and E, and add a new item G.

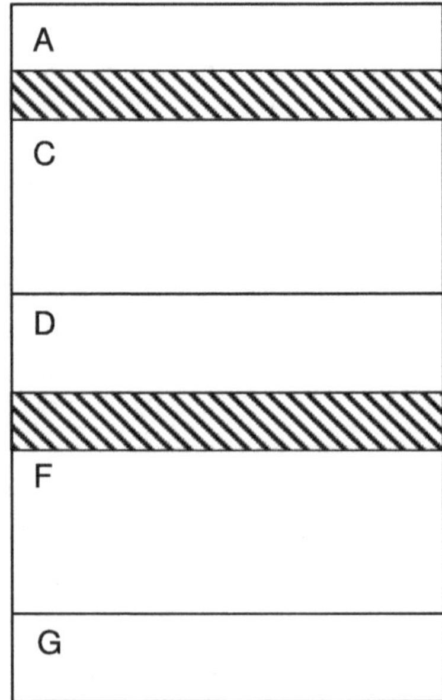

much larger than the size of the items. Unfortunately, the pathological case happens more frequently than you might expect.

In the discussion of rehashing the table, we mentioned that deleting the buckets can lead to fragmentation. Deleting bucket 1 is similar to freeing slot B above. Whether that slot can be reused later is very dependent on how memory is allocated in the time between when it is freed and when it needs to be reused. This is why we might as well leave empty buckets in place for future entries (unless the entire table is being thrown away or we are shrinking the table after deleting many entries).

Cache Lines

Another optimization related to memory fragmentation that should be considered when building hash tables is exploiting *cache locality*. Modern CPUs have a memory hierarchy. The fastest and smallest memories are registers. Next fastest are the memory cache layers, then RAM memory, and these days we should consider non-volatile memory (SSD or NVMe) as yet another layer. Cache layers contain data that also exists in memory (it caches the contents of the memory). When you access memory, the bytes (and some extra bytes as well) are saved in the cache so that if you revisit that memory location, the processor does not have to go "all the way back" to the memory to fetch it. The savings may seem insignificant (nanoseconds), but when accessing memory billions of times, it can lead to a dramatic difference in performance.

There are only a few registers and they are where arithmetic operations occur. The next level is the L1 cache. This is memory that exists on the CPU and is on the order of 100s of kilobytes to a couple of megabytes. The CPU can access the L1 cache about 100 times faster than RAM. L2 cache is larger, on the order of ten megabytes. Items in the L2 cache are accessed 25 times faster than RAM. L3 cache is slower still, but larger than L2 (10s of megabytes). L1 and L2 caches are part of a particular CPU; L3 cache spans multiple CPUs and is important for multithreaded applications where multiple CPUs are working on the same memory.

Finally, there is RAM which is typically measured in gigabytes.[6]

When a CPU fetches memory from RAM, it fetches a *cache line* of memory On Intel processors this is typically 64 bytes. Assume you have the following code:

```
1   int32_t a[16];
2   ...
3   int32_t total = 0;
4   for (int i = 0; i < 16; i++) {
5           total += a[i];
6   }
```

On the first access of a[0] (Line 5), the cache will be populated not only with a[0], but in fact the entire array.[7] It is likely that the access to a[1], a[2], … a[15] will be 100 times faster than that first access because the entries will already be in cache in the CPU. Exploiting cache lines is referred to as *cache affinity*.

---

[6] Memory size follows something like Moore's Law increasing exponentially. In 2024, some machines have terabytes of RAM.

[7] This isn't quite true; it depends somewhat on what the address of the first array element is. Regardless, a substantial amount of the array is likely to be read in with the first entry.

Note that we are grossly oversimplifying cache architectures. Just as caches can greatly enhance performance, there are pathological memory access patterns where the cache can actually degrade performance. For example, reading a few bytes that resolve to cache line X and then a different set of bytes not contiguous with the first set of bytes that also resolves to cache line X may require the old content of the cache line to be evicted before being populated with new content. The unreferenced bytes in the cache represent "lost opportunity" and therefore lost performance.

Cache architectures vary with processors and are non-trivial to exploit. Hennessy et al. (1990) has a reasonable introduction to caches; Processor-specific documents should be considered for maximum leverage of the cache.

Choosing memory layout can be dramatic. As discussed in the section on table structure, hash tables are frequently organized into buckets that contain entries that are the hash and the item the hash corresponds to.

Here is an example of two bucket structures. Both share the same entry structure and item structure.

```
struct Keyed_item {
    char *key;
    ... other data fields...
};


struct Entry {
    uint32_t hash;
    struct Keyed_item *item;
};
```

We can organize these entries in two ways. In the first case, we put the entries directly into the bucket.

```
struct Bucket {
    int num_entries;
    struct Entry  entries[MAX_BUCKET_SIZE]; // inlined entries
    struct Bucket  *next_bucket;
};
```

This bucket is an array of entries. Each entry is 12 bytes long (if pointers are 8 bytes): a hash and the Keyed_item pointer. The size of a bucket is MAX_BUCKET_SIZE $\times$ 12 + 4 (num_entries) + 8 (next_bucket).

In the alternative organization, we use pointers to entries in the bucket.

```
struct Bucket {
    int num_entries;
    struct Entry  *entries[max_num_entries]; // point to entries
    struct Bucket  *next_bucket;
};
```

Now the array contains pointers to entries. Our bucket is roughly a third smaller: MAX_BUCKET_SIZE $\times$ $8 + 4 + 8$.

We have very simple code to fetch an entry in a bucket:

```
7   struct Entry * Bucket_find_entry(struct Bucket *bucket,
8                          uint32_t h, char *k) {
9    for (uint32_t i = 0; i < bucket- > num_entries; i + + ) {
10     struct Entry *entry = &bucket- > entries[i]; // inlined entry
11          - OR -
12       struct Entry *entry = bucket- > entries[i]; // pointer to
entry
13
14       if (entry- > hash ! = h) {
15        continue;
16       }
17      if (strcmp(k, entry- > item- > key) = = 0) {
18        return entry;
19       }
20    }
21   return NULL;
22 }
```

To fetch a given item, we iterate over the entries in a bucket. In the case with inlined entries, we use line 10. In the second case where the bucket points to the entry (instead of inlining it within the bucket), we use line 12.

The rest of the code remains the same. The only difference between the two fetch codes is that in the inline case we take the address of the inlined entry in the bucket (line 10), and in the second case the pointer to the entry is directly accessed (line 12). The rest of the code is identical. The difference in performance (measured on an Intel i7-9700 CPU running at 3 GHz, compiled with gcc version 9.3 at optimization level 3)[8] is somewhat startling. The second case where we dereference a pointer to get to the key runs 50% slower than the first depending on how many buckets we use. It is likely that in the first case, when we iterate over the entries in a bucket, all the entries in the bucket are in cache after the first entry is accessed. In the second case it is likely that every entry fetched is actually a cache miss. While the difference per table access is less than 50 ns, when millions of accesses are made, the time truly adds up (Fig. 1.8).

You may ask yourself why anyone would create buckets of pointers to entries. Note that some languages (for example, Java and Python) make it difficult to store objects contiguously. By default, objects are only available through *references* and the notion of taking a pointer to an object isn't available. Understanding the cache

[8] The fact that we must provide this level of qualification to the performance result shows that exploiting features like cache affinity is a tricky tuning exercise.

Hash value Pointer to Item	Hash value Pointer to Item	Hash value Pointer to Item	Hash value Pointer to Item

Entries follow each other in memory and may share a single cache line (the dotted rectangle). Accessing the first will likely cause all the entries to be loaded into cache.

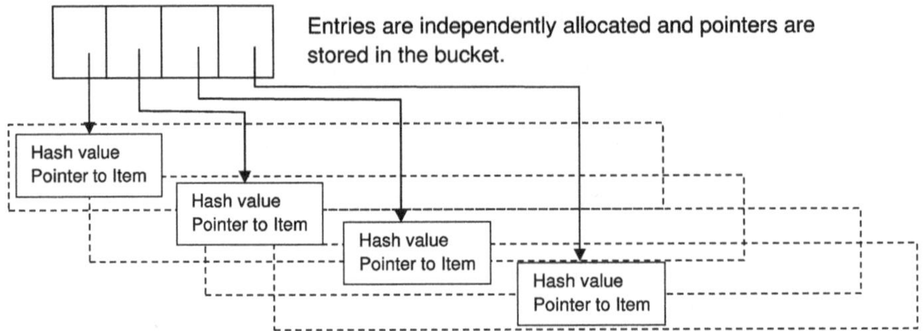

Bucket entries could be distributed so that none of them share a cache line. Each bucket entry accessed may require a cache load.

Fig. 1.8 Making buckets more "cache friendly"

behavior can help with understanding limitations of some languages when every nanosecond counts.

It is possible to take the bucket organization one step further as is done in *F14* (Bronson et al. 2019), Facebook's open-source hash table. In F14, multiple entries in a bucket are compared in parallel using a processor's vector instruction (for example, the Streaming SIMD Extensions instructions such as PCMPEQD, which allows comparison of four 32-bit values in one instruction). You can imagine, for example, aligning your hash values in the buckets so that a single instruction could compare four hashes at once.

When getting the last nanosecond of performance out of a hash table, it is important to understand the memory architecture and machine capabilities at hand.

Litwin's Linear Hashing

As we mentioned earlier, the key to maintaining constant performance (O(*1*)) in hash tables is to keep the number of entries in a bucket bounded. Using a fixed number of buckets for an unbounded number of items can lead to O(n) types of behavior instead of O(*1*). And as noted, resizing a table can be expensive. Imagine a table of a billion objects that needs to grow. Rehashing a billion entries will take a relatively long time. Imagine you are developing a real-time application where you must add objects to the table in less than 50 μs. Things go along swimmingly when all of a sudden the system seizes up for some number of seconds as it rehashes entries to grow the hash table. Your guarantee for 50 μs will not be satisfied for tens of thousands of transactions.

Litwin (1980) introduced a new kind of hash table originally used for database indices. Its primary goal was to make a hash table that could grow (or shrink) in a constant amount of time, be space efficient, and in LItwin's original design, require minimal disk accesses to reach a given item. This section presents Litwin's algorithm with some modifications because we are going to assume this hash table is in memory and that allocating and accessing large contiguous regions is not as necessary an optimization as when the table is stored on (slow) spinning disk.

In Litwin's approach, we start with a hash table of n buckets as described previously (to simplify the algorithm, assume n is a power of two). Buckets can hold an arbitrary number of items but we're going to try to cap a bucket to 4 entries (roughly a cache line's worth). A given hash table with n buckets would have a capacity of $4n$ entries. We also define a *load factor*. This is a threshold that, when reached, will trigger the hash table to expand. We express this as the percentage of the maximum capacity. For example, a load factor of 85% will trigger an expansion when the number of entries exceeds $0.85 \times 4n = 3.4n$ ($4n$ is the capacity of the table).

A quick note about double precision calculations. In the early days, integer calculations were much faster than floating point. Today, floating point calculations are still a bit more expensive (about 50%) but for incidental calculations (like the load factor), deciding whether to use floating point or integer representations is largely personal preference.

When the number of entries in the table exceeds the load factor, we split a bucket, establishing a new bucket at the end of the table. The next bucket to split is called the *split point*. The split point begins with the first bucket in the table. When a bucket is split, a new bucket is added to the end of the table. We then recalculate the index of each item in the bucket being split using one extra bit of the key's hash to determine whether the item is to remain in its current bucket, or moved to the new bucket. Half the items in the bucket are expected to stay in the current bucket, and half to go into the new bucket.

The split point has two roles:

1. it points to the next bucket to split,
2. to find the index of a bucket in a table of 2^k buckets, we take the lower k bits of the hash (effectively, modulo the table size) as the bucket index. If that index is less than the split point (i.e., refers to a bucket that has been split), then we take the lower $k + 1$ bits of the hash as the bucket index. This may index the original bucket or the new bucket depending on the value of the $k + 1st$ bit.

Once a bucket is split, the split point is advanced to the next bucket. When the last bucket in the table of 2^k buckets is split, we treat the original table and the 2^k new buckets as a new table of 2^{k+1} buckets (the original table and all the buckets created by splitting) and the split point is reset to the first bucket.

Note that the bucket being split is not necessarily (and probably isn't) the fullest bucket in the table. Key to the Litwin idea is that the split point advances monotonically through the buckets. The average capacity of the table should be the load factor times the capacity of the table and we hope that the hashing will distribute keys more or less evenly over the buckets.

Here is an example of the bucket layout before and after the first split. We are adding entry 372-21-4235 to bucket 2 (Fig. 1.9).

With the addition of **372-21-4235**, we need to expand the table. We expand the bucket at the split point (in this case, bucket 0). Note two important points:

1. Buckets 0 and 3 have *overflowed* (i.e., have exceeded the 4 entries/bucket we designated). We do not enlarge a bucket on overflow. Instead, the overflow is placed in an overflow bucket—another bucket that is linked to the bucket that is full effectively creating a larger bucket.
2. We split the bucket at the split point regardless of how full the other buckets in the table are. This is non-intuitive at first but is critical to the basic Litwin model and is discussed further below.

After the split, our table looks like as shown in Fig. 1.10.

Bucket 0 has been split into itself and bucket 4. The split point has been advanced to bucket 1. Now when we calculate the index to lookup an entry, we look at 2 bits of the hash (the original 4 entry table), and if the value of the index is less than the split point (just advanced to 1) then we use 3 bits of the hash to determine the new index. In this case, if the index calculated by taking the lower two bits is 0 (and therefore less than 1), we must consider three bits. The index will therefore either be 0 or 4 (the index $+ 2^2$). The capacity of the table has increased by one bucket, so the new threshold is $20 \times 0.85 = 17$ items. When the split point advances to bucket 4 (and hence the table is 8 items long, i.e., has doubled), the split point is reset to bucket 0, and we treat the table as a new table of length 8 using 3 bits of the hash to find the items.

Note that in this example, bucket three will eventually be split as long as items are being added to the table. And though we have an outlier, our buckets are meeting the average of 3 items per bucket (i.e., 85% of capacity of the table).

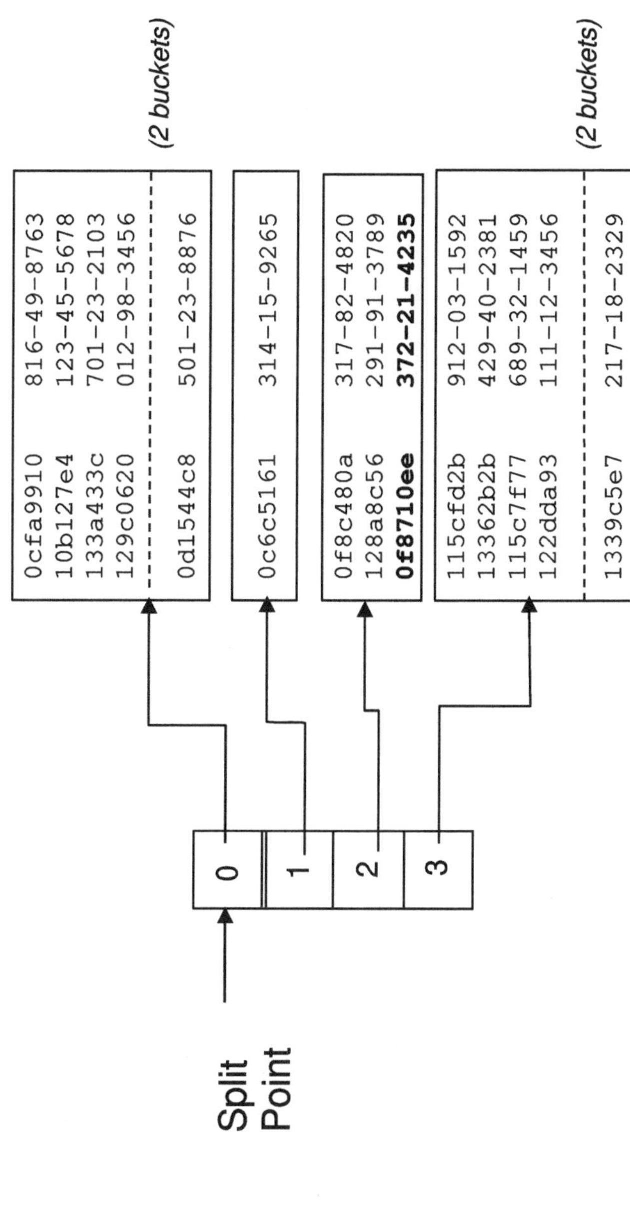

Fig. 1.9 Addition of **372-21-4235** puts the number of entries (14) over our load factor ($16 \times 0.85 = 13.6$)

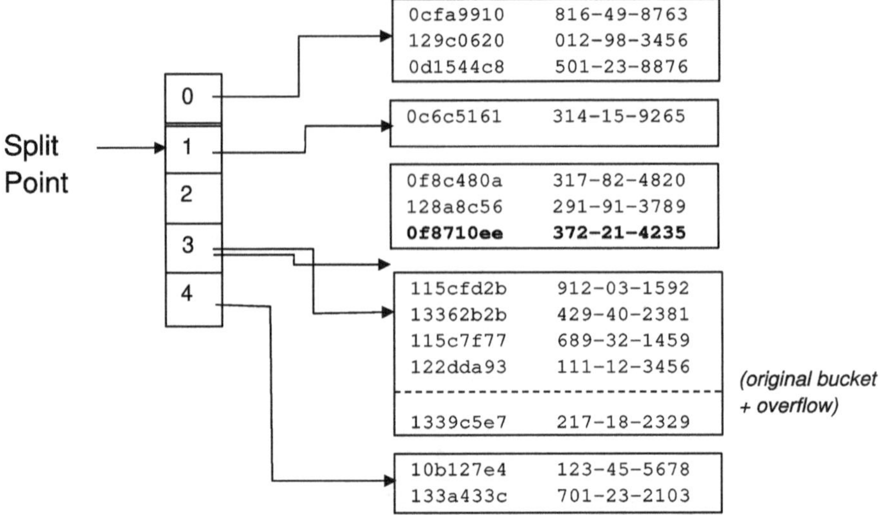

Fig. 1.10 Splitting bucket 0 advances the split point and creates bucket 4

The algorithm for insertion and retrieval follows.

```
1 struct Entry {
2   uint32_t hash;
3   Keyed_item *item;
4 };
5
6
7 struct Bucket {
8   struct Entry entries[MAX_BUCKET_SIZE];
9   struct Bucket *overflow;
10 };
11
12 struct Table {
13   Bucket **buckets;
14   uint32_t num_buckets;
15   uint32_t split_point;
16   uint32_t num_items_in_table;
17   uint32_t threshold;
18 };
```

Lines 1–4 An entry contains the hash for the key in the item, and a pointer to the item. In this model, the item must meet the `Keyed_item` format, i.e., a pointer to a null-terminated character string in its first field.

Lines 7–10 A bucket is an array of entries with a pointer to another bucket if the bucket overflows. An entry is considered empty if the item pointer in the entry is NULL. The bucket is not packed, i.e., empty entries may be interspersed with non-empty entries. This allows an entry to be removed from the table by simply setting the item pointer in the entry to NULL.

Line 13 A table contains a pointer to an array of pointers to buckets. When we have to double a table, this array is doubled. It will have enough room for the original buckets and the split buckets (e.g., if the number of buckets is 4, then the buckets array has room for 8 pointers to buckets. If bucket 2 is split, then a split bucket will be stored at bucket $2 + 4 = 6$). When all the buckets have been split, then this array must be copied into an array that is twice as large.

Line 14 Num_buckets is the number of primary buckets; it does not include split buckets. See the previous discussion of num_buckets.

Line 15 The split point is the index of the next bucket that should be split and will be in the range of $0 \leq$ split_point < num_buckets.

Line 16 The total number of items in the table.

Line 17 The number of items that, when the total number of items in the table exceeds this value, requires a bucket to be split.

```
1  struct Entry *Bucket_find_entry(struct Bucket *bucket,
2                   uint32_t hash, char *key) {
3   while (bucket ! = NULL) {
4     for (uint32_t i = 0; i < MAX_BUCKET_SIZE; i + + ) {
5       struct Entry *entry = &bucket- > entries[i];
6       if (entry- > item = = NULL || entry- > hash ! = hash) {
7         continue;
8       }
9
10      if (strcmp(key, entry- > item- > key) = = 0) {
11        return entry;
12      }
13    }
14    bucket = bucket- > next_bucket;
15  }
16  return NULL;
17  }
```

Lines 1–2 Find an entry in a bucket with a given hash and key. While the hash could be calculated from the key, it is almost always the case that the hash has already been calculated to figure out which bucket to access and its value should be reused.

Line 3 Loop over the bucket and any other overflow buckets.

Lines 4–5 Iterate over the entries in the bucket.

Lines 6–8 If the entry's item is NULL or the hash doesn't match the given hash, this entry can't match the item being looked for. Look at the next entry. Note: If the key doesn't exist in the bucket, all the bucket's entries (and its overflow bucket's entries) will be considered.

Lines 10–12 Just because the hashes match, doesn't ensure that the keys match. Check that here. If the keys match, return the entry.

Line 14 If no entries in this bucket match the key being searched for, then try overflow buckets, if any.

Line 16 If no entries were found, return NULL.

```
1  Void Bucket_add_entry(struct Bucket *bucket, uint32_t hash,
2                        struct Keyed_item *item) {
3
4    for(uint32_t i = 0; i < MAX_BUCKET_SIZE; i + + ) {
5     struct Entry *entry = &bucket- > entries[i];
6     if (entry- > item = = NULL) {
7      entry- > hash = hash;
8      entry- > item = item;
9      return;
10      }
11    }
12
13    if (bucket- > overflow ! = NULL) {
14      Bucket_add_entry(bucket- > next_bucket, hash, item);
15      return;
16    }
17
18    bucket- > overflow = make_Bucket();
19    Bucket_add_entry(bucket- > overflow, hash, item);
20  }
```

Lines 1–2 Add an entry to a bucket. An entry can be added multiple times to a bucket. We will address this below.

Lines 6–10 If an empty entry is found, replace it with the entry being added and return. This allows entries to be deleted and reused easily.

Lines 13–16 If there is no place to put the item in this bucket, try the overflow bucket.

Lines 18–19 And if there is no overflow bucket, then create one and add the item to it.

```
void Bucket_split(struct Bucket *this_bucket,
                  struct Bucket *other_bucket,
                  uint32_t mask) {
  struct Bucket *bucket = this_bucket;
  int32_t other_index = 0;

  while (bucket ! = NULL) {
   for (uint32_t i = 0; i < MAX_BUCKET_SIZE; i + + ) {
    struct Entry *entry = &bucket- > entries[i];
    if (entry- > item = = NULL) {
     continue;
    }

    if (bucket- > entries[i].hash & mask) {
     if (other_index = = MAX_BUCKET_SIZE) {
      other_bucket- > next_bucket = make_Bucket();
      other_bucket = other_bucket- > next_bucket;
      other_index = 0;
     }
```

```
20       other_bucket- > entries[other_index].hash = entry- > hash;
21       other_bucket- > entries[other_index].item = entry- > item;
22       other_index + + ;
23
24       entry- > hash = 0;
25       entry- > item = NULL;
26     }
27   }
28   bucket = bucket- > next_bucket;
29  }
30 }
```

Lines 1–3 We reallocate entries between `this_bucket` and `other_bucket` according to the mask. The mask will be a single bit and will govern if an element stays in `this_bucket` or is moved to the `other_bucket`. If an entry's hash, bitwise-ANDed with the mask is 1, then it will be moved from `this_bucket` to `other_bucket`. Typically, the mask will be the number of buckets in the table x 2. Upon entry to this function, `other_bucket` will be empty.

Line 7 We split all the chained buckets in a split operation.

Line 8 Iterate over all the entries in the first bucket of the chain.

Line 10 If the current entry is NULL, move to the next.

Line 14 Check if the hash qualifies for moving the entry to the other bucket.

Lines 15–19 If there is no room in `other_bucket`, then create an overflow bucket for it and reset the destination of moved elements to the overflow bucket.

Lines 20–22 Move the element to the overflow bucket.

Lines 24–25 Reset the element in the original bucket, making it available for subsequent storage.

Line 28 Continue until `this_bucket` and its overflows are split between `this_bucket` and `other_bucket`.

```
1 uint32_t Table_get_bucket_index(struct Table *table,
2                    uint32_t hash) {
3   uint32_t index = hash & (table- > num_buckets - 1);
4   if (index < table- > split_point) {
5     index = hash & (table- > num_buckets * 2 - 1);
6   }
7   return index;
8 }
```

Lines 1–8 We assume that the number of buckets is a power of 2. The mask created by `(table->num_buckets - 1)` determines the index of the bucket. If the index is less than the split point, it must be a bucket that has been split. In this case, we need to consider an extra bit `(table->num_buckets * 2 - 1)` to choose between this bucket or the bucket it was split into.

```
1  struct Keyed_item *Table_fetch_item(struct Table *table,
2                char *key) {
3   uint32_t hash = hash(key);
4   uint32_t index = Table_get_bucket_index(table, hash);
5
6   struct Bucket *bucket = table- > buckets[index];
7   struct Entry *entry = Bucket_find_entry(bucket, hash, key);
8   if (entry ! = NULL) {
9    return entry- > item;
10   }
11   return NULL;
12 }
```

Lines 3–4 Calculate the hash of the key and use it to determine the bucket index.

Lines 6–7 Find the entry in the chosen bucket.

Lines 8–11 If we find an entry, return the item in the entry. It is not allowed to store a NULL item since that is the indicator for an empty entry. If no entry is found, return NULL.

```
1  void Table_add_item(struct Table *table,
2            struct Keyed_item *item) {
3   Table_split_if_needed(table);
4
5   uint32_t hash = hash(item- > key);
6   uint32_t index = Table_get_bucket_index(table, hash);
7
8   struct Bucket *bucket = table- > buckets[index];
9   if (!bucket) {
10    bucket = make_Bucket();
11    table- > buckets[index] = bucket;
12    }
13    Bucket_add_entry(bucket, hash, item);
14    table- > num_items_in_table + + ;
15  }
```

Line 3 See if the table needs to be split before we add the item.

Line 5 It would be a good idea to make sure item is not NULL since that is an illegal value (and would cause a null pointer dereference here).

Lines 5–8 Get the bucket corresponding to the key. It may be a primary bucket or a split bucket.

Lines 9–12 If the index is to a split bucket, it is possible that the split bucket has not been allocated. Do it here if necessary.

Lines 13–14 Add the item to the bucket and update the number of entries in the table.

```
void Table_split_if_needed(struct Table *table) {
 if (table- > num_items_in_table < table- > threshold) {
  return;
 }
```

```
5   if (table- > split_point = = table- > num_buckets) {
6    Table_double(table);
7    return;
8   }
9  struct Bucket *bucket = table- > buckets[table- > split_point];
10   struct Bucket *other_bucket = make_Bucket();
11   table- > buckets[table- > split_point + table- > num_buckets]
=
12          other_bucket;
13   Bucket_split(bucket, other_bucket, table- > num_buckets);
14   table- > split_point + + ;
15    table- > threshold = (table- > num_buckets + table- > split_
point)*
16          MAX_BUCKET_SIZE * load_factor;
17 }
```

Line 1 Check if we need to split and, if so, split the next bucket. If the table must double, handle that as well.

Lines 2–4 If the number of items in the table is less than the threshold, then no split is necessary.

Lines 5–8 If all the buckets in the table have been split, then double the size of the table.

Lines 9–14 Split the bucket at the split point and advance the split point.

Lines 15–16 Recalculate the threshold based on the enlarged table.

Deleting Entries

The Litwin algorithm above is for finding an entry in the hash table and adding an entry with associated splitting and doubling of the table to try to maintain a given load factor. Notice that in the `Bucket_find_entry` operation, we skip over entries with NULL item pointers but nevertheless continue searching in the bucket and any overflow buckets. This allows us to delete an entry in a bucket by simply nulling out its item pointer. Moving an entry to a split bucket is a copy operation followed by nulling the original entry's item pointer. The disadvantage of this technique is that all the entries in a bucket (and any overflow buckets) must be interrogated before a "missing entry" can be declared. Since we hope that all the entries are in cache, this may not be as high a penalty as might be expected.

The advantage of this approach is that it is trivial to delete an entry from a table: Simply find the entry and null out its item pointer. Under conditions where items are being added and removed frequently, the theory is that:

- Deleted entries will be reused by new entries.
- Splitting keeps the chain of overflow buckets relatively short.

Nevertheless, it may be necessary to perform an occasional cleanup to reduce the sparseness of the buckets. There are applications that will fill a hash table, then delete a large fraction of the entries (often the pattern is to add entries, then process them, and as they are processed, remove them from the table).

One logical place to perform a cleanup is to "compress" a bucket when it is split by moving retained items to a previous open slot, filling in holes left by previous deletions. Another approach is to keep a count of the deleted items, and like the load factor for splitting, we could also have a load factor for deletions such that when a certain percentage of the table is empty, we can compress one or more buckets.

Doubling the Table Without Reallocation

So far, table-doubling has been mentioned but has not been described fully. A simple approach is to allocate a new bucket index that is twice as large, copy the old bucket index (the `buckets` field in the `Table` struct) to the top half of the new index and then set the `buckets` pointer to the new bucket index.

This sounds like a lot of work. It is but it also happens relatively rarely. By the time you reach the 20th doubling you have increased the table by a factor of a million. Doubling 32 times is a factor of 4 billion. With relatively few doublings you can get to very large table sizes. Nevertheless, copying 256,000 pointers to buckets will take around a millisecond which, depending on the application, can be considered a long time.

Using another level of indirection can eliminate the need to reallocate. Let's assume we never have more than 4 billion buckets (not counting overflow buckets which are not indexed by the bucket table). We create an array of 32 pointers with each pointer referencing a generation of the hash table. When a table is created, it has its original buckets, plus the buckets needed for splitting the table. When the split point returns to index 0, a new sub-table is added (where the split buckets will be allocated) and no other allocation needs to be made.

For example, assume we have doubled the table three times. The memory layout would appear as shown in Fig. 1.11.

Buckets are accessed by bucket index (as we did above). The index is converted into the correct pointer to the block of buckets containing the index, and the offset in that block of buckets of the desired bucket. Assume that the original number of buckets is 2^k. For a given bucket index b, the sub-table needed is found by a few bit operations:

```
uint32_t b_index = b >> k;
if (b_index == 0) {
  The sub-table index is 0, and the offset in the subtable is b.
}
else {
     uint32_t j = index of the high order bit of b_index where
       the least significant bit is index 0
     The sub-table index is j+1, and the offset is b − 2^(k+j)
}
```

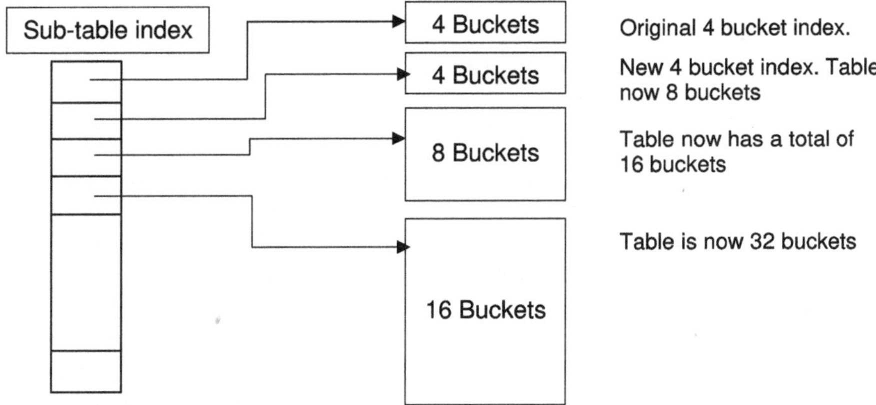

Fig. 1.11 Adding a bucket index

It is perhaps easiest to see what is going on here with a picture of how bits in the index align to the bucket tables, shown in Fig. 1.12. Assume $k = 2$ so that the first sub-table is 4 buckets long and that we've expanded the table two times (the first table began with 4 buckets + 4 split buckets, then it expanded to 8 buckets and 8 split buckets, and then 16 buckets + 16 split buckets). Here is how a bucket index b would map to a sub-table in this two-tier system.

Suppose we have a bucket index b of 423 and an initial table size of 4 buckets, i.e., $k = 2$.

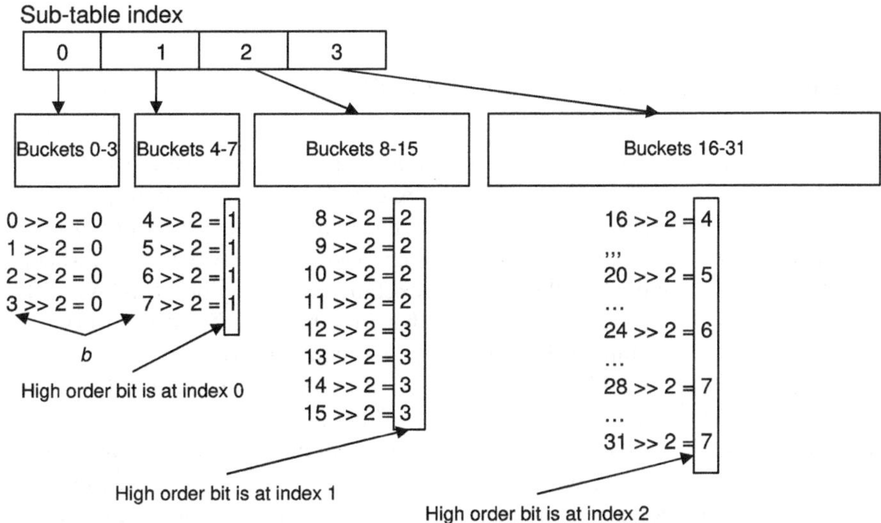

Fig. 1.12 Resolving a bucket index b to a sub-table index assuming initial table of size 2^2

```
423 = 0001 1010 0111 in binary
      0001 1010 0111 >> 2 = 0110 1001
Bit index                   7654 3210
High order bit is at index 6.
The index of the sub-array containing this bucket is (6 + 1) = 7.
```

The offset in this sub-table of buckets is simply the original bucket index without all the buckets in the previous sub-tables. For sub-table index j, the number of buckets preceding it is 2^{j+k-1}. In this example, there are $2^{7+2-1} = 2^8 = 256$ buckets in front of this sub-table so the offset in the sub-table is $423 - 256 = 167$.

Calculating the index of the most significant bit in the shifted index is not necessarily expensive. It turns out that Intel architectures have a set of instructions that return bit information of the operand. Using the GNU CC compiler, we can access one of these instructions with `__builtin_clz`, which returns the index of the most significant bit, with 0 being the highest order bit in the value being checked. Subtracting the `__builtin_clz` result from 31 results in the enumeration required above (i.e., the least significant bit set is 0). `__builtin_clz` is undefined for 0 which is why there is a special case for when `b_index` is 0 in the above algorithm.

With the usual performance caveats, the resolution of the sub-table index and bucket array offset is on the order of 3 ns. If an occasional millisecond (or more) delay for doubling the bucket table by copying is not acceptable, then the extra cost of the sub-table indirection is worthwhile. Note that it only takes a million accesses to accumulate 3 ms of additional execution time (albeit, spread over all of those accesses). In an application with many orders of magnitude more fetches versus adds, and if an occasional delay of a millisecond or so is tolerable, then simply reallocating the table index may be the most efficient approach to expanding it.

Thread-Safe and Multithreading Hash Tables

One of the challenges with the Litwin algorithm as presented is that it is not thread-safe. Multithreading will be addressed in more detail in Chap. 7. If multiple threads are accessing the same table, the table can get into an inconsistent state. For example, if two threads use `Table_add_item` simultaneously, they may both create a bucket for index 5 and each will store that in the bucket index but only one will "win." The loser will add the item to its bucket only to have the bucket effectively overwritten by the second, winning thread (i.e., last thread to update wins).

A simple way of fixing this problem is to *lock* the table on each action. This means that only one thread can read or write items in the table at a time. This makes the table *thread-safe*. The table will remain consistent but multiple accesses at the same time will be serialized (i.e., will not run at the same time). If the access rate isn't too great, then a thread-safe implementation may be sufficient. For example, a non-thread-safe version of this algorithm requires about 100 ns per fetch from the table. Adding a lock with no contention adds about 25% to the run-time. However, if there are multiple threads contending for the lock, the delay can increase substantially.

Making the table multithreaded, where multiple actions can occur simultaneously is much more difficult. Allowing multiple fetches simultaneously is not too hard; allowing multiple insertions and fetches, especially with the possibility of the table needing to double during these actions, is where the difficulty lies.

One attempt to multithread the hash table is to reduce the scope of the lock from the table to the bucket. That would allow two buckets to be accessed (either fetching or adding an entry) at the same time since they could not interfere with one another. For example, splitting a bucket does not change the access of another bucket. Adding a lock to each bucket where disjoint buckets can be accessed simultaneously would allow concurrent reads and updates of disjoint buckets. Unfortunately, bucket locks of the table are insufficient. Doubling the table in the middle of an operation can create an insertion in the wrong place or an access not considering the correct split point. In fact, synchronizing the threads that are accessing the table and simultaneously doubling can be nearly as expensive as simply locking the whole table, especially since the individual fetch and add actions are so fast.

Another approach could be to allow one writer (and therefore one splitter or one doubling) and no readers, or no writer and multiple readers. This is a classic read/write lock. A read lock can be taken so that multiple readers can operate on the table but block writers, and similarly a write lock can be granted that blocks readers. How much parallelism is possible is tricky based on the arrival of reads and writes. Depending on the underlying policy of the read/write locks, writes can be postponed for a long duration while reads are serviced more quickly. Again, the performance gain may be outweighed by the overhead of managing the read/write lock, especially when the time spent accessing the item is measured in nanoseconds.

In general, simply locking the table and performing the action is usually "good enough." More complex mechanisms to allow greater parallelism often introduce enough overhead that the increased parallelism is outweighed by the overhead of the mechanism. We will discuss alternate mechanisms for handling parallelism for hash tables below.

We will have more discussions about multithreading in Chap. 7.

Exercises

1. Create a simple fixed hash table. It should have a fixed but configurable number of buckets with a fixed number of entries per bucket, and extra entries accommodated by overflow buckets. Let N be number of buckets x number of entries/bucket: the capacity of the table. Insert N, $10N$, and $100N$ entries into the table and display:
    a. The minimum, maximum, and average number of entries per bucket (consider an overflow as part of the bucket).
    b. The time to insert. Graph the time it takes to insert an item as a function of the number of items that have been inserted.

2. Build an extensible hash table with whatever starting size you wish. Let's assume your starting size accommodates N entries. Insert N, $10N$, and $100N$ entries and display:

   a. The minimum, maximum, and average number of entries per bucket (consider an overflow as part of the bucket).
   b. The time to insert. Graph the time it takes to insert an item as a function of the number of items that have been inserted.

3. Using the hash table from Exercise 2, record all the keys of the $100N$ entries inserted. Delete a random set of $50N$ of the keys. Then insert $50N$ new keys and display:

   a. The minimum, maximum, and average number of entries per bucket (consider an overflow as part of the bucket).
   b. The time to insert. Graph the time it takes to insert an item as a function of the number of items that have been inserted.

   Compare the utilization and times with those of Exercise 2.

4. Using the hash table from Exercise 1, insert N keys ($N > 2500$) using the Knuth's multiplicative hash. Record the minimum, maximum, and average number of entries per bucket (with overflows counting toward the original bucket) and total time required. Repeat with the MurmurHash, SHA256, and a constant hash (i.e., $F(x) = k$). Compare.

Chapter 2
Finite State Machines

One of the most common activities in programming is recognizing patterns. It might be as simple as recognizing commands for controlling a system, or, more abstractly, the actions of pressing keys on a keypad.

This chapter introduces finite state machines and explains how to use them for simple parsing of text and processing more complex states and transitions to enhance program reliability. This chapter will not delve into the formalism and theory of finite state machines also known as finite automata. (McNaughton (1982) presents this level of detail.)

Finite State Machines at 30,000 Feet

A finite state machine is characterized by a set of *states* connected by *transitions*. The transitions represent some action that influences the state. For example, here is a finite state machine diagram for a push button switch (Fig. 2.1).

The round circles are the finite state machine's states and the arcs are actions causing the state to change (the transitions). Arcs are tagged with the condition that causes the transition from one state to another. In this case, the button can be in either the on or off state; pushing the button transitions it to the opposite state.

A vending machine's operation can be modeled as a finite state machine. Imagine a vending machine that only accepts quarters, and all of its items cost 50 cents. There are nine choices of items indicated by nine buttons labeled 1–9. A finite state machine for this simple vending machine would be (Fig. 2.2):

Supplementary Information The online version contains supplementary material available at https://doi.org/10.1007/978-981-92-0260-7_2.

M. Kilian, *Ten Software Patterns Every Student Should Know*,
https://doi.org/10.1007/978-981-92-0260-7_2

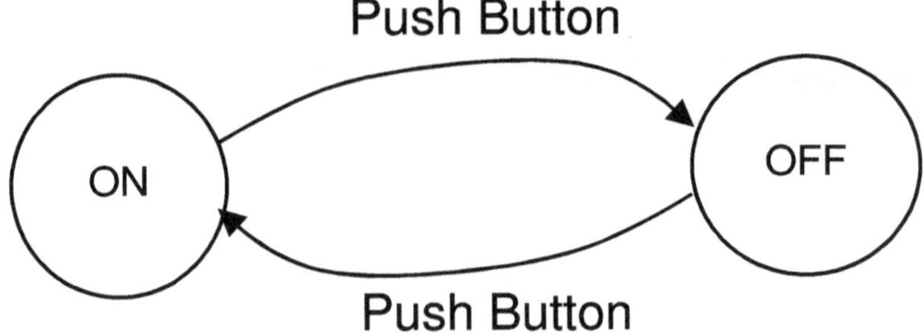

Fig. 2.1 Simple finite state machine

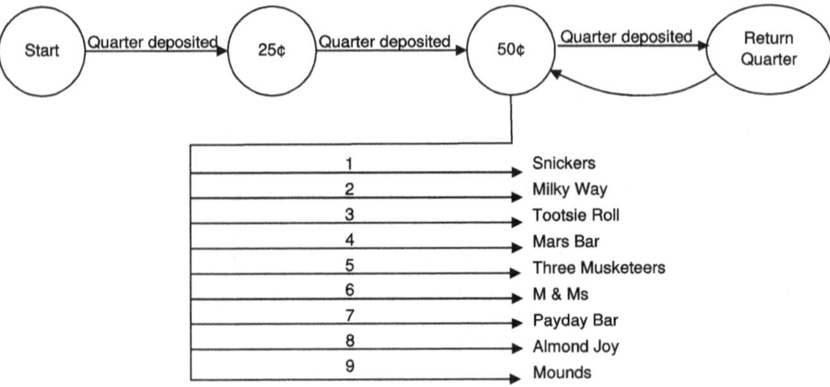

Fig. 2.2 A finite state machine for a simple candy machine

One of the most common uses of finite state machines is parsing text. Here is a simple example of a finite state machine that recognizes three words: *pat, paws, cat*. Note that *paw* is not matched (Fig. 2.3).

The empty circle is the beginning state. The double circles are final states (also called *accept* states). The symbol ε designates that the end of the input has been reached.

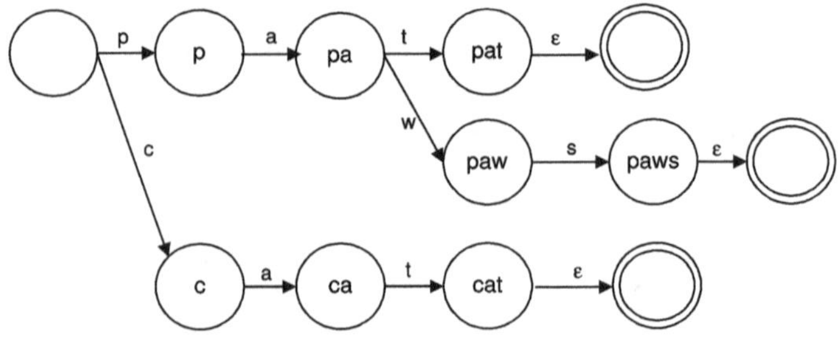

Fig. 2.3 Finite state machine that recognizes the keywords pat, paws, and cat

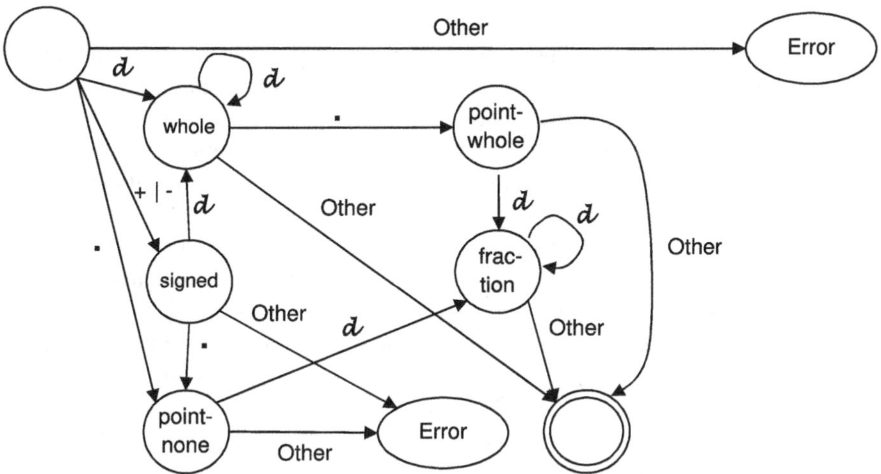

Fig. 2.4 Recognizing decimal numbers

"Walking" the graph means we start in the beginning state and take each subsequent letter in the word being matched and choose the arc labeled with that letter to the next state. The word `paws` would transition from the start state to **p** state, **pa** state, **paw** state, **paws** state and since we are at the end of the word, we would accept the word. The accept state could do whatever processing is necessary since it knows the word is `paws`. This might be returning an identifier (e.g., a small integer) designating `paws` as a special keyword.

Implicit in this transition graph is that if a letter is encountered that doesn't match an arc in the current state, then an error has occurred. In some cases, making error transitions explicit is required and the error state can take some action. One of the advantages of the finite state machine is that it is possible to make recommendations if a word fails. For example, if the word `car` were being processed, you would arrive at the **ca** state but not have an arc labeled **r**. The system might even be smart enough to produce an error message: "You typed `car`; did you mean `cat`?" It could even be smart enough to recognize that `t` is next to `r`, but if the word `cam` is being scanned, it might simply report "`cam` is not recognized" since `m` is far from `t` on the keyboard.

Here is a bit more complex example. It recognizes a number including integer and decimal numbers, signed or unsigned (Fig. 2.4).

In this case, `d` designates a digit (0–9). Consider the string "+123.45." The *starting state* is in the upper left corner (an empty circle). The "+" moves to state *signed*. The "1" causes a transition to state *whole* and remains there for "2" and "3." The "." transitions to state point-whole indicating the decimal point occurs after the whole part of the number. The "4" transitions to *fraction* and the "5" remains in this state. The "Other" transition matches any character that is not explicitly handled by the state. The end of the string matches "Other" and so transitions to the *accept state*.

The *point-none* state recognizes a decimal number with no whole part. This state requires a digit to follow it. This is different than the *point-whole* state that allows nothing to follow the decimal point since once the whole part is found, a fractional part after the decimal point is optional. Two states are required to parse decimal numbers to prevent a single decimal point from being recognized as a number: *point-whole* only recognizes a decimal point if digits precede it, and *point-none* only recognizes a decimal point if digits follow it.

Also, the character moving us to the accept state should be "pushed back" to be available for a subsequent analysis. For example, the finite state machine will parse the string "123..45" into 123. and end at the second decimal point. This decimal point should not be consumed; instead it needs to be the starting point for a subsequent run of the finite state machine. The result is that two numbers are recognized on consecutive runs of the machine: 123. and.45.[1] Similarly, the string "123.." would return 123. on the first run, but the second run would not be accepted since the second decimal point would be flagged as a solitary decimal point in the *point-none* to Error transition.

Simply recognizing a legal number (and we have not included exponentials, i.e., E notation) is a non-trivial state machine. It is a useful example if for no other reason to appreciate the need for error cases and the care required for completeness (like disallowing a single decimal point).

Implementing a Finite State Machine

There are many ways of implementing a finite state machine. If you need to identify more complex patterns (e.g., tokens in the C++ programming language), it is likely that a tool such as *flex* or its predecessor *lex* would be the appropriate tool. For example, the diagram for numbers would be recognized by simply specifying a pattern such as:

`("+"|"-")?{DIGIT}+`	signed whole numbers
`("+"|"-")?{DIGIT}*"."{DIGIT}+`	optional whole part, non-optional fraction
`("+"|"-")?{DIGIT}+"."{DIGIT}*`	non-optional whole part, optional fraction

You may be tempted to combine the second and third lines to become:

```
("+"|"-")?{DIGIT}*"."{DIGIT}*
```

Unfortunately, this would allow a single decimal point without any digits to be a legal number.

A particularly straightforward way to create a finite state machine to recognize strings is to use a *transition array*. There are as many columns as inputs to the graph

[1] It would also be possible to flag this as an error by explicitly detecting two decimal points as an error, i.e., point-whole and point-none could add a transition to error when detecting a '.'.

(e.g., recognizing numbers requires 10 digits, +, −, and decimal point "."). Each row is a state in the graph and the next state to go to is given by the cell at the intersection of the current state and the input designating the column). The Push Button is quite simple:

	Button	Push button
0	ON	1
1	OFF	0

The first row says that at state 0 our Button is ON and if we receive a Push Button event, then we will transition to state 1, where our Button is OFF. If the button is pushed again (a Push Button event) we return to state 0 and the Button is ON. The Button column is the label on the node, and the Push Button is the transition allowed from that node.

As you can imagine, the transition array for recognizing numbers is a little more complex.

	State	±	Digit	.	Non-digit or ε
0	Start	1	2	3	7
1	Signed	7	2	3	7
2	Whole	6	2	4	6
3	Point-none	7	5	7	7
4	Point-whole	6	5	6	6
5	Fraction	6	5	6	6
6	Accept	Character resulting in this transition is not part of the number			
7	Error	Character causing transition is bad			

Rows 0–5 are the parsing of the number. Row 6 indicates that a valid number has been parsed and that the character causing this transition should not be consumed from the input and is available for a subsequent parse. Similarly, Row 7 indicates an character now allowed in a number has been detected and the character causing the transition to this state is illegal.

Let's parse the number "+1.23". From state 0 (Start) we see that the value for the "+" column in this row is 1, so we move to state 1 (Signed). From state 1, the digit "1" moves us to state 2 (Whole). From state 2, the "." moves us to state 4 (Point-whole). The digit "2" moves us to state 5 (Fraction). We stay in state 5 with the digit "3" and finally the end of the string (ε) moves us to state 6 (Accept) and we know that +1.23 is a legitimate number.

Here is one way of representing the finite state machine for recognizing numbers and a simple function that simply returns true if the text submitted is a number or false if not.

```
1 enum Token {
2   TNUMBER = 1,
3   TERROR,
4 };
5
6 enum Character_class {
7   plus_or_minus,
8   digit,
9   point,
10    other
11  };
12
13  int Transition_table[5][4] = {
14  /* ± digit point other */
15  /* 0 start */ { 1, 2, 3, -TERROR},
16  /* 1 signed*/ { -TERROR, 2, 3, -TERROR},
17  /* 2 whole */ { -TNUMBER, 2, 4, -TNUMBER},
18  /* 3 point-none */ { -TERROR, 5, -TERROR, -TERROR},
19  /* 4 point-whole */ { -TNUMBER, 5, -TNUMBER, -TNUMBER},
20  /* 5 frac */ { -TNUMBER, 5, -TNUMBER, -TNUMBER}
21  };
22
23  enum Token Validate_number(struct Lexer *lexer, char *number)
{
24
25  int state_cursor = 0;
26  int text_cursor = 0;
27  do {
28    int c = number[text_cursor + + ];
29    enum Character_class c_class = get_character_class(c);
30
31    int transition = Transition_table[state_cursor][c_class];
32    if (transition > = 0) {
33      state_cursor = transition;
34      continue;
35    }
36    enum Token token = - transition;
37    return token;
38   } while (true);
39  }
```

Lines 1–4 This finite state machine identifies a number or an error and returns a token indicating that. Normally other things happen in processing the input (like converting the textual string to an internal floating point) but that will be left as an exercise to the reader.

Lines 6–11 Characters in the string being processed are classified as one of these classes.

Lines 13–21 This is the array representation of the chart above. Final tokens are negative with their token value being the absolute value of the item in the table. The value -TNUMBER means that a final state has been reached and the token to be returned is TNUMBER. Likewise, -TERROR is a final state that returns TERROR, i.e., an error. There is no attempt at communicating the cause of the error in this code.

Line 23 Validate number takes a Lexer structure and a character string to be parsed as a number and returns the token corresponding to the string (TERROR if the string does not match). We don't use the Lexer structure here but in "real-life" context is usually needed when parsing out characters (such as the last cursor position in the text undergoing lexical analysis) and this is carried in the Lexer structure.

Lines 25–26 The state-cursor indicates what row of the matrix we are referencing. The text cursor is the index of the letter we are looking at in the number string.

Line 27 Loop until we reach a terminating state (lines 36 and 37).

Lines 28–35 Get the character class of the next character to process in the number string. Character classes index the columns of the table. Find out what the next state is (the transition) from the transition table. For example, if we are in state 0 (the starting state) and the next character class is point (2) (meaning we have seen the decimal point), Transition_table[0][2] = state 3 (point-none) indicating that we have seen a decimal point with no whole number before it. If the next character is a number (character class digit = 1), then we transition to state 5 (frac).

Lines 36–37 We've reached a final transition. Return the token (which might be an error token).

`Validate_number` reads characters from the provided string, characterizes them as digits, points, non-digits, etc. and uses the character class to transition through the state transition table. The starting state is row 0. If the character class is digit, then the next row is 2 since Transition_table[0][digit] is 2. If the next state (given by `transition`) is negative, then the scan is complete and the token is the absolute value of the next state. The main program is simply:

```
struct Lexer *lexer = make_Lexer();
if (validate_number(lexer, number) != TERROR)
  printf("VALID NUMBER\n");
else
  printf("INVALID NUMBER\n");
```

Classifying the characters (as we did for Digit and non-Digit) is optional. We could simply have 128 columns (1 per ASCII character) and replicate the state transitions for each character. For example, in the Start row, we would have columns for "0," …, "9," and each would have the next state as 2. This allows the classification of the character and the determining the transition to be done in one step saving time at the expense of a much larger array. Using an expanded array instead of character classes is one of the fastest implementations of a finite state machine. This is not so convenient for character sets that don't fit conveniently in 7 bits!

One alternative to building a transition array is to literally create structures for nodes and arcs. Here is an example for the number finite state machine above.

```
struct Arc {
 struct Node *destination;
 enum Character_class transition;
};

enum Node_enum { normal_type, accept_type, error_type};

struct Node {
 struct Arc **arcs;
 struct Arc *other_arc;
 int num_arcs;
 int id_number;
 char *id_name;
 enum Node_enum node_type;
};

struct Node *run_machine(struct Node *initial_state, char *number) {
 int index = 0;
 struct Node *current_node = initial_state;
 while (current_node- > node_type = = normal_type) {
   char current_char = number[index + + ];
   enum Character_class current_class =
     get_character_class(current_char);
   bool found_it = false;
   for (int i = 0; i < current_node- > num_arcs; i + + ) {
     struct Arc *arc = current_node- > arcs[i];
     if (arc- > transition = = current_class) {
       current_node = arc- > destination;
       found_it = true;
       break;
     }
   }
   if (!found_it) {
     struct Arc *arc = current_node- > other_arc;
     if (arc ! = NULL) {
       current_node = arc- > destination;
     }
     else {
        return NULL;
     }
   }
 }
 return current_node;
}

struct Node *initialize_fsm() {

 struct Node *start_node = make_Node("start", 1, normal_type);
 struct Node *signed_node = make_Node(" ± ", 2, normal_type);
 struct Node *whole_node = make_Node("whole", 3, normal_type);
 struct Node *point_none_node =
 make_Node(".", 4, normal_type);
 struct Node *point_whole_node =
```

```
54  make_Node(".", 5, normal_type);
55  struct Node *fraction_node =
56  make_Node("fraction", 6, normal_type);
57  struct Node *accept_node =
58  make_Node("accept", 7, accept_type);
59  struct Node *error_node =
60  make_Node("error", 8, error_type);
61
62  add_Arc(start_node, make_Arc(point, point_none_node));
63  add_Arc(start_node, make_Arc(plus_or_minus, signed_node));
64  add_Arc(start_node, make_Arc(digit, whole_node));
65  start_node- > other_arc = make_Arc(other, error_node);
66
67  add_Arc(signed_node, make_Arc(digit, whole_node));
68  add_Arc(signed_node, make_Arc(point, point_none_node));
69  signed_node- > other_arc = make_Arc(other, error_node);
70
71  add_Arc(whole_node, make_Arc(digit, whole_node));
72  add_Arc(whole_node, make_Arc(point, point_whole_node));
73  whole_node- > other_arc = make_Arc(other, accept_node);
74
75  add_Arc(point_none_node, make_Arc(digit, fraction_node));
76  point_none_node- > other_arc = make_Arc(other, error_node);
77
78  add_Arc(point_whole_node, make_Arc(digit, fraction_node));
79  point_whole_node- > other_arc = make_Arc(other, accept_node);
80
81  add_Arc(fraction_node, make_Arc(digit, fraction_node));
82  fraction_node- > other_arc = make_Arc(other, accept_node);
83
84  return start_node;
85 }
```

Lines 1–4	An arc connects to a node and is triggered by a specific character class. A more sophisticated approach would allow multiple character classes to trigger the transition across this arc.
Line 6	Most nodes are "normal." Accept nodes and error nodes are also possible.
Lines 8–15	A node has outgoing arcs (lines 9 and 11) and if none of these arcs match the current character class being considered, then there is an optional "other arc" which is a catch all.
Lines 12, 13	The node has an identifier and label. This is actually unnecessary to execute the finite state machine but is very helpful for displaying information about the graph when debugging.
Line 14	Each node has a type: normal, accept, or error. Walking the finite state machine stops when reaching an accept or error node.
Line 17	This function runs the finite state machine to recognize a number given in the string `number`. The node the machine ends at is returned.
Line 18	`Index` will march through the number string.

Lines 21–23 Get the character being indexed in the number string and characterize it.

Lines 25–31 Go through the arcs of the current node, If the arc's transition class matches the current class then set the current node to the destination of the arc.

Lines 33–41 If an arc could not be found in the current node with a matching transition, then check for an "other arc" which is used if no other arc matches.

Line 43 It must be the case that we exit the loop eventually (as long as the graph is well formed). Additional checks can be made to prevent from advancing past the end of the string in case a bad graph has been constructed.

Lines 48–82 Construct the finite state machine. The nodes and arcs in this example correspond to the finite state machine in Fig. 2.4.

With this in place, a number can be recognized as follows:

```
struct Node *the_fsm = initialize_fsm();
struct Node *result = run_machine (the_fsm, test_string);

if (result->node_type == accept) ... the number was matched...
```

A common application for finite state machines is to recognize keywords. This is also called a *trie* (Knuth, Volume 3, 1998). It is possible to dynamically add entries to the trie allowing it to function much like a hash table for lookups with the advantage that a character need only be accessed once. For example, in a hash lookup, the string being looked for must be hashed, which means accessing each character of the string. When the candidate hash entry is found, a string comparison must be done to validate the match, which is another pass over the string. The trie avoids the second scan over a string. Hashing also cannot figure out if a word is "like another" word (e.g., the word found was "look" but the closest match is "loop") since the hash of even nearly identical words can be completely different.

However, the overhead of arcs and nodes and the addition of more and more arcs from a given prefix (e.g., there could be hundreds of entries starting with the letter s) makes it difficult to maintain its efficiency, especially compared to a dynamic hash table. Similarly, maintaining a compact array representation for a growing set of keywords, while still efficient even for many keywords, is non-trivial.

In practice, nodes and arcs are rarely used for text scanners; some form of state transition array is the norm. The fact that half the number of lines of code and a much more compact array is used in the code for the array implementation is a good indication of the greater simplicity of the array model. Tools such as lex and flex are commonly used for creating finite state machines based on transition arrays.

Recursive Descent Parsing

Often the state machines in the previous section are used to break a stream of characters into logical chunks called *tokens*, e.g., a number, a keyword, a string, etc. This happens for any programming language processing such as an interpreter or a compiler. It is also used for simple languages (like configuration languages) or data description languages (e.g., XML). The creation of tokens from characters is called *lexical analysis* and the finite state machine that performs that operation is called a *lexer*.

Tokens are then fed to a *parser*. A parser recognizes tokens according to a *grammar*. There are many variations of grammars and the rules for building a correct grammar depend on the parsing technology in use. Parsing rules generally appear like the following:

```
add_operation → number '+' number
```

An add operation consists of a number followed by a plus sign followed by a number. This is similar to *Backus-Naur* notation (Aho et al. 1978).

A good overview of parsing techniques can be found in Aho et al. (1978), which describes different parsing algorithms such as LR, LALR, and LL. For this section we are only going to consider LL(1) parsing and its implementation as recursive functions. The first L in LL(1) means that the tokens from the lexer are consumed as they are produced (the text is effectively read from left to right). The second L means that we match grammar rules left-most first. For example, when matching 1 + 2 + 3, 1 + 2 will be matched then + 3. This will not be discussed further. The (1) of LL(1) designates that only a single token is required to determine which grammar rule should be followed in the parse. This sometimes forces the grammar to look strange. For example, our simple grammar rule:

```
add_operation → number '+' number
```

would not be allowed since we cannot tell from the token "number" that an add operation will occur. Instead this will be typically written as:

```
math_operation_lhs   →   number math_operation_rhs
math_operation_rhs   →   '+' number
                     →   '-' number
```

In this formulation, we receive a number. Then we see either a + or − and know that we have a math operation. Each grammar rule is determined by the token we are currently looking at.

The following discussion of creating an LL(1) grammar will be cursory; a more complete discussion can be found in Lewis et al. (1976).

Here is an example of an LL(1) grammar for a simple scripting language that allows:

- variable assignment,
- arithmetic addition and subtraction,
- run a command,
- functions to be defined,
- calling a function,
- a trivial looping mechanism is also allowed where you can say loop 10 times.

For example, to execute the command "cat some.txt" (the Unix cat command which lists the contents of file some.txt) ten times would be:

```
loop 10
  cat some.txt
done
```

Here is a simplified LL(1) grammar for this simple scripting language. Tokens will be represented as uppercase words (e.g., LOOP is the token for the keyword "loop"), an italicized uppercase word for a non-keyword token (such as an identifier or number), or a literal symbol (such as an equal sign). Optional constructs (i.e., tokens that may or may not be present in the rule) are shown in square braces. The *STRING* token is a double-quoted string. A *PATH* is any legal file path for the operating system we are running on and is used to invoke a script. An *IDENTIFIER* is a variable identifier in the usual sense (starts with a letter followed by letter or number and isn't a keyword). The *rules* making up the grammar are as follows:

```
function        →  FUNCTION IDENTIFIER ( [ id-list])
                   statement-list
                   END
statement       →  LOOP expression statement-list DONE
                →  CALL IDENTIFIER ( [ expr-list])
                →  PATH [ expr-list]
                →  LET IDENTIFIER = expression
expression      →  term [ expr-tail]
expr-tail       →  + term [ expr-tail]
                →  − term [ expr-tail]
term            →  IDENTIFIER
                →  NUMBER
                →  ( expression)
                →  STRING
                →  PATH
expr-list       →  expression [, expr-list]
id-list         →  IDENTIFIER [, id-list]
statement-list  →  statement [; statement]
function-list   →  function [ function]
script          →  [ function-list] [statement-list] EOF
```

Each rule can be determined by looking at one token. We know that we are defining a function when we encounter the FUNCTION token. A loop statement always begins with LOOP. A term starts with *IDENTIFIER*, *NUMBER*, '(', *STRING*, or *PATH*. These tokens are called the *select set* of the rule. There are also a number of references to optional rules enclosed by square brackets (for example, the expr-list after the *PATH* token). To determine whether the optional rule exists, we consider the tokens that can follow the rule it is part of. This is called the *follow set*. The follow set of expr-list in the *PATH* statement, for example, is the follow-set of a statement: ';', END, DONE, and *EOF*. We will show how the select sets and follow sets are used to guide the parsing.

The grammar is another way of representing a finite state machine, and is particularly simple in the case of a LL(1) grammar. A function definition can be graphed as shown in Fig. 2.5.

A recursive descent parser for these rules is built by implementing a function for each of the rules. Here is the function for `statement`:

```
bool statement() {
  struct Token token = get_next_token();

  switch (token) {
  case LOOP: loop_statement(); break;
  case CALL: call_statement(); break;
  case PATH: path_statement(); break;
  case LET: let_statement(); break;
  default:
     ERROR - expected LOOP, CALL, PATH, or LET and
   found token instead.
    return false;
```

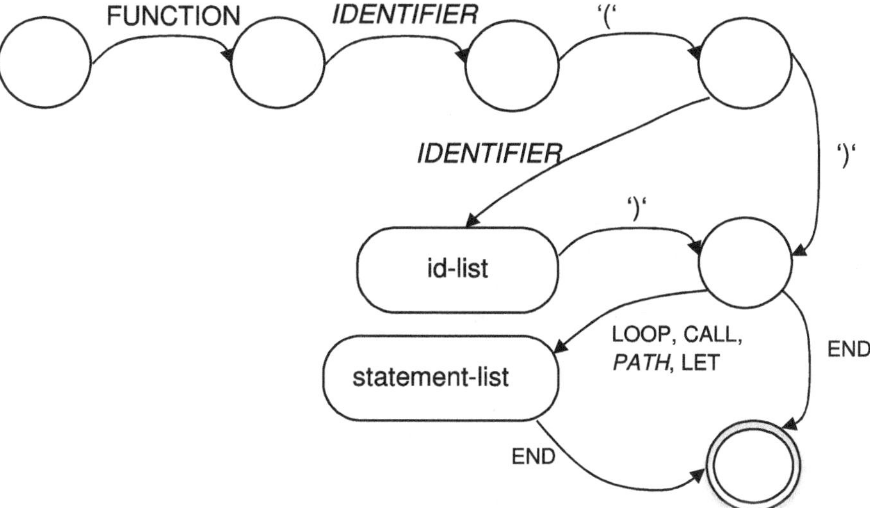

Fig. 2.5 Finite machine representation of the grammar given earlier

```
13   }
14   return true;
15 }
16
17 bool loop_statement() {
18    expression();
19    statement_list();
20
21    struct Token token = get_next_token();
22   if (token ! = DONE) {
23       ERROR - expected DONE but found token instead.
24       return false;
25   }
26   return true;
27 }
28
29 bool statement_list() {
30 do {
31    statement();
32    struct Token token = get_next_token();
33    if (token ! = SEMICOLON) {
34      push_back_token(token);
35      return true;
36    }
37   while (true);
38 }
```

Line 2 — A statement always grabs a token. This sometimes necessitates "pushing back" a token from a previous function (see line 34).

Lines 4–13 — Use the token to decide which statement we are processing. If the token isn't in the list of cases, it is an illegal token and an appropriate error message can be issued.

Lines 17–27 — A typical statement function. The LOOP keyword was already processed (that's how we got to this function), and we now process the expression following the LOOP keyword, and then the list of statements to be looped over. The statement list should end with the keyword DONE.

Lines 29–38 — A typical list of items. A statement is parsed. If the token after the statement is a semicolon, we expect another statement and continue the loop. Otherwise, the statement list is over and we push back the terminating token (for example, the keyword DONE) and return.

This style of parsing is called recursive descent because rules can be expressed in terms of themselves. The `statement` function calls the `loop_statement` function which calls the `statement_list` function which then calls the `statement` function again. Since each function typically consumes a token, the recursion must end with either a completed parse or an error when the tokens are used up.

Occasionally it is convenient to push a token back and re-read it. For example, a statement-list is a semicolon separated list of statements. If we don't find a semicolon at the end of a statement we assume it is the end of the `statement-list` and push that token back for the enclosing rule to process. This allows better error messages as well. If a `loop-statement` finishes processing a `statement-list` and doesn't see a DONE token following it, the `loop-statement` can report that "A Loop statement must be terminated by DONE and <insert erroneous token> was found instead."

Only one token ever needs to be pushed back and in fact with due care this slight inefficiency can be eliminated as well. For example, in the `loop_statement`, instead of `get_next_token`, we know that the LOOP token must have been processed to determine that the `loop-statement` function should be called. Care must be taken that all enclosing rules have the same expectation of where the lexer leaves off in the inner rules. While less efficient, it can be simpler to assume that we always grab a token at the beginning of major rules (e.g., expression, statement) and leave the rule with the lexer pointing to the last token of the rule (instead of the one token we may have had to "look ahead"). The inefficiency is that we may be getting a token and pushing it back several times as the recursive rules unwind themselves.

Note also in the example above that a do-loop is used for the body of a `statement-list` instead of recursively calling `statement-list`. A more strict grammar for statement list would be:

```
statement-list   →   Statement; statement-list
                 →   <empty>
```

This differs slightly from the "short-hand" notation in that it allows a statement list to be empty whereas the grammar with an optional repeating list requires at least one statement (though that can easily be remedied and should be).

In general, a rule that includes a `list [, ` *`other-rules`* *...]* can be implemented as a loop that repeatedly invokes the *other-rules* functions until the end of the list is found. In the `statement-list` function above, the `statement` function is repeatedly called until a semicolon is not found. At that point we assume that the next token belongs to the enclosing rule (for example the DONE keyword of a LOOP statement), push the token back and let the `loop-statement` function finish processing with that token.

For example, here is how a simple program would be parsed as shown in Fig. 2.6.

When parsing text, it is frequently necessary to carry extra information about the parse along. For example, we might want to "remember" the function identifiers and variable names introduced by the script we are parsing. A straightforward approach to this is to add a parameter to the functions implementing the rules that represents the state of the parser. For example, we could have a Parser struct that defines a pair of tables and accessors for them:

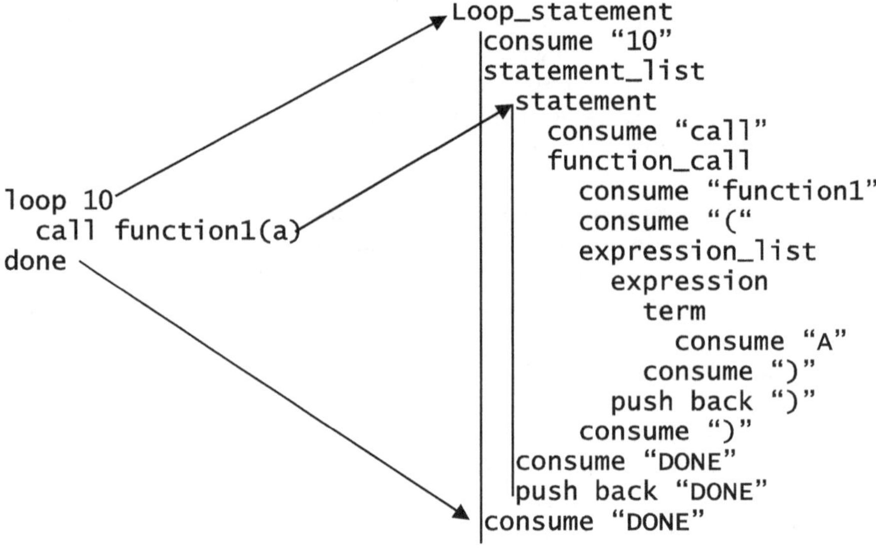

Fig. 2.6 Mapping text to recursive descent parse

```
struct Parser {
  struct Table *function_identifiers;
  struct Table *variable_identifers;
}
void Parser_add_function(struct Parser *parser,
              char *function_id) …
struct Function *Parser_get_function(struct Parser *parser,
                     char *function_id) …
…
```

And then in the rule function:

```
bool function(struct Parser *parser) {
    …
    struct Token function_id = get_next_token(parser);
    struct Function *prev_function =
             Parser_get_function(parser, function_id);
    if (prev_function != NULL) {
       ERROR… Redefining a previously declared function…
    }
    Parser_add_function(parser, function_id);
}
```

By including state capturing parsed text, parsing and execution can be combined as well. This is not as common; it is usually better practice to generate an intermediate representation (sometimes called *P-code*) that can be quickly executed, particularly when there are functions and loops involved. However, as an example, here is a simple calculator grammar that allows numbers to be added, subtracted, multiplied, and divided with proper precedence. The grammar is similar to the grammar above but includes an extra level to handle the precedence of multiplication and division over addition and subtraction.

expression$_z$ → term$_x$[expr-tail$_{x,y}$]
z = x if expr-tail is not used
z = y if expr-tail is used,
expr-tail$_{x,z}$ → + term$_y$[expr-tail$_{x+y,w}$]
z = x + y if expr-tail is not used
z = w if expr-tail is used
→ −term$_y$[expr-tail$_{x-y,w}$]
z = x-y if expr-tail is not used
z = w if expr-tail is used
term$_z$ → factor$_x$[term-tail$_{x,y}$]
z = x if term-tail is not used
z = y if term-tail is used
term-tail$_{x,z}$ → * factor$_y$[term-tail$_{x*y,w}$]
z = x*y if term-tail is not used
z = w if term-tail is used
→ / factor$_y$[term-tail$_{x/y,w}$]
z = x/y if term-tail is not used
z = w if term-tail is used
factor$_z$ → NUMBER
z = value of NUMBER
→ (expression$_x$)
z = x

The subscripts represent *attributes* that are passed down the parse tree as the rules are executed. For example, in `expr-tail`, two attributes are passed in: `x` and `z`. X is called an *inherited* attribute. It receives a value from an enclosing rule (i.e., `expression`). It is logical to think of this as an *IN* parameter to the rule. `Z` is called a *synthesized* attribute. It will be calculated by the rule and used in enclosing rules (i.e., `expression`). This can be thought of as an *OUT* parameter. In the case of `expression`, the value of `x` is synthesized in term, and then inherited by `expr-tail` which then synthesizes `y`. `Z` will be synthesized according to whether the optional `expr-tail` is present or not.

This allows syntax driven evaluation of expressions: as the expression is parsed, its value is calculated.

One code representation is:

```
1 struct Token {
2   enum Token_enum id;
3   double value;
4 };
5
6 void expression(struct Parser *parser, double *z) {
7   double x,y;
8   term(parser, &x);
9   expr_tail(parser, x, &y);
10  *z = y;
11 }
12
13 void term(struct Parser *parser. double *z) {
14   double x, y;
15   factor(parser, &x);
16   term_tail(parser, x, &y);
17   *z = y;
18 }
19
20 void expr_tail(struct Parser *parser, double x, double *z) {
21  struct Token plus_minus_token = get_next_token(parser);
22  switch (plus_minus_token.id) {
23  case TOKEN_PLUS:
24  case TOKEN_MINUS:
25    double y;
26    double t;
27    term(parser, &y);
28    if (plus_minus_token.id == TOKEN_PLUS) {
29      t = x + y
30    }
31    else {
32      t = x - y;
33    }
34    expression_tail(parser, t, z);
35    break;
36  default:
37    push_back_token(parser, plus_minus_token);
38    *z = x;
39    break;
40  }
41 }
42 …
43 double answer;
44 struct Parser *parser = make_Parse(expression_string);
45 expression(parser, &answer);
46 printf("The expression evaluates to %f\n", answer);
```

Lines 1–4 A token is created as part of the parsing. The parser object will be initialized with the text to parse and will produce tokens used by the recursive descent parsing.

Lines 6–11 As shown in the grammar, an expression is a factor followed by a term-tail. Synthesized attributes are represented by pointers in the function arguments (in this case, `double *z` for term, and the `&x` and `&y` for factor and `term_tail`.

Lines 21–35 Fetch the next token, and if it is '+' or '−' then process the expression, calculating either the sum or difference, setting the synthesized attribute to the result.

Lines 36–39 In this case, the expected token is not found so this rule does not apply and is empty. Return the token for an enclosing parse, and set the synthesized value to the inherited value passed in the parameter list.

The code for `term_tail` (which handles * and /) and `factor` are similar and straightforward (see Lewis et al. (1976) for complete examples). Note that there is no need to keep a stack of operands; the stack frames generated by the recursion combined with the grammar is all that is necessary to execute the arithmetic operations.

This model of execution also explains the use of expression, term, and factor in the grammar rules: these capture operator precedence as part of the parse. If we had * and / in the expr_tail rule, then calculations would be strictly left to right without regard to operator precedence. The additional level of parsing rules ensure that higher precedence expressions are parsed before completing the parse of the lower precedence expressions. This parsing structure can be generalized for other levels of precedence:

```
expression    →   prec-1 [ expr-tail]
expr-tail     →   + prec-1 [ expr-tail]
              →   - prec-1 [ expr-tail]
prec-1        →   prec2 [ prec-1-tail]
prec-1-tail   →   * prec-2 [ prec-1-tail]
              →   / prec-2 [ prec-1-tail]
prec-2        →   factor [ prec-2-tail]
prec-2-tail   →   ^ factor [ prec-2-tail]
factor        →   NUMBER
              →   ( expression)
```

Each prec-# rule is of a higher precedence, so that ^ has higher precedence than * or / which has higher precedence than + or −. The parse tree for the expression 1 + 2 * 3 − 4^5/6 is (the tokens consumed are in parentheses) (Fig. 2.7).

If we walk the parse tree left to right, depth first, we will calculate the answer with the right precedence, i.e., (1 + (2 * 3)) − ((4^5)/6). That walk is identical to the call chains when executing the implementation above.

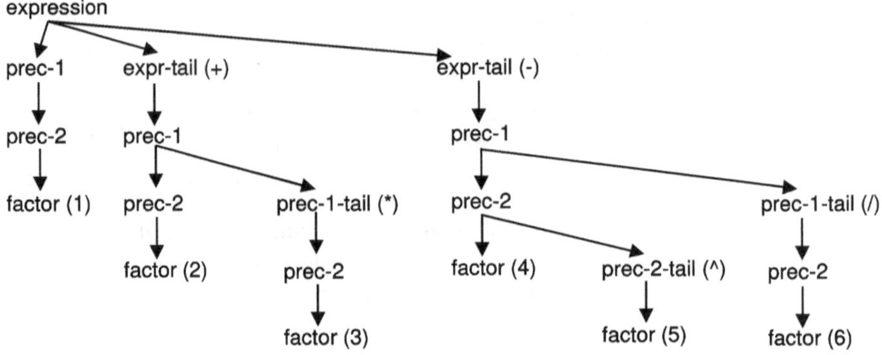

Fig. 2.7 Parsing arithmetic expressions with precedence

Keyword Processing

A keyword finite state machine such as the pat, paws, cat machine described at the beginning of this chapter is rather trivial and frankly a hash table is nearly as fast and simpler for keyword recognition. The advantage of the finite state machine in this case is that it can recognize keywords in the input without a separate stage to delimit a potential keyword (i.e., recognizing that the string "loop" in the text is a candidate keyword). For example, suppose we are parsing HTML response headers contained in a single buffer:

```
Accept-Ranges:     bytes
Content-Length:    17490
Content-Type:      image/gif
Date:              Fri, 29 Dec 2023 17:53:21 GMT
Etag:              "64e49ab3-4452"
Last-Modified:     Tue, 22 Aug 2023 11:23:31 GMT
Server:            nginx/1.18.0 (Ubuntu)
```

We want to recognize the keywords such as "Accept-Ranges" and "Etag." One way is to simply remember the start of a keyword (e.g., the position of 'A' in Accept-Ranges) and scan to the ':', and call lookup in our keyword hash table which will then walk the characters from "A" to "s" (in the case of Accept-Ranges) to generate the hash. Once the lookup arrives at the entry in the hash table, the characters are accessed again to compare with the key in the entry to check if the text and the keyword in the table match. That is three times the text in the buffer has been accessed. With the finite state machine, the 'A' starts the first transition and by the time the ":" is reached the keyword has been identified. The text in the buffer is only looked at once. And when complete, the cursor marking the scan in the buffer is at exactly the right place for further parsing. This use-case is one of the best examples of using a finite state machine for processing keywords.

A Word to the Wise

To be honest, using tools to generate a parser or lexer from a high level specification (including carrying state through the parse) is more common than hand generated code, especially for complex grammars. Bison (2021) is a tool for generating a parser (typically using LALR(1) (Aho et al. 1978) instead of LL(1)). A Bison specification, for example, is much more self-documenting and therefore more maintainable, since the text to express the input grammar is very close to the grammar formalism shown above. It also supports synthesized and inherited attributes.

Writing a lexer is also not conceptually very difficult. You may choose to build a transition matrix with a character classifier to help minimize the number of states in the lexer. Associating values to the tokens generated by the lexer (e.g., the floating point representation of a number, or the C-string representation of a quoted string), is added bookkeeping. But as with parsing, a tool such as Flex (Paxson et al. 2015) can generate a sophisticated lexer, including tokens and token values with an input specification based on regular expressions.

If using a lexer or parser generator is not the path taken, and a custom implementation is done, it is always the case that mistakes will be made. When implementing any lexer or parser, a tracing mechanism should be built into the system to show what tokens are created and how rules are being followed. An if-statement can test whether tracing is enabled. More discussion about creating this type of added infrastructure is in Chap. 10.

Program Organization

Finite state machines can represent fundamentally more complex states that simply processing grammar rules in a lexer or parser. Here is a diagram of a TCP network connection (Wright et al. 1995) (Fig. 2.8).

The only point we want to make with this diagram is that the states and transitions can be more complex than a string of characters and tokens. It also illustrates how something as seemingly simple as connecting two computers over a network can be very complex when all the states and transitions are mapped out (and only a subset of TCP is shown above!). The finite state machine aids us in:

1. Understanding the process.
2. Ensuring that all state transitions are handled.

While it is unlikely that an entire program will be represented as a state diagram, it is often useful to model core functions as a state diagram. This is especially true

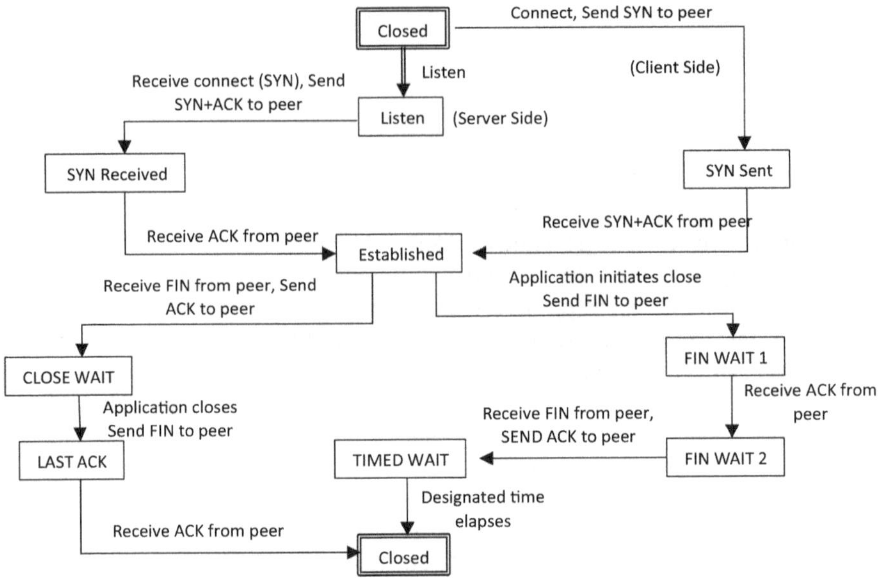

Fig. 2.8 Subset of the TCP protocol finite state machine

for real-time programs reacting to events occurring as a result of some set of inputs. Though the whole program might not be organized as a finite state machine, often a key component within the program can. This helps with the inevitable question of "Why is the program doing that?" while debugging. By having the state of key entities in the program explicitly represented and the transitions between states well defined, a program's behavior can be more precisely explained.

Exercises

1. Create a finite state machine that:
   a. Recognizes the words "cat," "catenary," "category," "dog," and "dogma" and rejects all others.
   b. Modify the finite state machine to include the words "dog", "dogma", and "dogmatic."
2. Write a program that:
   a. Given a list of words, automatically generates a finite state machine that recognizes those words and no others.
   b. Extend the program to allow words to be added dynamically, i.e., the initial machine is created, and later a word is added.

3. Implement a simple calculator using recursive descent parsing. Include operations for $+$, $-$, $*$, $/$, ^. Bonus: extend this to support unary negation. For example, $\mathrm{a} = \mathrm{b} + - \mathrm{c}$ would be allowed.

Chapter 3
Bloom Filters

The previous two chapters have involved fairly complex data structures and algorithms. This chapter will take a break from that and introduce a simple way to quickly determine if something is *not* in a set. This is most useful when finding an object in a system can be expensive, especially if the object is not there.

Consider a program where most of the data is stored on disk and accessed by unique ID. To resolve the ID to the object, one or more indices (also stored on disk) need to be interrogated. Let's assume there are three indices[1]:

1. The most recently accessed objects are found with an index in memory.
2. There are objects stored on disk locally and that index is stored on disk as well.
3. Objects are stored in some network repository that must be interrogated over the network to retrieve an object if not found in memory or disk.

Finding an object means traversing each of these indices (typically in order though that is not strictly required) until either the object is found or not. Finding the object, especially if it is in the first or second index, is relatively efficient. Not finding an object means that all the indices must be exhausted and that can be very expensive.

Looking for an object and not finding it is not that uncommon. Often a system will look up an object and create it if it is not found. This means all new objects will incur the full look-up expense.

Bloom filters provide a way of determining at least for a subset of objects whether an ID exists in the system. Adding an object in the system works as follows.

1. We start with no objects in the system. Create a bit vector V (i.e., a vector containing just 1 and 0 s) of some given size N (determined below) and initialize the vector to all 0 s.
2. For a given ID, calculate a hash H. From the hash, calculate an index into the vector with a simple modulo: $I = H \bmod N$.

[1] There are some key-value stores that have this structure. RocksDB (RocksDB, 2026) is an interesting example.

M. Kilian, *Ten Software Patterns Every Student Should Know*,
https://doi.org/10.1007/978-981-92-0260-7_3

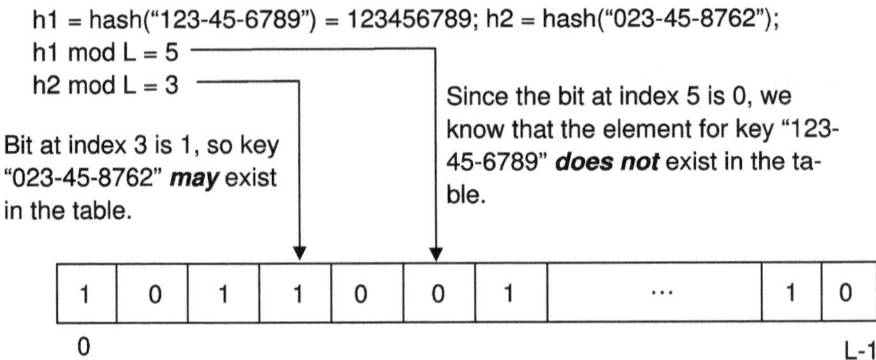

Fig. 3.1 Simple bloom filter

3. If *V[I]* is 0, then the object does not exist in the system. Proceed to add it to the system and set *V[I]* to 1.

Before accessing an object, *I* is again calculated and if *V[I]* is 0, the object cannot be present. Note the converse is not true. *V[I]* = *1* means that the object *might* be there. Multiple IDs can resolve to the same element in *V* even if they are different. Not only are hash collisions possible, but taking the hash value modulo the vector size increases the chance of collisions further. *V[i]* = *1* means we must go and verify that an object is really there.

The vector *V* is called a *Bloom filter* (Bloom 1970). In most cases it is implemented as a bit vector. Implementing a bit vector is pretty straightforward:

```
uint32_t bloom_filter[1024]
```

would be a bloom filter of 32 × 1024 = 32,768 bits.
Getting bit *i* is found by:

```
(bloom_filter[i/32] & (1 << (i % 32))) != 0
```

and setting bit *i* is performed with:

```
bloom_filter[i / 32] | (1 << (i % 32))
```

Here is an example of how a Bloom filter works (Fig. 3.1).

Improving Bloom Filter Accuracy

A Bloom filter is only effective if some of its elements are zero. The effectiveness of a Bloom filter is related to how many objects map to it. A 10-element Bloom filter is not terribly effective if 1,000,000 objects are mapped to it (it is almost certainly the case that all the bits of the Bloom filter will be set).

There are two variables that can be controlled in a Bloom filter to improve the accuracy of the result (reducing the rate of *false positives*): The size of the Bloom filter (i.e., the number of bits, *L* in the diagram above), and the number of independent hash functions used to probe the Bloom filter (a single hash function is used in the example above).

In the introduction, we calculated the index of a bit using a hash function over the key modulo the size of the table to generate a bit index. We can improve the probability of a correct answer if, instead of looking with one hash function, we use several (say *k*), independent hash functions. If the result of using any of the *k* functions results in a 0 element in the Bloom filter, then the result is 0. By using multiple hash functions we decrease the probability of false matches. For example, suppose H_1 hashes the identifier *I* to 10 and H_2 hashes *I* to 12. If the value at index 10 ***or*** 12 is 0, we know the item is not there. With a balance of the right size of vector and the right number of hash functions, the probability of a false positive is reduced.

The hash functions used must be *independent*. For example, if H_1 and H_2 both map odd identifiers to even hashes, the effectiveness of using two hashes is basically halved. Using a *seeded* hash function is an easy way to generate multiple, independent hash functions. A seeded hash function accepts a *seed* as part of its calculation. Multiple hash functions can be created by simply choosing multiple seeds. If *n* independent hash functions are required, generate *n* unique seeds, $s_1, s_2, \ldots, s_n$. $H(s_i, key)$ will generate a different hash (with acceptable probability) as $H(s_j, key)$ for $i \neq j$. The MurmurHash3 function is an example of such a seeded hash function.

There is a formula that can be used to size the Bloom filter (*m*) based on how many items we expect to put into the filter *(n)*, the number of hash functions (*k*), and the target probability of a false positive *(P)* (Bloom. 1970). The number of hash functions *k* for a given error rate is given by:

$$k = -\frac{\ln P}{\ln 2} \tag{3.1}$$

And the size is given by:

$$m = \frac{nk}{\ln 2} = -\frac{n \ln P}{(\ln 2)^2} \tag{3.2}$$

And *k* can be computed as:

$$k = \frac{m}{n} \ln 2 \tag{3.3}$$

These equations are estimates. Simply increasing the number of hash functions will eventually be self-defeating since it will effectively "use up" the bits in the Bloom filter. Note that Eq. 3.2 giving the size of the filter is based on *k* the number of functions.

To give some ideas about what this looks like, suppose we want to tolerate 1 in 5 random requests as a false positive (i.e., the Bloom filter reports the object being there, but it is actually not) for 10 million items (n = 10,000,000). P = 0.2. We are willing to hash twice (i.e., k is 2). The expected size of the Bloom filter according to Eq. 3.2 is (10,000,000 * ln 0.2) / (ln 2)^2 = 33.5 million entries with [(33,500,000/10,000,000) * ln 2] = two hash functions to meet this probability. That's around 4 megabytes of Bloom filter to avoid 80% unnecessary searches. In today's age of many gigabytes of memory this is not too bad a tradeoff. To get to 1 in 10 requires 5.7 megabytes with three hash functions. If you want to only use a single hash function, it requires nearly double the number of bits (11.3 megabytes). This is a classic space/time tradeoff. Less space requires more time both in the number of false positives and/or increased hashing.

Shortcomings of Bloom Filters

Bloom filters excel when the number of identifiers that will be hashed to the filter is bounded, and the identifier is not removed from the filter. Unfortunately, it is rare that the problem is this simple.

Deleting an Identifier

When an identifier is deleted (for example, an object in the database is removed) the bit representing that identifier cannot be automatically zeroed in the Bloom filter. The reason is that a single bit in a Bloom filter may represent multiple entries. Clearing a bit could inadvertently signal that multiple identifiers don't exist in the filter instead of only the identifier being deleted. Remember, Bloom filters guarantee that if a bit is zero, the identifier corresponding to the bit is not in the filter.

One approach to solving this problem is to replace the single bit in the Bloom filter with a count of identifiers that resolve to this bit. When an identifier is added to the filter, the count at the corresponding entry is incremented (and this is repeated for each hash function used). The entry is now counting how many identifiers are mapped to that entry in the Bloom filter. When an identifier is deleted, the count(s) corresponding to that identifier are likewise decremented.

What happens if more identifiers map to an entry than can be represented by the counter. For example, if we use 4-bit counters, then up to 15 identifiers may share that entry. If the size of the Bloom filter is given by Eq. 3.2 above then with high probability four bits (15 identifiers colliding on the same bit) should be sufficient. (Mitzenmacher 2006) shows that with recommended filter size and number of hash functions, the probability is on the order of 10^{-16} that an entry of four bits will overflow.

Note that this model assumes we aren't adding the same identifier over and over again which would defeat the counting. A basic approach is that if the count is already greater than 0, we search for the item in the corresponding table, and only if it is not there (and subsequently added) is the Bloom filter count incremented.

What happens if the improbable happens and 16 different identifiers collide on the same entry? One simple approach is that if an entry reaches a count of 15 (binary 1111) in our 4-bit counting, then it is permanently set. We cannot decrement the count and will expect to get more false positives for identifiers mapping to this entry. As long as the probability of overflow is rare (and 10^{-16} would indicate it is rare!) then this safety catch is sufficient.

Scalable Bloom Filters

The other problem with Bloom filters (either counted or not) is that if the number of identifiers mapped to the Bloom filter greatly exceeds the number that the filter was allocated for, then the number of false positives will make the filter ineffective. How can this be handled?

Unlike the extensible hash table, there is no simple way of dynamically adding "more bits" to a Bloom filter. We can't rehash the bits into a bigger vector. Instead, scalable Bloom filters are implemented as stacks of Bloom filters.

When a Bloom filter fills up, a new larger, Bloom filter is created that sits "on top" of the smaller Bloom filter. Entries are added to this filter. To check the filter, the layers are each interrogated. If a 1 is found, then the search is positive. If all layers return 0 for the hash(es), then the search is definitively negative. As with the regular Bloom filter, a bit is set when the object is actually added to the set. Incrementing and decrementing counts is similar: when adding an object we increment the count where it was found (or create a new count in the top-most layer). If a lower layer's count would reach its threshold, it is possible to create a count in the upper layer. Again, we expect this to be an exceedingly rare event so this optimization may not be worth the additional step.

When should a new layer be added? The simplest and often most effective approach is to keep track of how many elements are occupied in the top-most Bloom filter. When that exceeds some cutoff point (for example, 50%), then create a new layer. The cutoff point and the initial size of the first vector become the controls for how resistant to false positives the Bloom filter is. In one experiment, we insert 40,000 keys into a Bloom filter and then look for 20,000 keys that we know are not there. The question is: How often did we report that a key existed when it should not have (a false positive)? With an initial vector of 32,000 bits, and a threshold of 50% ones, the false positive rate was 0.25. If the initial vector is set to 64,000 that rate drops to 0.18. In both these cases, a single Bloom filter sufficed. If the initial vector is 32,000 vector but with a threshold of 40% the false positive rate drops to 0.16 at the expense of an extra layer of Bloom filter being created.

Counting ones is effective and fairly deterministic in performance and size. What is harder is to try to use it to automatically reach a given probability of false positive. We can use a different policy for expansion to achieve this.

The probability of a false positive in a Bloom filter of size m with k hashes and n entries inserted is given by (Almeida et al. 2007):

$$P = \left(1 - e^{-kn/m}\right)^{k} \tag{3.4}$$

We want to know how many items can be placed in the vector based on the vector size, probability, and number of hash functions. Solving for n in Eq. 3.3, we obtain:

$$n = \frac{-m \ln\left(1 - p^{1/k}\right)}{k} \tag{3.5}$$

If the initial vector is 100,000 bits long and we use 3 hash functions then the number of entries to be added to the vector and remain at around 0.3 probability of false positive is:

$$\frac{-100,000 \ln\left(1 - 0.3^{1/3}\right)}{3} = 36,898$$

Once we reach that number of entries in the vector, we need to layer a bigger vector on top of the current vector. Note that n is *not* the number of 1 s in the vector. It is the number of entries we've added to the vector even though the position calculated for the entry may already be set to 1.

It has also been observed if the overall false positive probability is to be kept across the scalable Bloom filter as a whole, then each successive layer should have a tighter probability factor so that the total probability is better bounded. See Almeida et al. (2007) for more discussion of this.

A threshold can now be calculated using Eq. 3.5 for a Bloom filter of size m with k hash functions and expected false positive probability P. When that threshold is reached, a new vector can be created. How much larger is dependent on the application. Doubling the vector size might be appropriate, at least to a limit. The key is to balance size of vector(s) with number of layers. Smaller growth during high insertion rates may lead to a very deep stack of Bloom filters. High growth may use too much memory.

Here is a sketch of a simple scalable Bloom filter that uses the probability of false positive as the metric for adding a layer.

```
struct Bloom_filter {
  uint32_t *filter;
  uint32_t size; // m in the documentation
  uint32_t population; // n in the documentation
  uint32_t saturation; // calculated from above.
};

uint32_t get_bf_bit(struct Bloom_filter *bf, uint32_t i) {
```

```
  return bf- > filter[i/32] & (1 < < (i%32));
}

void set_bf_bit(struct Bloom_filter *bf, uint32_t i) {
  bf- > filter[i/32] |= (1 < < (i%32));
}

bool is_saturated(struct Bloom_filter *bf) {
  return bf- > population > bf- > saturation;
}

uint32_t get_bit_from_hash(struct Bloom_filter *bf,
                                 uint32_t hash[]) {
  for (int i = 0; i < NUM_HASHES; i + + ) {
    uint32_t index = hash[i] % bf- > filter_size;
    if (get_bit(bf, index) = = 0) {
      return 0;
    }
  }
  return 1;
}

void set_bit_from_hash(struct Bloom_filter *bf,
                              uint32_t hash[]) {
  for (int i = 0; i < NUM_HASHES; i + + ) {
    set_bit(bf, hash[i] % bf- > filter_size;
  }
}

struct Scalable_Bloom_filter {
  struct Bloom_filter *bfa[32];
  uint32_t bfa_index
};

void Scalable_Bloom_filter_expand(
         struct Scalable_Bloom_filter *sbf){
  struct Bloom_filter *current = sbf- > bfa[sbf- > bfa_index + + ];
  uint32_t new_size = current- > filter_size * 2;
  sbf- > bfa[sbf- > bfa_index] = make_Bloom_Filter(new_size);
}

uint32_t get_sbf_bit(struct Scalable_Bloom_filter *sbf,
                          uint32_t hash[]) {
  for (int i = sbf- > bfa_index; i > = 0; i-) {
    uint32_t bit = get_bit_from_hash(sbf- > bfa[i], hash);
    if (bit ! = 0)
      return 1;
  }
  return 0;
}

void set_sbf_bit(struct Scalable_Bloom_filter *sbf,
                      uint32_t hash[]){
```

```
62      uint32_t bit = get_sbf_bit(sbf, hash);
63      struct Bloom_filter *bf = sbf- > bfa[sbf- > bfa_index];
64      bf- > population + + ;
65      if (bit = = 0) {
66        set_bit_from_hash(bf, hash, history);
67      }
68      if (is_saturated(bf)) {
69        Scalable_Bloom_filter_expand(sbf);
70      }
71    }
```

Lines 8–19 Single Bloom filter operations to retrieve a bit at a given index, set a bit, and determine if the filter is saturated.

Lines 20–35 Take an array of hashes and get or set the bits corresponding to those hashes. In the case of getting a bit, if any of the bits are 0, we know the item is not there. To set the bit, we simply set for all the hashes.

Lines 38–41 A scalable Bloom filter is a stack of Bloom filters. The lowest (smallest) Bloom filter is at index 0. The highest (largest) is at `bfa_index`. We search from `bfa_index` to 0 when retrieving a bit.

Lines 43–48 Expanding a scalable Bloom filter simply means putting a new filter that is larger than the previous one on top of the previous one. In this case, we double the previous size (Line 43).

Lines 50–58 Iterate over the stack of Bloom filters, starting with the most recent and see if the bit exists. If any of the filters return nonzero, then there is a match. If all of them return zero, then we definitely don't have the item. Note that this is the converse of the multihash lookup in Lines 21-35.

Lines 60–71 Set the bit in the highest Bloom filter in the stack if it is not there. Since this is not a counting Bloom filter we don't need to mark items that already exist in the filter since these will congest the filter more rapidly. Increase the population count, which will be used to determine if the Bloom filter is saturated (in which case we expand it with `Scalable_Bloom_filter_expand)`.

Summary

Bloom filters are extremely useful when looking for something and not finding it is very expensive. In many cases, a fixed size Bloom filter with a single hash function is "good enough." This is especially true when, instead of growing a set of objects in unbounded fashion, growth is managed by bounding the number of items in a set and creating a set of sets. Each set then has a well-behaved Bloom filter. More about this approach will be discussed when we address *sharding* in Chap. 7.

Exercises

1. Create a Bloom filter with 32,000 bits with a single hash function. Generate a set S of 5,000 unique integers that will be hashed and placed in the bloom filter. Generate a second set R of 5,000 unique integers such that $S \cap R = \emptyset$. Access all the items in set R in the Bloom filter and count how many false positives there are (i.e., the Bloom filter returns 1 for an element in R).

   Repeat with 10,000 and 15,000 integers. See if the false positive rate matches the expected when Eq. 3.2 is solved for P.
2. Create a Bloom filter with 32,000 bits with a configurable number of independent hash functions (a set of MurmurHash functions with different seeds will suffice).Generate a set S of 10,000 unique integers and hash and place them in the bloom filter with 1 hash function. As in Exercise 1, generate a set R of 10,000 integers such that $S \cap R = \emptyset$. Access the elements of R and count the false positives. Repeat with 2, 3, 4, and 5 hash functions and note the false positive rate. Plot the number of hash functions on the x axis and false positive rate on the y access and describe the shape of the curve.
3. Implement counted Bloom filters using 4 bits for the counter and 8,192 entries. Use one hash function to insert 40,000 unique random numbers, and then delete 20,000 of these. Now access the 20,000 numbers that remain and see how often the filter reports that a number does not exist in the filter.

Chapter 4
Network Programming

In this chapter, we introduce some basic patterns of network programming. This is an overview—see (Stevens, 2003) for a much more complete treatment. The goal of this chapter is to provide exposure to writing a program that can communicate reliably over a network. It will focus on a basic client–server model for network transactions though many others are possible. Chapter 5 will leverage this model to allow a single server to handle many simultaneous connections.

The Linux model of socket programming is used; the concepts are general enough that they can be applied to other APIs (e.g., Windows WINSOCK). Even if you have a system that hides much of the low-level mechanism discussed in this chapter, it is useful to understand the underpinnings of networking to make the best use of it.

What Is Network Programming?

These days, nearly every interaction with a computer isn't with just the computer you are sitting at. When you look at email or go to a website, or frankly, just log on to the computer, communications are almost certainly happening between one computer and another. Most of this communication is via TCP/IP: Transmission Control Protocol/Internet Protocol. Web sites in particular use Hypertext Transfer Protocol (HTTP) over TCP/IP.[1]

[1] There are now emerging HTTP protocols that use a different protocol: UDP. We will briefly discuss UDP later in this chapter.

M. Kilian, *Ten Software Patterns Every Student Should Know*,
https://doi.org/10.1007/978-981-92-0260-7_4

What is TCP/IP? The key characteristics of this protocol are:

- It is based on creating a reliable connection between two entities. Your web browser is *connected* to a web server.
- Information can flow in both directions. TCP/IP checks that the information is accurately received by the destination and will retransmit if data is damaged or missing.
- Once connected, the two ends of the connections act as peers. Either end can send data to the other, and both can send and receive data simultaneously.
- The connection will handle flow control. If one peer sends data faster than the other can receive it, the sender will be automatically throttled. The sender must be prepared to be told: Sorry, the connection could not accommodate your request!
- Because of this flow control, there are a host of ways to modify the underlying policy of the flow control when the default policy is not appropriate for the application.
- When the connection is no longer needed, it is explicitly closed by both peers.

The state diagram of a TCP/IP connection is shown in Fig. 2.8. Much of the complexity of this diagram is to ensure the robustness of a connection: Making sure that a bidirectional connection is established, ensuring that data is received properly, and that sent data doesn't overrun a receiver. A simplified picture of a TCP/IP session is (Fig. 4.1):

The section "Client Connecting to a Server" will outline the basics of establishing the connection, transferring data, and closing the connection.

The diagram model above is a convenient way of capturing exchanges between two (or more) computers that illustrates the transactions and the ordering of the transactions. It is really a shorthand for the finite state machine representing the state

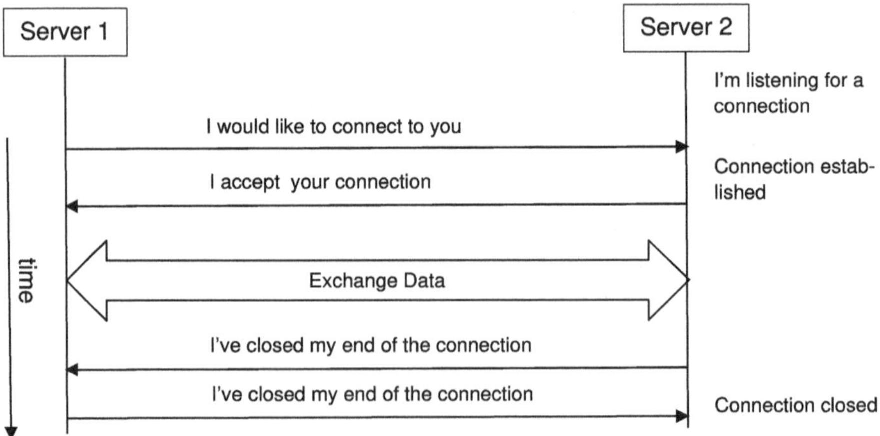

Fig. 4.1 *Basic client–servernetwork interaction*

of each computer (e.g., listening state, connection established state, receiving data) and the transitions (e.g., accepting connection).

A common structure is to have computer 1 be a *client* of computer 2 (referred to as a *server*). This is a classic *client–server* architecture where the client connects to a server, typically asks for some information, and the server responds. A server may be connected to many clients and clients may connect to multiple servers, but a common pattern is that a client sends a request, the server responds with an answer, and the process repeats until the connection is closed.

While client–server is very common, it is not the only way to organize programs interacting with one another over the network. Peer-to-peer where any connected program can initiate a request to any other participant is another architecture. We will only focus on client–server in this chapter.

Peeling back a layer, the data that flows across ethernet networks (the most prevalent kind of network in the world) is organized as *packets*. Packets typically carry up to 1500 bytes of data (the choice of 1500 seems to be an empirical decision made sometime in the dim past of ethernet).[2] Each packet includes information on where it should go, where it is coming from, and a checksum[3] that ensures that the packet hasn't been corrupted. This is the Internet Protocol layer [it is in the *Network Layer* in the OSI Network layer model[4] (Stevens, 2003)]. TCP/IP adds more metadata including information about the ordering of packets (since packets can be received out of the order they are sent; TCP sorts the packets on receipt), and data around creating a connection, and acknowledging that data has been received. TCP is the Transport Layer in the OSI Network model. The result is each packet can carry 1448 bytes.

A more detailed view of a connection and sending 2500 bytes is:

The first three horizontal arrows of Fig. 4.2 show the *three-way handshake* of packets to establish the connection. This ensures that both peers know the connection has been established. Data is then chopped into 1448-byte data packets and sent from client to server. Each packet has a sequence number giving the order of the packets (since they need not necessarily be delivered in order over the wire; TCP will order them at the recipient's end). Periodically an acknowledgement is sent saying all the packets up to a given sequence number have been received. If the client sends 5 packets of data and only receives an ack for the first 2 then it may infer that the data

[2] It is possible to have larger packets. Jumbo frames can provide up to 9000 bytes and are useful in high throughput applications. Unfortunately, the network switches and interfaces must be configured end-to-end to allow jumbo frames to travel the entire connection. As applications span larger and larger networks (or even provide services over the Internet), the opportunity to use jumbo frames has diminished.

[3] A checksum is the result of combining all the bytes to arrive at a single number. In this respect it is a type of hash. In this case, the checksum is calculated over the data and sent along in the packet. The receiver recalculates the checksum and if it doesn't match what is transferred in the packet, a corruption has occurred and some sort of error recovery needs to occur.

[4] The OSI Network Model has seven layers beginning with the Layer 1 the Physical Layer at the bottom which is the hardware used to send and receive bits to Layer 7 the Application Layer where applications manipulate the data over the network. IP is Layer 3 and TCP is Layer 4.

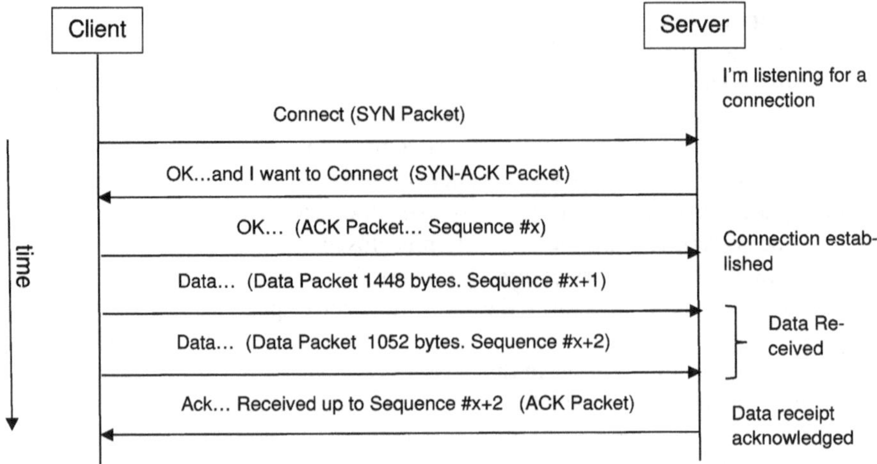

Fig. 4.2 More detailed view of how TCP creates a connection and exchanges data

has been lost and it should retransmit those packets. There are other error correction mechanisms at play to ensure that every data packet is ultimately delivered.

There is an exchange of packets for closing the connection that is similar to establishing the connection. This is discussed further below.

The following sections will explain how to program a basic client–server application using TCP/IP connections. We will be using the POSIX[5] API for Sockets.

Client Connecting to a Server

Each end of a connection is capped with a *socket*. A socket is somewhat analogous to a phone jack in the old-styled wired phones: You plug a phone into it, it is attached to a wire that ultimately connects to another jack that also has a phone plugged into it. The jack is the interface between the phone and the network that connects to another phone. A phone jack also has a phone number associated with it (yes, it really isn't the phone jack that has the phone number, but it helps with the analogy) that is used to establish the phone connection between two parties. Similarly, a network socket has a name associated with it that allows it to be found on the network and to be available for a connection.

With TCP connections, a server will *listen* for connections from its clients, which will *connect* to the server. Once the server *accepts* a connection, the bidirectional communication channel is established, and data transfer can proceed.

---

[5] POSIX stands for Portable Operating System Interface. It is a relatively old standard (established in 1988) that governs many APIs, commands, and applications used across operating systems. (POSIX, 2018).

A socket on Linux, once created, masquerades a lot like a file. You can read from it like a file. You can write to it like a file. You can close it like a file. However, the setup and ultimate control of the socket is very different from a file.

Unlike a file, a socket has two items identifying it: a name and a port number. The name may be an *IP address*. This is a number that looks like this: `192.168.86.1`. This is an IP version 4 (IPv4) address. There are also IP version 6 (Ipv6) addresses that look like this: `fde8:e131:67c2:cfc3:d14a:8bf7:da66:6378`. IPv6 addresses were developed because IPv4 could only represent a couple billion addresses and the world was in danger of running out of addresses for all the interconnected servers and devices. Other measures have mitigated this crisis, but you will see IPv6 addresses increasingly being mandated. These numeric addresses eventually are translated to the address at the hardware level (called a MAC address—*media access control* address) that looks like 80-32-53–85-F9-F7 and can enumerate around 280 trillion devices.

When you type a website address, you rarely type in an IP address (though you can). Instead, you enter a name such as www.google.com. A mechanism has been built called the Domain Name Service (DNS) that catalogs all of these names and translates them into the IP address of the device (server, Ring doorbell, internet connected washing machine) that bears the name. DNS allows a program wanting to connect a socket to translate the name (e.g., www.google.com) into the underlying IP address that is then used to identify the endpoint.

The other identifying item of a socket is a port number, which is a small integer (0–65, 535). A server might have a given name like www.google.com that allows many kinds of connections. Common kinds of connections are for web servers (and there are secure, https, and insecure, http, connections), file transfers (File Transfer Protocol: FTP), and remote terminal sessions (Secure Shell: SSH). Each of these is assigned a different *port*, the small integer number mentioned above. For example, when you connect to http://www.google.com port 80 is used for insecure web traffic. If https://www.google.com is given (note the https), port 443 is used. Each kind of connection is given a port number. Ports 0–1023 are reserved as *well-known* ports. We've already shown two of these (80 and 443). FTP is port 21 and SSH is 22.

A socket therefore connects to a name (that ultimately resolves to an IP address) and a port number. Because of the layers of translation involved to go from some name to a combination of IP address and port number, creating the structure to identify the socket is non-trivial. Here is a typical code fragment for connecting to a server given by `address` and its associated `port`. It is ugly and we will deconstruct it line-by-line:

```
char *host = "somehost";
char *port = "80";
struct addrinfo hints;
memset(&hints, 0, sizeof(struct addrinfo));
hints.ai_family = AF_INET; // IPV4
hints.ai_socktype = SOCK_STREAM;
struct addrinfo *resolved_address;
int retcode = getaddrinfo(host, port, &hints,
                          &resolved_address);
```

Line 1 The name of a host we want to connect to. It can be an IP address or a name like `cnn.com`.

Line 2 The port we want to connect to. Port 80 is the standard port for HTTP traffic. In some documentation this is listed as the *service*; port 80 represents the HTTP service for example.

Lines 3–6 Address resolution is very comprehensive. It can resolve all sorts of protocols and address formats (for example, there are half a dozen socket types). These lines provide guidelines to more precisely resolve the host and port to an underlying address. In this case the AF_INET resolve IPV4 addresses but not IPV6 (or APPLETALK, or DECnet, or a host of other protocols that might be present). We also want a SOCK_STREAM socket which is TCP/IP - a reliable connection that presents an ordered stream of bytes.

Line 7 A list of addresses will be placed in the pointer we supply. The memory for this list is allocated by the system (and must be ultimately freed by the application when it is no longer needed).

Lines 8–9 And finally we can get one or more addresses that we can use to connect to the peer. `Getaddrinfo` takes the host and port information along with the hints and returns a linked list of address structures (discussed below). It is not unlikely that multiple addresses will be returned. `cnn.com` resolves to at least four IPV4 addresses.

If `getaddrinfo` succeeds, it will return 0 and set the pointer to a linked list of address information structures (the struct addrinfo above):

```
struct addrinfo
{
  int ai_flags;                /* Input flags. */
  int ai_family;               /* Protocol family for socket. */
  int ai_socktype;             /* Socket type. */
  int ai_protocol;             /* Protocol for socket. */
  socklen_t ai_addrlen;        /* Length of socket address. */
  struct sockaddr *ai_addr;    /* Socket address for socket. */
  char *ai_canonname;          /* Canonical name for service. */
  struct addrinfo *ai_next;    /* Pointer to next in list. */
};
```

The fields we're most interested in are:

`ai_family` This distinguishes between different protocols, e.g., `AF_INET`, `AF_INET6`. It is used to interpret the address in the `ai_addr` field. If `AF_UNSPEC` (unspecified address family) is used in the hints of the request, then multiple address families can be returned, otherwise this should match what was requested initially.

`ai_socktype` Like `ai_family`, this will usually match what was specified in the `getaddrinfo` request. If `ai_family` is not specified (i.e., it is 0), then it is possible to get multiple results for the different socket types, e.g., stream sockets, data gram sockets, and raw sockets. Usually SOCK_STREAM is used to specify a TCP/IP socket.

`ai_addr` This is the address that is filled in by `getaddrinfo`. It is the translation of host and port into a usable address given the hints specified. The format of this depends on the ai_family. An IPv4 address has family `AF_INET` and is typically represented by four numbers separated by periods, e.g., `192.168.1.1`. An IPv6 address is specified with ai_family AF_INET6 with address like `fde8:e131:67c2:cfc3:9620:20d5:a0ce:493e`. Less common formats are also possible. The type of `ai_addr` is a pointer to a `struct sockaddr` which is an abstract type. The actual type will depend on `ai_family`: an IPV6 socket will have `ai_addr` pointing to a `struct sockaddr_in6`. If you need to dig into the specifics of what `ai_addr` points to (as opposed to just handing the pointer to a specific function), then you must be sure to cast `ai_addr` to the correct specific type for the address family given by `ai_family`.

For example, if `getaddrinfo` is used with host "cnn.com," port 80, and an unspecified address family or protocol, then multiple entries will be returned since multiple servers can service cnn.com, some accessed with IPv4 and some with IPV6, some with streaming protocols, and some with datagram protocols.

There is a special IP address: 127.0.0.1. This is the *loopback* address and represents the address of the local host and can only be used from that host (i.e., using the loopback address from one host to access another host will be fruitless). For example, we might want to test client and server programs on the same host. The IP address 127.0.0.1 can be used without having to worry about what the host's actual IP address is on the network. All traffic to this address will remain local. The hostname *localhost* can also be used to indicate that the connection should be restricted to the loopback address.

For most connections where data will be sent and received reliably, limiting the connection to `SOCK_STREAM` (as in line 6 above) will eliminate many extraneous addresses. If `ai_family` is left as unspecified (`AF_UNSPEC` or 0), then both IPv4 and IPv6 addresses will be returned. It is good future proofing to include IPV6 addresses as candidates for connection.[6]

Note that `getaddrinfo` is doing a lot of work behind the scenes. It has a series of places it looks to find the address information for a given host. It may have information locally, or it may need to resolve a name (like `cnn.com`) to its address by interrogating DNS. That means it needs to do its own network transactions behind the scene to find the address. As an example, performing `getaddrinfo` on the address localhost (which it can resolve locally), takes microseconds. Resolving

---

[6] While it is certainly a good idea to anticipate IPv6 it is often problematic to ensure IPv6 is actually supported on the systems you work on. Often it is simpler to at least focus on AF_INET connections (by either specifying AF_INET or filtering out the IPV6 addresses after the getaddrinfo).

cnn.com requires a request to the DNS service and can take a thousand times longer (milliseconds).

All of this simply gets a handle to a remote system, not an actual connection. As mentioned above, we connect sockets. To create a socket to connect to another server is relatively simple. Continuing the example code from above:

```
10  int my_socket = socket(AF_INET, SOCK_STREAM, 0);
11  struct addrinfo *connect_address = resolved_address;
12  while (connect_address) {
13    int result_code = connect(my_socket,
14                              connect_address- > ai_addr,
15                              connect_address- > ai_addrlen);
16    if (result_code == 0) {
17      break;
18    }
19    connect_address = connect_address- > ai_next;
20  }
21  freeaddrinfo(resolved_address);
22  if (connect_address == NULL) … we failed to connect on any address.
```

Line 10: This creates a socket. It is used very much like a file descriptor created by the open function for C. We plan on communication to another socket using TCP/IP (SOCK_STREAM) over an IPv4 connection (AF_INET).

Line 11 We will iterate over the addresses we resolved earlier with getaddrinfo. We must preserve resolved_address to allow us to free it at line 21.

Line 12 We loop over the addresses that we resolved in lines 8-9 of the earlier code.

Line 13–15 We connect using the address resolved in the getaddrinfo.

Line 16 If we connect, that's great and we exit the loop.

Line 19 We couldn't connect to this address, try the next.

Line 21 getaddrinfo allocated the address information structures. At this point we don't need them anymore so to avoid a memory leak we free them.

Line 22 Either we exited the loop with a connected socket or we ran out of candidates and failed to connect.

We now have a socket (my_socket) that is connected and is ready to read and write data. There are many reasons that a socket might not connect so it is important to check whether the connect does eventually succeed.

Also note that connections are not instantaneous. How long a connection takes depends on the network path it must traverse to get to the destination. Sitting in my office, connecting to google.com requires traveling through 25 network elements (routers, switches, gateways) traveling from Massachusetts to a server in Virginia. Yet the connection is still completed in under 20 ms (and at least 5 ms is required for signals to travel at the speed of light round-trip). The internet infrastructure is quite efficient after millions of man-years of effort to optimize it.

Server Accepting a Connection

The previous section connected a client to a server. That's half of the connection. The server at the other end of the connection needs to *accept* the client. This happens in three steps:

1. A socket is created that *binds* to a particular address and port. Using the same `getaddrinfo` used above, we establish the address that another program can connect to. For example, we might have
   `getaddrinfo("myhost.com", "80", &hints, &my_addr_info);`
   This will create the address info in `my_addr_info` for myhost.com:80 to use to attach to a socket so it can be found by that name by clients.
2. Once we have a socket bound to an address, the socket needs to *listen* for connections.
3. When a client tries to connect to the socket listening at the address we are bound to, the server *accepts* the connection. Once the server accepts the connection, the server connection will be assigned to a new socket and can read and write on that connection while the original socket can return to listening for further connections.

Binding a Socket

Our first step in accepting connections is to establish a socket that is bound to a particular network location contained in a `sockaddr`. One way is to create a `struct sockaddr_in` for the `AF_INET` address we are going to connect on, populating it correctly and then using that directly. In this case, the programmer is responsible for making sure the address is correct, matches the address family, and is in correct byte ordering for network transport. Another approach is to use `getaddrinfo` as shown above to create the `struct addrinfo` that will contain the address information of this network location. Now the system will fill in the fields correctly and this is the mechanism used in the examples below.

The hostname parameter in `getaddrinfo` can take on special forms. For example, you can specify "localhost" to refer to the server the program is running on. A NULL pointer for the host will also resolve to the host the program is running on. The port parameter for getaddrinfo can also accept the value "0." In this case, a random *ephemeral* port will be assigned to the address.

It may seem strange to have a socket bound to a random port. How can you connect to the socket if the port is some random number? Random ports for servers are not common but do have value.

- Some ports are not available to "ordinary" programs. All ports less than 1024 can only be used by privileged programs. That means if a program wants to listen on port 80 (the standard http port), it must be considered privileged. Most programs don't (and shouldn't) have this privilege.
- Only one program may listen on a port at a time. An attempt to use a port already in use is not allowed. In some applications, a random port is chosen and then communicated to the potential clients through some other mechanism to allow the same server code to be instantiated multiple times without creating a port conflict.

Once the address is established in an `addrinfo`, the `bind` function associates that address with the socket. For example:

```
1   char *host = "localhost";
2   char *port = "8000";
3   struct addrinfo hints;
4   memset(&hints, 0, sizeof(struct addrinfo));
5   hints.ai_family = AF_INET; // IPV4
6   hints.ai_socktype = SOCK_STREAM;
7   struct addrinfo *resolved_address
8   int retcode = getaddrinfo(host, port,
9                             &hints, &resolved_address);
10  int my_socket = socket(AF_INET, SOCK_STREAM, 0);
11  struct addrinfo *address = resolved_address;
12  while (address) {
13    int retcode = bind(my_socket, address- > ai_addr,
14                       address- > ai_addrlen);
15    if (retcode == 0) {
16      break;
17    }
18    address = address- > ai_next;
19  }
20  freeaddrinfo(resolved_address);
21  if (address = = NULL)
22    // Error... we could not bind the socket.
23  my_socket is now bound to localhost:80.
```

Line 1–9 As before, we create address structures for the address we are going to bind to (localhost:8000).

Line 10 The socket is created but it is unconnected and, until we bind it, not reachable.

Line 12–19 We iterate over the resolved addresses (which is usually a list of length 1 in this case) trying to bind to the socket to an address returned from `getaddrinfo`.

At this point, the socket is created and bound to an address. It is visible to the clients. The next step is to accept connections to it.

Listening and Accepting a Connection

Once a socket has been created and bound to an address, the server is ready to listen for clients. The code is straightforward:

```
1  listen(my_socket, 10);
2  sockaddr_in who_connected;
3  socklen_t who_length = sizeof(who_connected);
4  int connected_socket = accept(my_socket, &who_connected,
5                                              &who_length);
```

Line 1 "Listen" for connections on the socket that was previously created above. The second parameter to listen is the number of connections that can be queued. More about this later.

Lines 2–3 When a connection is accepted, we can capture who is on the other end. `Who_connected` is where this information will be placed, and `who_length` is how big a buffer we've allocated for this.

Lines 4–5 The server side socket accepts a connection from a client. The second and third parameters allow the server to record the address of the end point connecting to it. A pointer to a buffer and the buffer's length are passed in and the address information (a struct sockaddr_in in this example) are placed in the buffer. We can ignore this address (it is informational and not needed to establish the connection) by specifying a NULL buffer.

The `connected_socket` above is *not* the same as `my_socket`. `My_socket` is just used for listening for connections. When a connection is accepted, a new, connected socket is created that the program can use to interact with the client. As we'll see, this allows a server to accept connections from multiple clients from a single address. Think of a web server handling many browsers connecting to it. Each browser is connecting to the same address, for example `myhost.com:8000`. This is the role of the listening socket. The web server uses the socket returned by `accept` to communicate with the client. It is possible then to process multiple connections simultaneously. Much more about that below.

Reading and Writing on a Socket

Now that the client and server are connected, data can be written to and read from the peer on the other end of the connection. Either end of the connection can write data to its socket and the pattern of the reads and writes is dictated by the application. Frequently a client connects to a server and sends a request for some data which is then returned by the server to the client and the process repeats until the client no longer needs the resources at the server.

In C and related languages, writing is performed with the standard write function:

```
ssize_t amount_written = write (connected_socket, buffer,
                                buffer_length)
```

(size_t is the integer type for "amount of stuff" in POSIX, ssize_t (signedsize_t) means that a negative value can be returned, in this case -1 if the write fails. Generally size_t is the same as uint64_t and ssize_t is int64_t.)

Unlike files, it is often the case that the amount written is not the same as the amount in the buffer. There is a finite amount of memory associated with a socket for queuing data. If the connection is slow or the receiver is not reading at the same rate as the data is being written, then at some point the internal buffer for the socket will become full.[7] In this case, the write may return less than the amount requested, even 0.

A common pattern for writing a buffer to a socket is:

```
ssize_t total_to_write = buffer_length;
char *buffer_to_write = buffer;
while (total_to_write > 0) {
  ssize_t amount_written = write(connected_socket,
                                 buffer_to_write,
                                 total_to_write);
  if (amount_written < 0)
    handle error…
total_to_write -= amount_written;
buffer_to_write += amount_written;
}
```

Each time through the loop "uses up" some of the buffer until it is all written. It may be done in one shot or require multiple iterations. Often this while loop is placed in a function with a similar signature as the system write function (though we'll see in event processing where this is not the case). We will assume a function write_completely is available to write everything in a buffer to a network connection.

Like writing, reading from a socket may require multiple invocations reading a piece at a time.

An application writing to a socket typically knows the boundaries of the records it is writing. However, when reading from the socket, the application must be able to figure out the logical structure of the stream of bytes. From a socket's point of view, bytes are continuously streamed across the connection with no explicit boundaries between records. A single read might read one record or a dozen even if the records were written with individual write invocations. The application must determine the boundary of a request (unless you only make one request per connection which is highly unusual). Typically, there is an agreement between the client and server about what a request and response look like. This agreement is called a *protocol*. Standard

[7] Note that this is true for TCI/IP sockets. It is not true for other network protocols (for example, UDP) where data may be simply dropped into the void if it cannot be immediately sent.

protocols will be discussed below; often a bespoke protocol will suffice. For example, we might send the number of bytes in the request/response in the first four bytes of the transmission.

Suppose the client wants to send a list of strings to the server (to be stored somewhere). Let's assume there are a pair of routines `write_completely` and `read_completely` that each take a socket, a buffer and the length of the buffer, and ensures that the entire buffer is sent or received. We could then do the following to write the length of the string followed by the string itself, and likewise, read the length of the string and then read exactly that number of bytes.

Client:

```
write_completely(client_socket, length_of_string,
                 sizeof(length_of_string));
write_completely(client_socket, the_string, length_of_string);
```

Server:

```
read_completely(server_socket, &length_of_string,
                sizeof(length_of_string));
read_completely(server_socket, buffer, length_of_string);
```

The server receives the length (e.g., a 4-byte integer) and then reads the string following the length.

There are some interesting points to observe here. The first is even though we are doing two writes, the number of network transactions may only be one. This is because TCP/IP, the underlying network streaming protocol we are using (`AF_STREAM`), tries to fill a packet before sending it out. TCP uses *Nagle's algorithm* to maximize packet utilization. This algorithm (part of the underlying TCP protocol) holds off immediately sending data providing a chance that more data will fill in the packet. This means that writing to a socket does not mean that the data is immediately flowing.

The time taken from sending data to the time it is received is referred to as the *latency*. If a write call is made at 1.0 s and received at 1.2 s, the latency is 0.2 s (1.2–1.0). If the write is 2048 bytes, then the *throughput* (the measure of how much data is transmitted per unit time) is 2048/0.2 = 10,240 bytes/second. An analogy is how fast water flows downstream (the latency) and the width of the stream (the bandwidth). The wider stream may flow more slowly (has longer latency) but carries more overall water (the bandwidth). With the Nagel algorithm, the latency of the data may increase, but the overall throughput improves. This is a rather classic trade-off of better throughput for higher latency and can lead to non-deterministic performance for any given write to a socket.

Received data is buffered on the receiver side (the *server* in the example above). TCP/IP allocates buffers that are filled up asynchronously as the data flows in from the network. Two consecutive reads by an application are likely to access the same buffered data so that once the first read completes, the second can complete almost immediately.

Even though Nagle helps in combining the multiple writes, the write call is not completely free. A write function needs to happen in the kernel of the operating system (it is a *system call*). System calls are more expensive than "regular" calls and so combining multiple writes into a single write can have some impact on performance in very write-intensive applications. For example, creating a structure that combines the length of a string and the string into one contiguous memory location would allow a single write to send the data (even if the server receiving it uses multiple reads). Another approach is to use a *scatter–gather* write call which allows multiple non-contiguous pieces to be sent. In POSIX this is `writev`. It takes the form:

```
1    unint8_t *buffer;
2    uint32_t buffer_length;
3
4    … set buffer to some content
5    … set buffer_length to the length of that content
6
7    struct iovec the_iovec[] = {
8        {&buffer_length, sizeof(buffer_length)},
9        { buffer, buffer_length}};
10
11   writev(my_socket, the_iovec, 2);
```

Line 7–9 We define two separate chunks of memory we want to transfer: The first is the length of the buffer, and the second is the buffer itself.

Line 11 Send the two chunks of memory (the buffer length and then the buffer). The writev will not allow other data (from other threads for example) to interleave between the separate elements of the iovec transfers so it is assured that the buffer defined in the_iovec[1] will immediately follow the length of the buffer (the_iovec[0]).

`Writev` will generally save time by eliminating multiple kernel transits. It is not quite as fast as a single write of contiguous data but probably "good enough" in most cases. It also has the advantage that you are guaranteed that the pieces being sent are contiguous; as we will see in the two concurrent programming patterns, this is not always the case with two independent write calls. The disadvantage of `writev` is that it is much more complex to use in asynchronous transfers, which will be covered in the next chapter "Network Event Processing."

There is a corresponding `readv` for reading into multiple buffers. However, this is less useful in the case of reading counted buffers because we don't know a priori how many bytes will be transferred—that's in the first four bytes received. Two reads really are required for handling a record with a prefix length.

"Endianness"

When sending numeric data across a network such as the length of the record, it is possible that the byte orders of numbers can be different between the client and server. For example, Intel processors are *little-endian* which means that the least

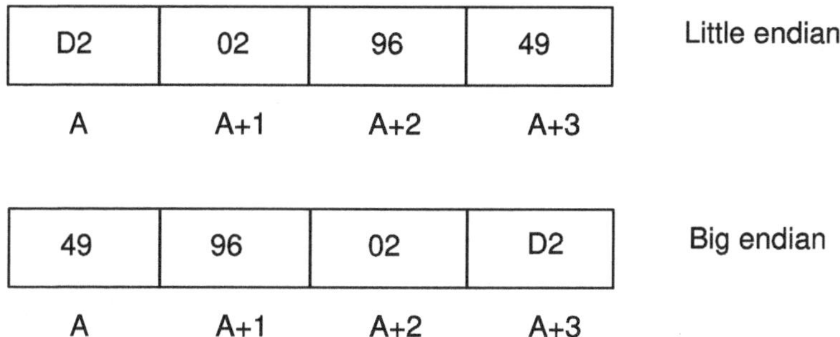

Fig. 4.3 "Endian" refers to the order of bytes for a multibyte numeric value

significant byte of a number will be stored at a lower address. Motorola processors are *big-endian*: the most significant byte is at the lower address. Here is a diagram illustrating endianness (Fig. 4.3):

Network protocols use a number of functions that convert numbers to a canonical format for transport called *network byte order*. For example, to convert an integer to the network form of that integer, the `htonl` (host-to-network-long) function is used:

```
uint32_t network_form = htonl(native_form);
```

The `network_form` representation would then be sent across the wire where the recipient would turn it back into native form using the `ntohl` (network-to-host-long) function:

```
uint32_t native_form = ntohl(network_form);
```

Now for a bit or reality: while we admit it is possible that two machines may have different endianness, it is increasingly unlikely. All Intel processors are little-endian. IBM mainframes and Motorola processors are big-endian so if you need to exchange data with these types of processors and Intel processors then using network byte ordering is required. Apple- and ARM-based processors (which includes Google's and Amazon's processors) are little-endian. If network byte ordering is required, the cost is fairly small; in an optimized build it will typically add a couple of instructions: one to swap the bytes, which is a single Intel instruction, and one to store the swapped bytes somewhere so they can be transferred.

Note that some fields in the network structures are in network byte order. For example, inside `struct sockaddr_in` there is a field:

```
unsigned short sin_port;
```

(`unsigned short` is the same as `uint16_t`). This value must be in network byte order, i.e., if you want to store port 80 into this field "by hand" (instead of using `getaddrinfo`), you *must* use `htonl(80)` as the assigned value, and likewise, use.

`ntohl(x- > sin_port)` to convert to a native form when accessing it.

Isn't This Old Fashioned?

Why should anyone bother learning about this addrinfo stuff, and the details of binding and accepting connections? Don't modern languages make this simpler?

This is partly true. Java, for example, makes it a little easier. You can simply create a "ServerSocket" specifying a port number. The creation of an address and binding to it are under the covers. Java still requires listen and accept functions that follow the model presented.

Connecting a socket to a server in Java is again similar to the Posix model. A socket is created and then connect is called to connect to a remote server. As with ServerSocket, the connect need not go through a getaddrinfo, and similar functions; these are done behind the scenes.

In the case, where more sophisticated control over the socket is required, the low-level functions described above begin to manifest themselves. For example, Java's InetAddress is used to resolve addresses. The fact is that, at least on Linux (and Linux variants) and, for the most part, Windows, the high level functions are using the getaddrinfo, bind, listen and accept functions described above. Understanding their use will help generalize to other models and will become important for more sophisticated network processing such as event-processing discussed in the next chapter.

HTTP Requests and Responses

How the client and server interact is completely dependent on the application. For example, a client requesting an employee record might connect to the server managing the employee database and simply send the employee ID as a counted-string (i.e., a string with the length preceding it similar to the model shown above). The response can be some encoding of the employee record (e.g., a combination of counted strings, numbers, etc.). Chapter 8 will discuss encoding in more detail.

A popular interchange form is based on HTTP (Gourley,et al., 2002). HTTP is the ubiquitous protocol for accessing content on the web. It uses name-value pairs to send and receive information, frequently from a web browser. For example, an HTTP request might be:

```
GET /homepage.html
Host: www.myhost.com
Accept: text/html
```

This is used to get the content of homepage.html from www.myhost.com and that we expect the response to be html text.

The response might be:

```
HTTP/1.1 200 OK
Content-Type: text/html
Content-Length: 767431
        <767,431 bytes of content>
```

A protocol has been built from HTTP called *Representation State Transfer (REST)* (Fielding,2000). The notion is to adapt the model of how HTTP accesses information and use that for invoking functions on a server. The server may be an actual web server, or some other software that interprets a minimal subset of the HTTP protocol.

For example, if a client needs the employee record for ID 123,456, it may send the HTTP request:

```
GET employee/id/123456
```

The server may respond with:

```
Http/1.1 200 Ok
 Content-Length: 172
 Content-Type: application/json
 { "employee": "Michael Kilian", "id": "123456", "address": {
   "street": "Broadway", "street-number": 34, "city": "New York",
   "state": "New York", "zip": "12123" } }
```

The format of the response is a header saying, "The request has been handled correctly," that it has 172 bytes, and it is encoded as a JSON string (JSON stands for JavaScript Object Notation and originated from JavaScript scripts needing to exchange information other than web pages). The actual 172 bytes of the JSON encoding follows. Different forms of encoding including more details on JSON will be discussed in the section on message formats in Chap. 8.

REST is very popular. One reason is that as "standard" HTTP, it can be sent over standard HTTP channels and play "nicely" with various network infrastructure such as firewalls. Often a web server hosts the code executing the service and that web server can handle complexities like transport over TLS (Transport Layer Security—what is used when https is used instead of http in the URL) so that the transaction is secure over the network.[8]

---

[8] Using TLS when networking is more complex than the network programming we've shown in this chapter. A TLS connection requires additional handshaking and will sometimes inject extra exchanges during a data exchange to ensure there is no one eavesdropping on the connection. See (OpenSSL, 2026) for more information. Using a library like cURL (cURL, 2026) can automatically manage both "regular" and TLS connections carrying HTTP on both the client and server side. cURL can also allow much of the fine-grained control described above.

REST is not really a standard but more of an approach. How requests are structured vary widely. For example, arguments to the function being called can be passed as part of the path (as above), query parameters (text separated from the URL by a ? on the request), or even as the request body. An alternative to the GET line above could use a query:

```
GET employee?id=123456
```

More complex requests can be sent in the request body:

```
GET employee
Content-Length: 93
{ "id" "123456",
  "subsidiary": "acme",
  "response": "summary" }
```

In this case, the server will parse the content body and return a summary of the employee "123,456" that is in subsidiary "acme".

Note that there are many libraries for managing JSON representation. Java and Python have very simple ways of converting from JSON to native objects and back again. Using JSON in C is difficult unless the JSON being generated is very fixed, i.e., corresponds directly to a struct that both sides agree upon. In that case, it may not be worth using JSON and creating a bespoke representation for the parameters and responses might be simpler in the end, especially if no web components (e.g., browsers, web servers) are involved.

A Word to the Wise

One of the nice features of using even a minimal HTTP protocol for passing information is that there are many tools for generating HTTP requests (even complex ones with multiple parameters and complex request bodies). And if you want to extend the server for use by something like JavaScript in a web application, it is fairly straightforward. Of course, if you are building a high-performance distributed system where the actions are self-contained in the system, then the overhead of parsing through HTTP is likely to be too expensive and a completely custom protocol is more appropriate.

Closing a Connection

When a connection is no longer needed, it should be *closed*. This frees up the network resources associated with the connection such as the port number in use, and system memory for buffering data for the connection.

Closing a connection requires both the client and server to close their sockets. Closing the server side of the connection, for example, does not necessarily mean the client side is automatically closed, and vice versa. It is therefore important for a program to recognize when a peer has closed its connection and for the program to correspondingly cleanup its connection. There are several ways of detecting a connection has closed but a common mechanism is when a read on a socket returns 0 bytes.

```
while (true) {
  ssize_t amount_read = read(socket, buffer, 1024);
  if (amount_read == 0) {
    close(socket);
    break;
  }
  // process buffer
}
```

In these simple examples where we are synchronously reading and writing to sockets, closing both ends of the socket is straightforward. When we have more sophisticated socket mechanisms (as discussed in Chap. 5: Network Event Processing) closing a socket can be a little more problematic.

Exercises

1. Create client and server programs. The server program can listen on 127.0.0.1 port 8000. The client program can connect to the server using this address. Implement a simple protocol: SET < integer > sets a stored value in the server to < integer >. GET will cause the server to return the value in the server. How this protocol is represented (text, binary, HTML) is unspecified.
2. Create a server program that listens on 127.0.0.1 port 8000 that will accept a connection, process a stream of bytes until it sees the string "`*END*`" and send back the number of words in the string (where a word is any string of characters not including a space. Note that "`*END*`" must be preceded by a space. Once the number of words is written back to the client the server should close the connection and then wait for the next connection (only one connection is processed at a time).
3. It is possible to do Exercise 2 without an explicit marker. In this case, the read and write sides of the socket can be shutdown independently with the `shutdown` API (see Chap. 5's section on Closing a Connection). In this case, the client will only shut down the writing part of the socket after sending the stream of bytes. It will still read the response and only then will it close the socket. The server will read until it reaches EOF, write the response back, and then close the socket.

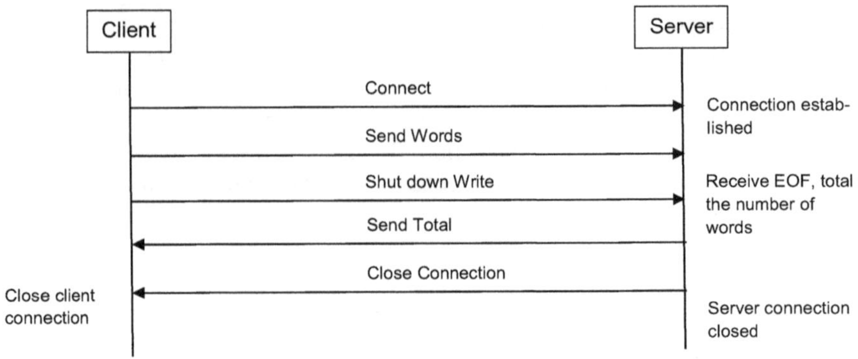
Client
Server
Connect
Connection estab-
lished
Send Words
Shut down Write
Receive EOF, total
the number of
words
Send Total
Close Connection
Close client
connection
Server connection
closed

Chapter 5
Network Event Processing

In many applications, a server application may need to handle multiple, simultaneous connections. The way the `listen` and `accept` functions operate anticipates this. The structure of these two calls is:

```
listen(listening_socket, 10);
while (true) {
   accepted_socket = accept(listening_socket, NULL, 0);
            // do something with my_accepted_socket asynchronously
}
```

The `listen` function tells the system that it can receive connections on the given socket. The second parameter specifies how many connections can be pending before new connection attempts are refused. This value will depend on how fast the loop accepting connections can run and how likely hordes of connections may flood the server.

The `accept` function waits until a client connects and then proceeds to hand off `accepted_socket` (a new socket that is different from `listen_socket`) to something that processes the connected socket while the main loop waits and connects to a new client.

No data ever flows over the listen socket. It is simply where connections are made. Once a socket is accepted, reads and writes to the socket returned by `accept` will transfer data from and to the client socket that initiated the connection.

There are many ways of asynchronously processing the accepted socket. The next sections present two approaches: Multithreaded, and event-based handling of the connections.

> You may want to peruse Chap. 7 if you are unfamiliar with threads. The current chapter assumes a basic understanding of multithreaded programming and common data structures such as thread-safe queues.

M. Kilian, *Ten Software Patterns Every Student Should Know*,
https://doi.org/10.1007/978-981-92-0260-7_5

Creating a Multithreaded Server

A program thread is one stream of instructions that the processor executes. Every program has at least one thread (i.e., the main program that is being executed). A program can have multiple threads each running independent streams of instructions but sharing the same data such as global variables containing tables, file descriptors.

> How to use and control multiple threads will be discussed in Concurrent Programming with Threads. If you are completely unfamiliar with threading, it may be useful to skim over Chap. 7 before continuing with this section.

For the rest of this chapter, we will assume we have multiple worker threads that perform the following task:

```
Loop-forever {
  Dequeue a connection from the "connection queue"
  Process the connection completely using reads and writes
  Close the connection.
}
```

Another thread contains the listen loop described above:

```
Loop-forever {
  Accept connection on listening socket
  Enqueue connected socket on the "connection queue"
}
```

The connection queue is a first-in-first-out (FIFO) data structure where the listening thread enqueues connections, and one or more action threads dequeue the connected connection to process. The queue is "thread-safe," i.e., it is guaranteed that either one thread is putting a connection on the queue or one thread is taking a connection off the queue but not both simultaneously. If no item is enqueued, the dequeue operation will wait until an item arrives.

Each worker thread is responsible for a connection. The worker dequeues a connection and then processes it, for example, by reading requests and sending responses until the transactions with that client are completed (often signaled by the client closing its side of the connection). The worker can then dequeue another connection and work on that. If all the workers are busy, then newly enqueued connections may need to wait until previous connections have been completely processed. A simplified picture is (Fig. 5.1):

Managing multiple connections with this multithreaded approach is quite common and suitable if the number of connections (and therefore the number of threads) is modest (10 s to 100 s, not 1000 s). In general, most of the threads will be waiting for a read or a write to complete. During that time, other threads will have a chance to process what they had previously read. The number of resources is modest and the CPU will be used fairly efficiently (although the amount of time to switch between

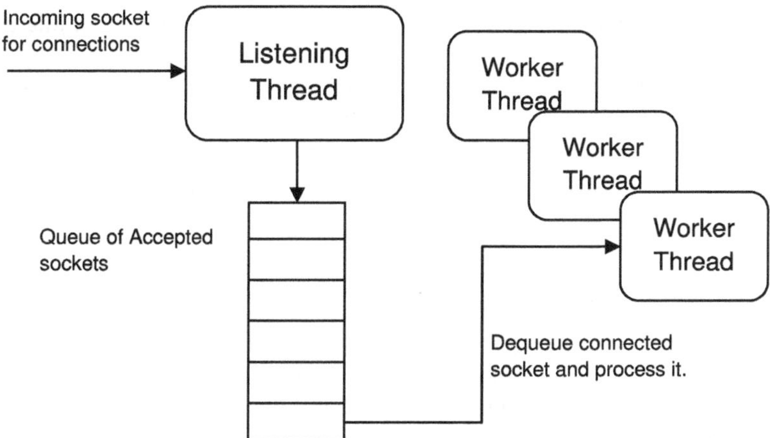

Fig. 5.1 Distributing connected sockets to worker threads

threads will increase and represent an inefficiency in the system). Let's say there are 100 worker threads and 10 CPUs (also called *cores*). Each thread will process data on a given core (e.g., transfer data from the socket), and wait for either some more packets to arrive or packets to be written. While the thread is waiting, the OS can run a different thread on that core. However, this can lead to the following sequence of events:

Core A: Runs Thread 1 until it needs to wait for some I/O (read/write/connect).
Core A: Thread 1 is suspended and Core A starts running Thread 2.
Core B: While Thread 2 is running on core A, Thread 1 needs to resume processing and switches to Core B. Core B is now running Thread 1.

The 100 threads end up jumping around the 10 cores (this is called an *involuntary context switch* in the Linux world). Functionally this is not a problem. However, remember the discussion of caching in the discussion of hash tables in Chap 1? The fastest caches are specific to cores. When a thread moves from one core to another (say from A to B), the cache it was exploiting on A is not on B and so the cache effectiveness is highly degraded.[1] This includes the thread-state that must be migrated from one core to another.

One way around this is to pin threads to cores. In our example above, 10 threads would be pinned to Core A, 10 threads pinned to Core B, and so forth until all the threads are assigned to a corresponding core. This is called setting *thread-affinity*. The disadvantage with locking threads to cores is that there are pathological workloads where all the threads assigned to a core are waiting for some I/O (and the core is essentially idle), while other cores are completely busy with multiple threads

[1] There is a L3 cache that does span the cores but each layer of cache (L1, L2, L3) is slower than the previous (though its capacity is also usually larger).

performing calculations, some of the busy threads could migrate to an idle core, if they were not pinned.

Note that handling 100 connections with a single server is a very modest load in some applications. Modern web servers can handle more than 100,000 connections on a multicore system. It is impractical to use threads for this. The next section will present a different architecture for scaling to very large numbers of connections.

Event-Based Networking

Imagine a used car dealership that acquires used cars, refurbishes them, and then sells them. Each car requires certain parts and can't be sold until the parts are acquired.

The multithreaded approach is akin to making cars by having lots of assembly lines (i.e., threads), each one refurbishing a complete car. If a part is unavailable, that assembly line stops until the part becomes available. Other assembly lines can proceed, but ultimately the production is limited by the number of assembly lines and the availability of parts. This is analogous to the previous section where each thread processed a connection to completion.

A way to keep the workers busier (and therefore the system able to get more done more efficiently), is to park the cars in a parking lot and install parts as they become available. 100 workers may be working on 1000 cars, and it is even possible that different workers may work on the same car depending on who is available to work. The work is driven by which cars have parts available to be installed. Continuing our thread analogy, the threads (workers) can now process multiple connections (cars) simultaneously.

In the *event-based* model, our events are the availability of data to be read or sent (similar to the car parts becoming available for a car). When connection A has some bytes to read, Thread 1 can read them. The bytes are equivalent to the car parts in our example. Thread 1 can then move to connection B and processes the bytes it has available to read. When connection C is ready for more data to be sent to its client, the thread can write pending bytes to it. The thread can therefore hop between connections processing whatever data is available. A single thread can therefore process many connections.

One problem is if a thread issues a read and the data is not there on the socket, the read blocks and the thread is suspended. Likewise, if a thread tries to write to a socket and the system write buffer for that connection is full, then the thread will be suspended. If the thread is suspended during a socket operation, how will it process the other sockets it is responsible for?

What is needed is a way to multiplex network operations across multiple network connections on a single thread. Instead of waiting for the read, the thread should be told that a socket has data that can be read (a *read event*). In the car analogy, the worker doesn't wait for the part but instead is notified that the part has arrived. There are many approaches to this. Linux has `epoll`, `select`, `poll`, `kqueue`, and asynchronous I/O. Epoll is a very popular facility and is available for most server network implementations. Windows has its own approach that uses asynchronous I/O. See (Stevens 2003) for more details on how Windows performs multiplexed I/O on a single thread.

This section will use a simplified model of event processing.[2] At a high level, event-based socket programming looks like this:

1. The thread maintains a list of connected sockets that it is processing.
2. Sockets have events such as "I have content that can be read" or "I am ready to have content written to me" associated with them.
3. A thread can get a list of all of the sockets that have pending events.
4. The thread then iterates over the sockets and processes the events.
   a. All I/O will be non-blocking. A socket with a "read-ready" event will have data to read without having to wait. Similarly, if "write-ready" then a socket will be able to handle the write I/O immediately.
   b. Only sockets having an event are presented to the thread. If only 5 sockets out of 10,000 registered to a thread have I/O then only 5 sockets need to be processed by that thread.
5. The program repeatedly waits for events and then processes them. This is a classic *event loop.*

Another key aspect of this model is that when a socket indicates it has data that can be read it could be one byte or one million bytes. The program reading the data cannot be sure that all the expected data is there in one I/O. Similarly, when a socket is ready to write, it might be able to accommodate 1 byte or 1,000,000 bytes. The application must be ready to do what it can and then pick up the rest when the socket is ready.

Here is an example that illustrates the difference between a threaded model and an event I/O model. Let's consider a model where records are represented by a 4-byte length n followed by n bytes. In the threaded model, it is relatively simple to receive a record and process it:

```
read_completely(f, &length, 4);
read_completely(f, buffer, length);
process_record(buffer, length);
```

The thread can wait for the length and then wait for the record to completely arrive. It is simple. Once the record is complete, it can be processed (for example, added to a database).

The event model is not so simple. There may be events for many sockets. One socket could receive one byte in the length of the record, another socket could have an event for data that represents five records. As the worker handles an event, it must be aware of what was done previously. Using our car assembly analogy, the car worker must install parts according to the plan of record for the car being built, marking off

[2] It is based on a simplified epoll model.

what has been done to ensure no step is missed and to know where to pick up when a part arrives.

There can be many different events. For now we will focus on just two possible events: Read-ready, and write-ready. When a read-ready event occurs, it means there are bytes ready to be read from a socket. If the thread reads from the socket, it is guaranteed to be able to read some data without waiting. It is not guaranteed how much data can be read. It could be 0 bytes (which means that the socket on the other end has closed) or 10,000 bytes. It is therefore important to be able to read a logical record in a piecemeal fashion. A write-ready event is similar in that it means the socket can accept data without blocking though it is unknown how much data it can accept. Again, writing data will usually be a piecemeal affair and this needs to be handled by the underlying data structures in the application.

> The sockets manipulated in event-based systems are typically marked as *non-blocking*. This means that any attempt to read or write that would cause the thread issuing the read or write to wait for the operation to complete would instead return an error (in POSIX it is the error EWOULDBLOCK) and no data would be transferred. See `setsockopt` in POSIX for how to set the non-blocking option on a socket.

Here is an example of processing counted records in an event-based system. Counted records contain the number of bytes in the record in the four bytes preceding the record. We will assume that the count is in little endian form and that our processor is also little endian. The outer loop is the *event loop*. It repeatedly waits for one or more events and then processes each read or write event. In this example, the event data structure is associated with each socket descriptor (the integer from the `accept` or `socket` call). In addition to the event-type that has occurred (e.g., read-ready, write-ready), the event structure contains a buffer that contains bytes that have not been processed. As bytes are read from a socket, it is appended to this buffer. When a complete record is received, those bytes are removed from the buffer and handed, as a record, to a routine that processes the record.[3] We are going to refer to this cose as the *event loop example* in discussions below.

```
struct Event_system event_system;
struct Event events[1000];
char buffer[4096];

for (;;) {
 int n = Event_system_wait_for_events(event_system,
                                      events, 1000);
  for (int i=0; i<n; i++) {
     struct Event *ev = events[i];
       if (Event_is_read(ev)) {
```

[3] This is a simplification of the Linux epoll model. It combines the application model of records with the physical transfer of bytes from the network.

```
11       int l = read(ev->socket, buffer, 4096);
12       if (l == 0) { // EOF… the other side closed the socket…
13        close(ev->socket);
14        Event_system_remove_socket(event_system, ev->socket);
15        continue;
16       }
17
18       Event_copy_to_buffer(&ev, buffer, l);
19
20       while (Event_has_complete_record(ev)) {
21           struct Counted_record *r = make_Counted_Record(ev);
22           Process_Record(r);
23           Event_consume_record(ev);
24       }
25     } // if (Event_is_read…
26
27       if (Event_is_write(ev)) {
28        if (!Event_write_buffer(ev)) {
29         close(ev->socket);
30         Event_system_remove_socket(event_system, ev->socket);
31       }
32       if (Event_write_buffer_empty(ev)) {
33        Event_system_remove_socket(event_system, ev->socket);
34       }
35     }
36  } // for (i…
37} // for (;;)
```

Lines 1–3 An Event_system is a container of sockets on which events occur. Events that occur (e.g., Socket 10 is ready for reading) will be placed in the events array. This is typically a subset of the sockets within the Event system. We allow up to 1000 events to be handled at a time (this is arbitrary and specified by the array size in Line 2 and Line 7). If there are more than 1000 concurrent events, we will handle 1000 and then loop to process the remainder (1000 at a time). There is little reason not to get many events at one time.

Lines 6–7 Wait for one or more events. Events either indicate that content is ready to be read, or a socket is ready to have content written to it.

Lines 8–9 Loop over the events that are ready for I/O.

Line 10–11 If the socket has content ready to read, then read it into a buffer. We limit the transfer to 4K bytes. If more than 4K of data is available, then a new read event will occur on another iteration of the outer loop (line 5) to read the extra bytes. This ensures fairness across connections (see below).

Lines 12–16 If the socket was marked as ready to read but received 0 bytes, this is an indication that the socket was closed by the other end. Close our end and remove the socket from the event system since it will no longer supply events.[4]

[4] This is an oversimplification. Sockets can close the read side while maintaining the write-side and vice versa. A not uncommon pattern is to send a CLOSE message from the client to the server

Line 18 Copy the data from the buffer to the socket structure associated with the event. This may be adding to a partial record previously transferred, reading one or more entire records, or creating a partial record.

Line 20 There may be no complete records, one complete record, or multiple complete records in the buffer we just received. The while loop continues until all of the complete records in the buffer have been accounted for.

Lines 21–23 With a complete record in hand, create the Counted Record structure from the buffer and process it. It is the responsibility of Process_record to free the memory associated with the record; it will not be released in the network handling code. Consume the record from the buffer in the event structure to make room for other records.

Lines 27–34 In the case of a write event, we assume that some other thread has placed content in the socket's write buffer using a routine not shown. Simply write as much as possible to the socket without causing the socket to block. If the write generates an error (for example, by having the other side close the socket while we are processing the write), then close the socket and remove it from the event system. If we've written all we can write, then remove the socket from the event system to avoid spurious events. Processing non-blocking writes is discussed more fully below.

The choice of 1000 events to capture at each call to `Event_wait_for_events` on Lines 2 and 7 is somewhat arbitrary. It is not a limit to how many sockets can be monitored. It is simply how many events we can process at one time. If 1500 sockets have events available, then the first call to `Event_wait_for_events` will return 1000, and, assuming no other events have arrived, the next 500 events will be returned in the subsequent call to `Event_wait_for_events`. The choice of this size can have some impact on load balancing when multiple threads share the event structure and that is discussed below.

There are some assumptions made in the event system. Suppose the socket receives 8,000 bytes of content (this is possible since a cycle of the outermost loop can take long enough that several packets arrive at the socket(s) between subsequent calls to `Event_system_wait_for_events`). The read will only process 4096 bytes however. The event system is smart enough to realize that the entire I/O has not completed and when `Event_system_wait_for_events` is called again, it will signal a read event containing the remaining $8000 - 4096 = 3904$ bytes.[5] This

which then closes the read side and sends a CLOSED message to the client and only when it writes the CLOSED message is the write side of the socket closed and the socket removed from the event system.

[5] There are multiple approaches to processing events. This is an example of *level-triggered* events where the event is signaled when there is a nonzero number of bytes to read. There are also *edge-triggered* event styles where adding bytes to the amount available is the trigger and once any amount of bytes are processed, the event is considered complete. Edge-triggering requires care to make sure that data is not missed for processing. For example, if there are 8000 bytes available, an event will

has the advantage that very long transfers for a single socket do not starve the transfer for other sockets, balancing the load across the sockets.

We also assume that `Process_Record` is fast. If Process_Record is slow, then the event loop may queue the action to be processed by another thread. We will discuss this in more detail below. The goal of the event loop is to rapidly process the I/O from the sockets and, depending on the work required, either immediately process the record or hand it to another thread.

Writing to the socket. `Event_write_buffer` will write as much as it can to the socket without causing the write to block because it has run out of internal buffer space. This is done by setting the socket to *non-blocking*. In Linux, a socket option is set after the socket is created (for example, after it is accepted). On a non-blocking socket, a write function call will return an error if the write cannot be completed without waiting for I/O to complete and no data will be transferred. The `Event_write_buffer` could write 4K chunks of the buffer (or however many bytes are available) until either the buffer is exhausted or the write blocks. Those bytes successfully written are removed from the buffer and the remainder will be picked up the next time the socket has a write-ready event.

Write events also have a small complication that read events do not have. A connected socket is typically always ready to write so that the check at line 27 will always be true even if there is no content to be written. This can lead to the outer `Event_system_wait_for_events` loop to spin (A socket could always be ready to write each time through the iteration even though we have nothing to write to it). Instead, the socket to be written to should only be added to the list of events (`Event_system_add_socket`) when there is content ready to be written, and once the content is fully written, then remove the socket (`Event_system_remove_socket`) as in Lines 32–34. Note that concurrent adding and removing sockets and content need to be governed by synchronization which is covered in Chap. 7.

A further optimization can be made: When asking to write to a socket, write to the socket until it blocks and only if it blocks, queue the data to the internal buffer and add the socket to the list of sockets to be processed in the event loop. Here is an example of this:

```
ssize_t write_buffer_to_socket(int fd, uint8_t *buffer,
                               size_t buffer_size) {
  ssize_t amount_written = write(fd, buffer, buffer_size);
  if (amount_written < 0 && errno == EWOULDBLOCK) {
    struct Event *ev = Event_get_event(event_system, fd);
    if (ev == NULL) {
      ev = make_Event(fd);
      Event_system_add_socket(event_system, fd, ev);
    }
    Event_add_to_write_buffer(ev, buffer, buffer_size);
    return buffer_size;
  }
```

occur and if only 4096 bytes are read, and no further data becomes available, 3904 bytes might go unprocessed.

```
13     return buffer_size;
14 }
```

Lines 1–2 This function will either directly write the buffer to the socket or queue the content to be written when the socket is write-ready.

Lines 3–4 Write the buffer out. We assume that fd is a non-blocking. If the buffer can't be written in its entirety, none of it will be written and the error EWOULDBLOCK will be indicated.

Lines 5–11 It is possible that other data has been buffered for this descriptor in the event system. If not, create a new event object, and associate it with the file descriptor.

Line 13 In all cases, we have either directly written buffer_size bytes or have queued buffer_size bytes to be written. There are no partial writes with this routine.

Using Event-Based Networking to Accept Connections

The previous section assumes a connection has already been established. Events can also manage the initial connection. In this case, a listening socket will have a read-event present indicating that a connection is ready to be accepted. The change to the event loop is fairly straightforward. Assume there is a single listening socket (remember, accepted sockets are different than a listening socket). When an `Event_is_read` returns true for the listening socket, it means that a connection can be accepted. This newly accepted socket can then be added to the list of sockets in the events structure. Here is a modification to the event loop example above to handle new incoming connections:

```
10 struct Event *ev = events[i];
11 if (Event_is_read(ev)) {
12   if (ev->socket == The_Listening_Socket) {
13     int new_socket = accept(ev->socket, NULL, 0);
14     Event_add_socket(event_system, new_socket,
15                              make_Event(new_socket));
16     continue;
17   }
18   int l = read(ev->socket, buffer, 4096);
19   if (l == 0) { // EOF... the other side closed the socket...
20     close(ev->socket);
21     Event_remove_socket(event_system, ev->socket);
22     continue;
23   }
```

Line 12 If the read event is on the one and only listening socket, we can accept a new connection.

Lines 13–15 Accept the connection and add it to the event system. It can now be processed normally.

Line 16	Done accepting a connection. If multiple connections on the listen socket are pending, separate events will be processed for each of them.
Lines 18–23	The rest of the socket processing remains the same as above.

Given that sockets can be added and removed as part of an event loop, the event loop can handle many simultaneous connections without requiring any additional threads (assuming, as mentioned above, that processing a given event is very fast).

Managing Load

In the case, where the event-loop queues work to another thread, I/O can actually be processed too quickly. Suppose the `Process_Record` call enqueues the record to be processed to another thread. It is conceivable that a queue could get quite large. As of the writing of this book, single network interfaces can deliver 100 Gbps or around 150 million 64-byte records per second (NVIDIA 2026). That means that if the workers consuming records from the queues only process 100 million records/second while the event-loop queues 150 million records, that in one second there will be an excess of 50 million records in the queues which, at 64 bytes/record, is 3.2 GB. At that rate, it would not be long before memory is exhausted.

Part of the reason for this is that by quickly reading (or writing) from the sockets and transferring the content to the queue, the event loop has removed any back-pressure in the TCP network protocol. System buffers will be cleared out when the record is read in the event loop, and the clients will be capable of writing more data to the network. If the processing is unbalanced, you may find yourself queuing gigabytes of records. There are several ways to address this.

One way is to make the event-loop aware of the backlog of work. The event loop should ask: Is the queue length for processing records more than some maximum number of items. If so, stop processing reads from the socket and let the content remain in the TCP buffers. It will build up and eventually the client on the other end of the socket will not be able to write. The downside of this approach is that as long as content is present in the buffer, the event system will keep waving the "I have data" flag. This can lead to a tight spin of the event loop.

A way out of this is to put a condition variable on the work queue. If the work queue gets long, the event loop must wait on the condition until the workers consume the entries on the queue and the queue drops to an acceptable number of entries. There needs to be an appropriate hysteresis implemented: The high-water mark for the number of queued entries to suspend the event loop and the low-water mark for when the event loop can be resumed should be sufficiently separated so that the event loop is not thrashing between waiting and being able to proceed. Condition variables (and the mutexes associated with them) are covered in Chap. 7.

A similar approach to flow-control can be used for writing to the socket. Suppose we have a `Write_to_Socket(Event, buffer, length)` routine that normally transfers the buffer of length bytes to an internal Event write buffer.

Like the interaction with queue length and read, `Write_to_Socket` can look at the buffer in the event and determine if it has grown past some maximum size. If so, `Write_to_Socket` can return an error code indicating that there is too much buffered and the caller will have to retry later.

Unlike the case with throttling reads, the event loop will not spin uselessly in this case. The write buffer will continue to be written to the socket as the socket transfers the content to the socket's peer. However, when the routine calling `Write_to_socket` receives a response that indicates that the socket is congested and the write has failed, the worker needs to back off. It can't simply retry or it risks spinning uselessly. How the worker thread backs off and retries is highly dependent on the application being developed and this is left as an open design question.

Another dimension to managing load is distributing the socket reads and writes across multiple processors. It is not necessary to have only a single event loop. There are two ways to handle dividing work among multiple event loops, each running in separate threads (or processes). The first is to simply have multiple event systems for each thread/process. They will get their own set of sockets and process them independently. This statically divides the load. In some pathological cases, one thread (or process) can get all the "heavy hitting" connections that could be better served if they were distributed over multiple threads.

It is possible to share a single event system among multiple threads. The event system is designed such that an event is delivered to only one of the threads waiting for an event (otherwise a read-event might be seen by multiple threads with only one successfully gathering up the data). This allows I/O to be randomly distributed over the threads. The advantage is that the pathological case above is avoided. However, it also means that the context for a connection (e.g., the buffers being used to send and receive) may bounce around the threads and create cache misses.[6]

Distributing Interrupts

Interrupts create another interesting problem when handling high volumes of network traffic. Each network interaction creates an interrupt. An interrupt is when the processor is literally interrupted from its computing to handle some hardware event like the arrival of a packet on a network interface card. In I/O intensive applications like those handling network traffic, the time processing the interrupts can be non-trivial. You can use a utility to see how much time is being spent processing interrupts. On Linux, the `top` command can be used to look at the per CPU performance and the "hi" field is the time spent processing hardware interrupts.

Often one CPU is swamped by interrupts and it fundamentally gates the throughput of the system. If a single core is managing the interrupts for an entire computer that has many cores, it will be a bottleneck to delivering the data to the other cores of

[6] If you are mapping the event-loop discussion to the Linux epoll API, then you want to associate the EPOLLEXCLUSIVE event to the socket in the epoll that is being shared by the threads.

the system. In Linux, it may be necessary to use a facility such as `irqbalance` to distribute the interrupts over multiple cores to avoid any one of them becoming a bottleneck. On extremely network-bound applications, such as network proxies, this can have a dramatic effect on the overall throughput of your system.

Much has been done to reduce the overhead of interrupts. Network interface cards can handle some of the memory traffic and process the packet correction codes (the packet *checksum)* without interrupting the processor. It is worthwhile to look out for cases where interrupts are limiting system performance and balancing the interrupts over more cores can be very beneficial.

Closing a Socket and TCP states

The TCP protocol transitions through several states in its finite state machine both for opening a connection and closing a connection. Here is a simplified view of the states that occur when a connection is closed. While the two participants are marked "Client" and "Server" they are really peers: Either participant can initiate the close of the socket. It is also the case that a socket can be closed just for reading or just for writing (Fig. 5.2).

The steps in closing a socket are:

1. The client application decides to close the socket. The client starts the close by sending out a close packet (a packet marked FIN) to the server. The client waits to have the FIN packet acknowledged by the Server.

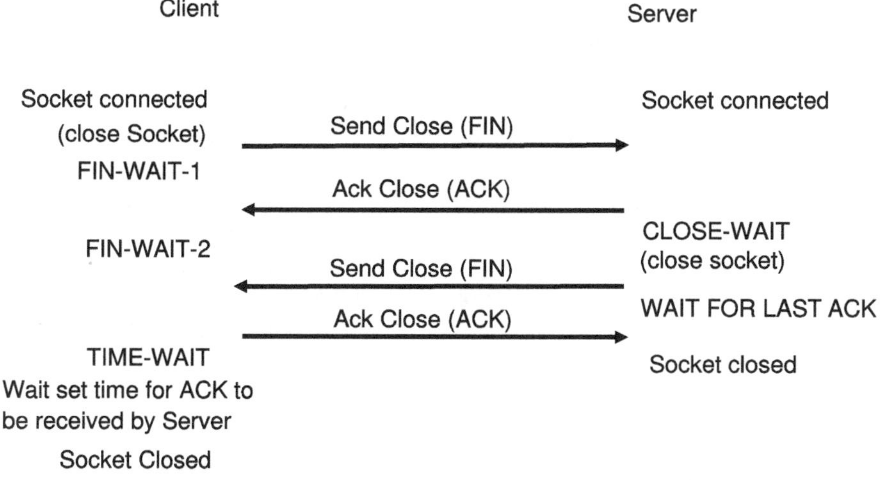

Fig. 5.2 TCP states for connection closure

2. The server acknowledges the FIN by sending an ACK to the client. It then enters the CLOSE-WAIT state. The server is waiting for the server application to see that the client has closed, and to close its side of the socket.
3. The server application closes its end of the socket and closes its end. The server tells the client it has closed by sending a FIN packet to the client.
4. The client acknowledges that it has received the FIN packet.
5. The server receives the ACK and closes its socket.
6. The client enters the TIME-WAIT state and waits to make sure the ACK ultimately gets delivered and to make sure any stray packets sent to the client for the now closed socket are thrown away. This wait time is on the order of 1 min for Linux systems.

Applications can encounter two problems based on the close protocol. The first is if the server application doesn't close its connection to the client when it receives a close. The symptom of this problem is that sockets will be stuck in the CLOSE-WAIT state.

A server applications detects that a client has closed its end of the socket by receiving a signal that a read is ready but 0 bytes are transferred. In our event loop example, we had the lines:

```
int l = read(ev->socket, buffer, 4096);
if (l == 0) { // EOF... the other side closed the socket...
  close(ev->socket);
  Event_remove_socket(event_system, ev->socket);
  continue;
}
```

This should avoid the problem. Note that there are more complex scenarios where a socket can't immediately close when it receives an EOF. Sockets have independent read and write channels. You can close the read part and leave the write part open. In C, this is done with the POSIX `shutdown` function. For example:

```
shutdown(ev->socket, SHUT_RD);
```

shuts down the read side of the socket (no more read events will be available) but leaves the write side open. The application can finish writing to the other side and then close the socket (or even shutdown the write side using `shutdown(ev- > socket, SHUT_WR)`. Determining when to shut down the write side of the socket (and close the socket) is often application specific. For example, a web server may receive an EOF from a client and shut down the read side. Once all the corresponding responses have been sent from the server to the client, the server can shut down the socket completely.

TIME-WAIT State Problem

Another problem that occasionally crops up is a side effect of TIME-WAIT. At the end of the close protocol, a client sends a final ACK to the server's close and then waits. This wait time is to ensure that the client has received any straggling packets from the server before retiring the port used to connect to the server for another connection.

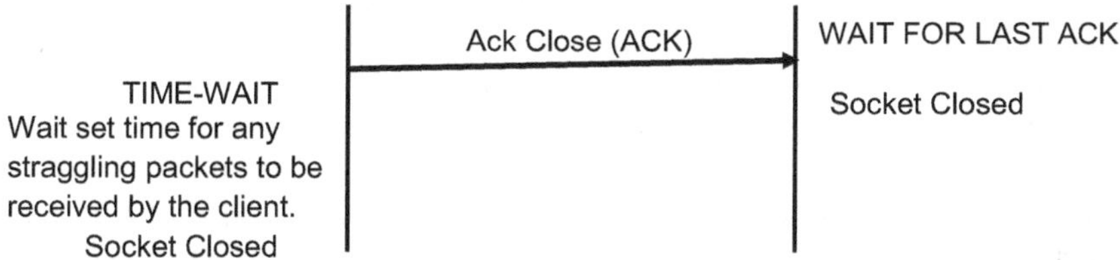

Going back to our discussion of a client connecting to a server, we see that a connection is composed of the IP address of the client, an outgoing port for the client (usually assigned by the system and called an *ephemeral* port), the server's IP address and the port used to connect to that IP address. These four pieces of information uniquely identify the connection. There are roughly 64,000 ports. If a client with address 1.2.3.4 is connecting to a server at 5.6.7.8 on port 80, then at most the client can make 64,000 connections (give or take) to that server before running out of ephemeral ports.

When a client enters TIME-WAIT at the close of the connection, the quadruplet representing that connection becomes unavailable until the TIME-WAIT interval expires. The goal is to prevent straggling packets arriving at a client from being applied to a different connection because an ephemeral port has been reused. While in the TIME-WAIT state, the system will hold onto the port that the client used to connect to the server and the combination of client IP address—outgoing port server IP address will be unavailable for reuse.

Normally this is not an issue. But suppose there is a test where a server accepts a connection, receives an HTTP request, processes the request, and returns an answer as an HTTP response. We want to write a script to test as many simultaneous requests as possible. The script connects to the server, issues the request, receives the response, and closes the connection to the server.[7] We might run 32 scripts at the same time on a multicore system and as soon as one finishes another one begins. The result is that 2000 scripts might complete in a second. Each of these script executions creates a connection, exchanges data, and closes the connection, going through the closing handshake and ending in TIME-WAIT. That would be roughly 120,000 executions per minute (this is a very reasonable number for a multicore system).

Here is the problem. TIME-WAIT is often configured to be 60 s. All of our connections have the form <client-ip-address>:ephemeral port → <server-ip-address>:80. Since client-ip-address and server-ip-address are fixed, and all the clients are connecting to port 80 on the server, this means that there are only around 64,000 unique quadruplets. At 120,000 connections per minute, we will run out of ephemeral ports in about 30 s and have to wait about 30 s for the first terminated connections

[7] Many tools can do this. cURL is a popular one.

to actually release their resources for reuse. In this case, the scripts will begin to fail around the 30 s mark with errors such as "Resource not available."

There are several ways to address this (see (Bernat 2014) for a list of configuration options). The first is to issue more requests per connection. That can be tricky if only off-the-shelf tools are available but it is the most effective way of solving this problem. For example, the cURL command can support multiple URLs on a single connection. It means that parsing the result is more complex (instead of getting a single result, multiple results must be parsed—see Chap. 2—Finite State Machines).

It is possible to allow sockets in TIME-WAIT to be reused by changing system parameters. In Linux, setting `net.ipv4.tcp_tw_reuse` to 1 (and in Windows the corresponding registry variable is `TcpTimedWaitDelay`) on the client will immediately reuse sockets when possible. This is useful in testing but can have issues in production (out-of-sync packets can be delivered to a client). Since the TIME-WAIT problem often manifests itself in testing, setting the `tcp_tw_reuse` parameter can be limited to test environments but otherwise left in its default state.

Another approach is to bypass the TIME-WAIT. If the server sends a RST (Reset connection) instead of a FIN (the normal close), the socket is immediately closed without a subsequent ACK or TIME-WAIT. This is not the "normal" end of connection (and can result in a client complaining that the peer reset the connection). If the client is under your control or doesn't care about receiving a RESET, then providing this as an option in your server is one way of avoiding the TIME-WAIT state, at least in testing. It is not, however, recommended for production.

A Word About Secure Connections

Throughout Chaps. 4 and 5, we have made no assumptions about the security of the connections between servers. Data written by server A destined for server B could be intercepted, read, perhaps modified, and forwarded to server B without server B being aware of the malevolent third party.

Increasingly, even traffic within a data center is required to be resistant to hacking. This includes eves-dropping and man-in-the-middle attacks. To counter this, traffic is encapsulated by a layer of encoding called Transport Layer Security TLS (a successor to SSL—Secure Sockets Layer). TLS creates a new connection protocol on top of TCP/IP that authenticates the two parties to one another to make sure that when server A connects to server B it is actually server B and only server B that is at the other end of the connection. All traffic over the connection is encrypted so that only B can see what A sends it. Other steps are taken so that other forms of impersonation (like server C replaying packets at a later time pretending to be A) are prevented.

Unfortunately, we cannot simply read and write to the socket governed by TLS. There is a new set of APIs for communicating with TLS. OpenSSL is one such API (the SSL is retained from when it implemented SSL; it is now compliant with TLS). It includes functions like: SSL_connect, SSL_accept, SSL_read, SSL_write, and SSL_ get_error. Though similar to the generic connect, accept, read, and write functions, there are important differences.

- Connections require certificates that authenticate the endpoint's server (e.g., server B). A connection can be accepted but the authentication can fail.
- A read-ready doesn't necessarily mean data is available. TLS inserts handshake and periodic exchanges between servers to ensure integrity. It is possible that a socket may be read-ready but only for the underlying handshake protocol that should remain invisible to the application. In this case, SSL_read may return an error that indicates that it still doesn't have data and the application should wait for a subsequent read event.
- New kinds of errors can creep up such as a client not having a sufficiently sophisticated encryption algorithm to meet the server's requirements.

While most of the discussion of Network Event Processing holds true for TLS, there are important differences and having to handle these will become a more ubiquitous requirement in network programming.

Exercises

1. Create a server that will accept up to 100 connections with a single thread. Each connection will accept a piece of text and the server, when it sees *END*, will send back the number of words and close the connection. The server must recognize when a client closes the connection prematurely. Test the server with 100 concurrent clients and make sure that if 101 connections are attempted that one connection is not processed until an existing connection completes.
2. Enhance the server in exercise 1 to automatically disconnect a connection if it is idle for more than 10 s without sending *END*.
3. Create a trivial web server. It will receive requests of the form:

```
GET /<filename> HTTP/1.1<CR><LF>
Host: 127.0.0.1<CR><LF>
User-Agent: <some string><CR><LF>
Accept: */*<CR><LF>
<CR><LF>
```

The filename is a file that can be accessed by the server. Each line is terminated by a carriage-return character (<CR>, octal 015) and a line-feed character (<LF>, octal 012). Two successive <CR><LF> sequences mark the end of the request.

The response should be:

```
HTTP/1.1 200 OK<CR><LF>
Content-Length: <length of file><CR><LF>
<CR><LF>
<contents of file>
```

The cURL utility can be used to test, e.g.,

```
curl https://127.0.0.1:8000/test-file
```

Start by processing a connection synchronously in a single thread.

4. Enhance the server in #3 to support multiple connections using an event loop. The event loop will read some fixed amount from the designated file and then write that content in response until all the content has been read and transferred. This will require a context object to be associated with each socket to hold the content that was read from the file that needs to be written to the socket. When the event system needs to write, it will use the buffer in the context.

Chapter 6
Digital Fingerprinting

We have already seen the usefulness of hashing in Chap. 1—Hash Tables. We will now look at some other ways hashing can be exploited. Some of the examples are of less general use (for example, finding the longest palindrome in a string of letters) but will illustrate how what appear to be lexical problems can be viewed through a numeric lens.

Finding a Fixed String

In Chap. 2, we showed how a finite state machine can be used to find strings. This is quite effective especially when the strings being searched for are fixed beforehand. A set of keywords is a good example. But generating a state machine dynamically for a provided string and then using that machine to find the string is more complicated. The finite state machine can be fairly complicated, especially if the search is to be $O(n)$ where n is the length of the text we are searching through. For example, consider searching for the target string "ababe" in the source string "ababfababe." The finite state machine will start at the first "a," match four characters ("abab") and detect a mismatch between the "f" and "e" in the target string. Now what? Do we restart the search at "b" (the second letter in the source string), and quickly fail, and advance to the second "a" (the third letter) and start again and so forth. Without adding prefix matching states to the finite state machine so that partially matched substrings can be excluded, the cost of the search is $O(m \cdot n)$ where m is the length of the target string and n is the length of the source string. That is equivalent to simply walking the source string and comparing the target string at each character position (Fig 6.1).

Supplementary Information The online version contains supplementary material available at https://doi.org/10.1007/978-981-92-0260-7_6.

M. Kilian, *Ten Software Patterns Every Student Should Know*,
https://doi.org/10.1007/978-981-92-0260-7_6

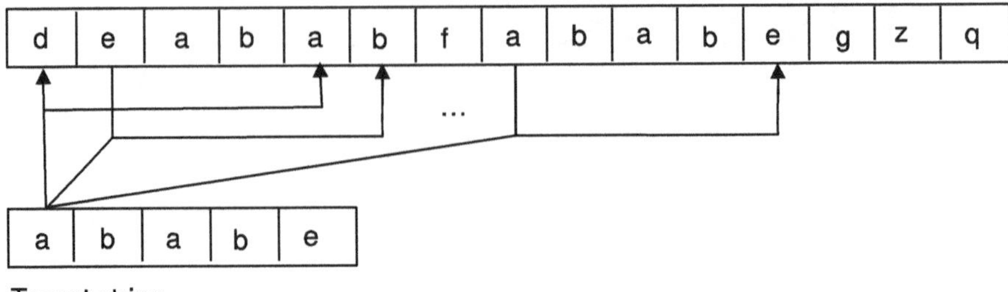

Fig. 6.1 Byte-by-byte comparison of the target string with the source string

In the next section, we show a relatively simple way to find a fixed string in some text that is $O(n)$ (with a caveat that we explain below).

Rolling Hash

In Chap. 1, the hash function mapped a string of bytes to a number. The intent was that the hash did a good job of mixing up the bytes so that two strings of bytes, even if differing only slightly, would with high probability map to different numbers.

The rolling hash (Karp et al. 1987) also derives a number from a string of bytes. However, it has a unique characteristic: A byte can be added or removed from the string of bytes, and the new hash can be computed from only the previous hash and the new byte (or removed byte). If I have the hash of "abcd" (say H) and want to calculate the hash of "abcde," the new hash will be $f(H,$ *"e"*) where f is a simple function (for example, it only uses integer add and multiply). Similarly, calculating the hash of "bcde" from H is equivalent to $f(g(H,$ *"a"*), *"e"*), where g removes the first letter ("a") and f adds the 'e').

The rolling hash can allow a sliding window of hash values to be calculated very quickly. For example, the hashes of all the five-character substrings in a 2,000-character source string can be done by examining each character in the source string only once. For example, a naïve hashing solution would hash characters c_1, c_2, c_3, c_4, c_5 to get the hash of the first substring, and then hash c_2, c_2, c_3, c_4, c_5, c_6 for the next, and so on. The result is that we must "touch" 2000 × 5 characters to get all the hashes. In the case of the rolling hash, H_0 = Hash of (c_1, c_2, c_3, c_4, c_5) and H_1 = Hash of (c_2, c_3, c_4, c_5, c_6) = f(g(H_0,,c1), c_6) where f and g are again simple functions involving only addition and multiplication. The original 2,000 characters must be only accessed twice: Once to add to the hash, and once to remove them.

A common rolling hash function has this form to hash a string of k bytes: $c_1..c_k$.

$$H = c_1 \cdot a^{k-1} + c_2 \cdot a^{k-2} + \cdots + c_k \cdot a^0 \tag{6.1}$$

All the arithmetic is performed according to some modulus, typically a large prime and designated as *p* below, and *a* is a value greater than (but close to) the largest value of *c*, and also prime, and is called the *base*. For example, if we would like H to fit into a signed 32-bit number, and the bytes are limited to ASCII values (i.e., $c_i < 128$), then choosing the modulus *p* to be 1,000,000,009 and the base *a* as 131 works well.

Modular Arithmetic Much of this section depends on *modular arithmetic*, in which the operations are performed and then reduced by a modulus. Reducing a number *n* by modulus *p* (abbreviated n mod p) is done by dividing *n* by *p* and taking the remainder. For example, 21 mod 8 = 5 since 21 / 8 is 2 with a remainder of 5.

There are some helpful rules when calculating mod *p*:

$$(a \times b) \bmod p = ((a \bmod p) \times (b \bmod p)) \bmod p$$

$$(a + b) \bmod p = ((a \bmod p) + (b \bmod p)) \bmod p$$

$$(a - b) \bmod p = ((a \bmod p) - (b \bmod p)) \bmod p$$

There is no corresponding rule for division, i.e., (a / b) mod p ≠ ((a mod p) / (b mod p)) mod p-a mod p = p – (a mod p) (and so it is possible to have all negative numbers be converted to positive ones).

a^b mod p can be calculated in multiple ways. A simple way is to use a loop:

```
c = 1;
for (i=0; i<b; i++) c = (c * a) mod p;
answer is c.
```

This is linear in the power b. A faster way is to square a, then square that result and so forth for $\log_2 b$ times. Repeat for the remainder of the exponent so that the overall cost of raising the power is O(log(b)).

In practice, it is helpful to create "mod_plus" and "mod_times" operations to replace conventional addition and multiplication operators. Also, it is important to avoid overflow when performing modular arithmetic. When performing (a × b) mod p, the wrong result will occur if a × b overflows. For example, if two 32-bit numbers are multiplied creating a 64-bit result, the operation has effectively been done modulo 2^{32} before applying the intended modulus. That will not be the correct result. In this case, perform the operation using 64 bits and then take the modulus to return the value to a 32-bit number. Likewise, be careful with subtraction. If a–b will result in a negative number, it might be reasonable to first convert b to a "negative" number modulo p, i.e., (p-b). and then add it to a. The representations can be unsigned in this case.

Of course there are libraries available for efficient modular arithmetic.

Using Rolling Hash to Find a Fixed String

Let's say we are looking for a target string $T = t_1, t_2, \ldots, t_m$ in a source string $S = c_1, c_2, \ldots, c_n$ ($m < n$). Using the rolling hash, we can find the target in the source string by just looking at each character in the target string once, and each character in the source string once. Our first step is to use Eq. (6.1) to calculate the rolling hash of the target string:

$$\text{Hash(T)} = t_1 \cdot a^{m-1} + t_2 \cdot a^{m-2} + \cdots + t_m \cdot a^0$$

(and again, all arithmetic operations are done modulo p).

We then calculate the rolling hash of the first m characters of the source string.

$$\text{Hash(S1..m)} = c_1 \cdot a^{m-1} + c_2 \cdot a^{m-2} + \cdots + c_m \cdot a^0$$

If Hash(T) = Hash($S_{1..m}$) then we have found, with high probability, a match of T in S at position 1. But if there is no match, then we move to the characters $c_2..c_{m+1}$ but hashed with same exponentiation of the base, i.e., $c_2 \cdot a^{m-1} + \cdots + c_{m+1} \cdot a^0$. This is equivalent to:

$$\text{Hash}(S_{2\ldots m+1}) = \left(\text{Hash}(S_{1\ldots m}) - c_1 \cdot a^{m-1}\right) \times a + C_{m+1}$$

In short, we remove the first character, and shift the hash left (because we have removed the first character) by multiplying the hash by the base. We then add the new character. All operations are modulo p.

Now we compare this hash against the target hash Hash(T), and if it matches, we have a high probability of being done; otherwise, we repeat the process, removing the contribution of the left character and adding a character to the right.

Here is the gist of the algorithm. We use the type `MOD_VALUE` to explicitly delineate where a value should be mod p, where p is our modulus. The variable `rolling_base` corresponds to a in the discussion above.

```
MOD_VALUE calc_rolling_hash(char *s, size_t k) {
 MOD_VALUE hash = 0;
 for (size_t i=0; i<k; i++) {
 // If this is to be case insensitive, convert s[i] to lowercase.
  hash = mod_add(
                 mod_mul(hash, rolling_base),
                 (MOD_VALUE) s[i]);
 }
 return hash;
}

MOD_VALUE shift_window(
                    MOD_VALUE prev_hash, MOD_VALUE left_byte,
                    MOD_VALUE right_byte, MOD_VALUE multiplier) {
 MOD_VALUE drop_left_byte_hash =
           mod_sub(prev_hash,mod_mul(left_byte, multiplier));
```

```
17  MOD_VALUE new_hash =
18          mod_add(mod_mul(drop_left_byte_hash, rolling_base),
19                   right_byte);
20  return new_hash;
21 }
22
23 int32_t find_substring(char *string, char *substring) {
24  size_t l = strlen(string);
25  size_t k = strlen(substring);
26
27  MOD_VALUE target_hash = calc_rolling_hash(substring, k);
28  MOD_VALUE current_hash = calc_rolling_hash(string, k);
29  MOD_VALUE multiplier =
30                         mod_power(rolling_base, (int32_t)(k-1));
31
32  size_t i = 0;
33
34  do {
35     if (current_hash == target_hash) {
36       if (strncmp(&string[i], substring, k) == 0) {
37         return i;
38       }
39     }
40
41    if (i + k == l) {
42      return -1;
43    }
44    current_hash = shift_window(current_hash,
45                                 string[i],
46                                 string[i+k],
47                                 multiplier);48    i++;
49  } while (true);
50 }
```

Line 1 Given a string s of k characters, calculate the rolling hash. All operations are performed modulo p (which is intrinsic to the mod_xxx operations used).

Line 4 In this case, we multiply the previous hash by our base (*rolling_base*) and add in the next character. This automatically creates the a^k that we show in the explanation above. For example, we start with hash = 0, and the next iteration will be hash × a + s[0] = s[0]. The next iteration will be s[0] × a + s[1], the next iteration becomes s[0] × a^2 + s[1] × a + s[2], and so forth so that in the end we have s[0] × a^{k-1} + ··· + s[k-1].

Lines 11–20 We drop the first byte's (left_byte) contribution to the hash, multiply the remainder by the base, and add in the new byte (right_byte). We are going from

$$s[i] \times a^{k-1} + s[i+1] \times a^{k-2} + \cdots + s[i+k-1]$$

to

$$s[i+1] \times a^{k-1} + \cdots + s[i+l-1] \times a + s[i+k]$$

where s[i] = left_byte and s[i+k] = right_byte. The `multiplier` passed in is a^{k-1} the multiplier of the first term of the rolling hash.

Lines 23–30 We are looking for a string of length *k* that matches target_hash. We kick off the search with the hash of the first *k* characters of the source string (current_hash). The multiplier of the character that we drop is fixed to a^{k-1} (rolling_base is equivalent to *a*).

Lines 35–39 If the hashes match, then verify the match. If correct, then return the index of the match; otherwise, continue the search.

Lines 44–48 Move the search window over one byte. We visit each byte twice: once to add it to the rolling hash and once to remove it, so the complexity is *O*(*n*) where *n* is the length of the source string.

Note that we find a match with *high probability.* We are comparing hashes to determine if two strings match. If the hashes are different, then it is 100% certain that the strings do not match. But if they do match, there is a probability of a hash collision. The probability of collision is roughly:

$$P = \frac{1}{p}, \text{ where p = the modulus.}$$

In the example above, p = 1,000,000,009, so the probability of a hash collision is roughly one in a billion. False matches are unlikely. However, to eliminate even this uncertainty, the match can be verified with a final string comparison (as we do in line 31). This does not change the overall complexity of the algorithm, i.e., it is still *O*(*n*).

If you are searching for a match to a fixed set of keywords, then a finite state machine effectively searches for a match to all of the keywords simultaneously and is more effective. But when the keyword being searched for is unknown (e.g., a user enters it as a search term), the rolling hash method is quite efficient and relatively simple to code.

Finding the Longest Palindrome

This section is an amuse-bouche of sorts. You will almost never need to find a palindrome (let alone the longest palindrome) in a string in "real life" (with the exception of a programming challenge in an interview and some bio-computing cases where palindromic amino acid sequences are important to regulating gene expression and even cancer (Miklenic et al. 2021)). The reason to include this is to show how rolling hashes can be applied in innovative ways to create a fairly simple algorithm that is more efficient than a traditional approach. A more practical example follows in the section on synchronizing content.

What is a Palindrome

A palindrome is a string of characters that reads the same forward or backward. For example, the phrase "A man a plan a canal Panama" has the same order of characters going forward or backward.

```
A man  a  plan  a  canal  Panama
```

Palindromes can be even or odd, depending on the number of characters in the string. The string "abba" is an even palindrome; "aba" is an odd palindrome. In the case of the odd palindrome, there is no mirror for the middle character.

The challenge is to find the longest palindrome in some arbitrary text of length n. Creating an $O(n^3)$ algorithm is straightforward. You walk the source string and check for all the palindromes at each character position (taking into account both odd and even palindromes), recording the longest one found so far. The longest one found so far when you reach the end of the source string is the longest palindrome. Searching for a palindrome is $O(n^2)$ and we are doing that at each character, so the final complexity is $O(n^3)$.

It is possible to find the longest palindrome with an $O(n)$ algorithm (Manacher 1975). This algorithm exploits the property that longer palindromes contain shorter palindromes, and once the shorter palindrome is found, it need not be revisited (the longer palindrome is built from it). The algorithm is not completely straightforward, but if getting the fastest time is critical, then it would be the choice.

Using Rolling Hash to find Palindromes

With rolling hashes, we can find an $O(n \log n)$ solution to finding the longest palindrome in a string. This is better than $O(n^3)$ for the brute force approach, but not as good as the Manacher algorithm. If for some reason you really need to find palindromes very efficiently, the $O(n)$ algorithm is the way to go. We present the rolling hash solution because it is an ingenious application of a numerical algorithm and shows how knowing a little math can help in solving what appears to be a problem of text recognition.

A Slightly Different Rolling Hash

In the palindrome finding algorithm, the rolling hash changes slightly. The rolling hash of a string of *m* bytes will be:

$$\mathrm{Hash(S)} = c_1 + c_2 \cdot a^1 + \cdots + c_m \cdot a^{m-1} \tag{6.2}$$

Again, all arithmetic is performed modulo p as above. The multipliers increase with character position rather than decreasing as in Eq. (6.1) above. We also stipulate that the hash of an empty string is 0. Adding a character to the rolling hash is a little different than above:

$$\mathrm{Hash(S_{k+1})} = \mathrm{Hash(S_k)} + c_{k+1} \cdot a^{k}$$

This rolling hash has an interesting property. Let S_k be the string $c_1, c_2, \ldots, c_k$ (k > 0) with S_0 being the empty string (and $\mathrm{Hash}(S_0) = = 0$). $S_{j..k}$ will be the substring from j to k: cj, $c_{j+1}, \ldots, c_k$. The rolling hash of a substring $S_{j..k}$ ($j > 0, j \leq k$) is:

$$\mathrm{Hash}\left(S_{j..k}\right) = \mathrm{Hash}(S_k) - \mathrm{Hash}\left(S_{j-1}\right)$$

and as usual, all arithmetic is done with a common modulus. In short, the hash of any substring is the hash of the whole string up to the end of the substring minus the hash of the characters before the substring. Given the string "abcdefg," the Hash("cde") will be Hash("abcde")—Hash("ab"), a simple subtraction (modulo p) once the rolling hashes are calculated (Fig 6.2).

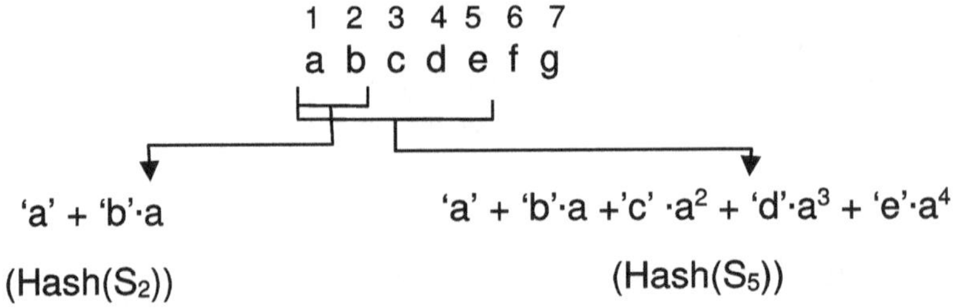

1 2 3 4 5 6 7

a b c d e f g

'a' + 'b'·a

(Hash(S_2))

'a' + 'b'·a +'c' ·a^2 + 'd'·a^3 + 'e'·a^4

(Hash(S_5))

(Hash($S_{3\text{-}5}$)) = Hash(S_5) - Hash(S_2) = 'c' ·a^2 + 'd'·a^3 + 'e'·a^4

Fig. 6.2 Computing hash of a substring using rolling hashes over the string

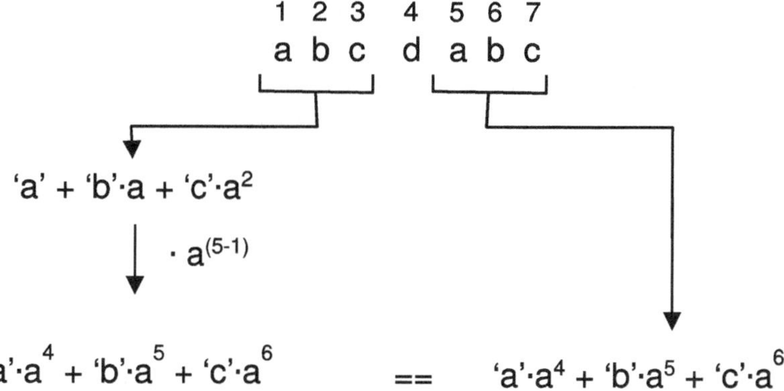

Fig. 6.3 Comparing two substrings using rolling hashes. Match is probabilistic

By traversing the string once and recording in a table the rolling hash at each character position in the source string, we can subsequently calculate the hash of any substring in constant time by simply subtracting the hash of the prefix of the string from the hash of the string up to the last character.

Two substrings Sj..k and Sp..q are the same if

$$\mathrm{Hash}\left(\mathrm{S}_{\mathrm{p..q}}\right) == \mathrm{a}^{\mathrm{p-j}} \times \mathrm{Hash}\left(\mathrm{S}_{\mathrm{j..k}}\right) \quad (\text{assuming } \mathrm{p} \geq \mathrm{j}) \tag{6.3}$$

The extra multiplier accounts for a different starting point in the string (and hence different exponent). We can think of it as shifting the first substring to the position of the second substring. Comparing the first three characters of "abcdabc" with the last three characters would be performed with (Fig 6.3):

$$\mathrm{Hash}\left(\mathrm{S}_{5,7}\right) == \mathrm{a}^{(5-1)} \times \mathrm{Hash}(\mathrm{S}_{1..3})$$

Reverse Strings

We introduce one more bit of notation. Up to now, we have denoted a substring as $S_{i..j}$ with the implicit assumption that $i \leq j$. If we instead write $S_{j..i}$ $(j \geq i)$, this denotes the substring with characters in reverse order: $c_j, c_{j-1}, \ldots, c_i$. The hash of this is similar to above, except that the characters are treated in reverse order (i.e., from right to left).

$$\begin{aligned} &\mathrm{RHash(S)} = c_m + c_{m-1} \cdot a^1 + \ldots + c_1 \cdot a^{m-1} \\ &\mathrm{RHash}\left(\mathrm{S}_{\mathrm{j..i}}\right)(\mathrm{j} \geq \mathrm{i}) = \mathrm{RHash}(\mathrm{S}_{\mathrm{i}}) - \mathrm{RHash}\left(\mathrm{S}_{\mathrm{j}}\right) \end{aligned} \tag{6.4}$$

When comparing the Hash of $S_{i..k}$ with Rhash of $S_{q..p}$ (q > p) the multiplier is also calculated slightly differently. The multiplier of the leading term of $S_{i..k}$ is a^{j-1} and the multiplier of the leading term of $S_{q..p}$ is a^{n-p} (where *m* is the length of the string) When comparing the two, we must multiply $H(S_{q..p})$ by the ratio of the two multipliers: $a^{n-p} / a^{j-1} = a^{n-p-j+1}$. A forward hashed string $S_{j..k}$ is therefore the same as a reversed hashed string $S_{p..q}$ if:

$$\mathrm{RHash}(S_{p..q}) == a^{m-p-j+1} \times \mathrm{Hash}(S_{j..k}) \tag{6.5}$$

(This assumes that the $p + j < m + 1$, otherwise, we use j-m + p-1 as the exponent and multiply Rhash.)

For the string "abba," we can compare the Hashes to see that

$$\mathrm{Rhash}(\text{“abba”}) == a^{(4-4-1+1)}\mathrm{Hash}(\text{“abba”})\,.$$

We now have a way to gather, in linear time, the hashes of all the substrings of a given length *n* from left to right, and the hashes of all the substrings from right to left. We can also compare these for equality with high probability in O(1) time.

> To achieve O(1) time in comparisons, the *m* powers of *a* need to be precalculated and saved in a table such that multiplier[1] = 1, multiplier[2] = multiplier[1] * a = a, multiplier[3] = multiplier[2] * a = a^2, …, multiplier[m] = multiplier[m-1]*a = a^{m-1}). This can be constructed at the same time the table of rolling hashes is generated. This table and the rolling hash tables represent O(*m*) space required for this algorithm).

Finding a Palindrome of Length k

With this machinery at hand, we can find a palindrome of length *k*. Consider the source string of *n* characters. The basic outline of the approach is to generate a table of the rolling hashes over the source string as well as a table of the reverse rolling hashes. Then iterate with i = 1 to n – k over the table, calculating the $\mathrm{Hash}(S_{i,i+k-1})$ and $\mathrm{Rhash}(S_{i+k-1,i})$ and compare the values using Eq. (6.5). If the values match, then there is likely a palindrome at position i, and it can be checked with a character-by-character check (Fig 6.4).

Here is the rolling hash algorithm for finding a palindrome of length k for a given string *S* of length *n*. It begins with calculating the forward and reverse hashes:

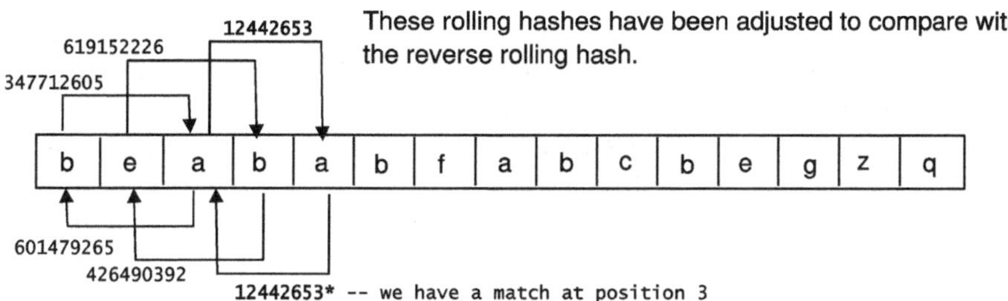

Fig. 6.4 Rolling hash of a three-letter sequence in a string. All hashes can be calculated in linear time

```
1 MOD_VALUE *calculate_forward_hashes(char *s) {
2
3  int32_t l = (int32_t) strlen(s);
4  MOD_VALUE *hashes = new MOD_VALUE[l+1];
5  hashes[0] = 0;
6  MOD_VALUE power = 1;
7
8  for (int32_t i=0; i<l; i++) {
9   hashes[i+1] = mod_add(hashes[i],
10                                  mod_mul((MOD_VALUE) s[i], power));
11    power = mod_mul(power, rolling_base);
12  }
13
14  return hashes;
15 }
```

Lines 1–5 Given a string, we return an array of the hashes of the substrings. Prefixes[0] = 0 which represents the hash of the string after 0 characters. Prefixes[1] = hash of the first character. Prefixes[2] = hash of the first two characters, and so forth. The hash of a substring i..j is Prefixes[j] – Prefixes[i-1] where i,j > 0 (i.e., 1-based string, not 0).

The use of MOD_VALUE is to indicate that the value should always be mod the rolling hash modulus. We use mod_add instead of +, mod_mul instead of * to perform arithmetic modulo our rolling hash modulus.

Line 6 Power will be 1, a (denoted as rolling_base in the code), a^2, a^3, … It is calculated as the hashes are constructed, so there is no repeated raising of a to ever-increasing powers. These values can be saved if we want to avoid recalculating a^k when performing the comparison function.

Line 8–10 Simply loop through the bytes of the string and calculate $\text{Hash}(S_{1..j+1}) = \text{Hash}(S_{1..j}) + S_{j+1} \times a^j$.

Line 11 Note that a^j is represented by power which has its exponent increased each iteration.

A similar function can be used for the reverse hashes.

To find a palindrome of length k is now basically walking the indices and looking at the forward and reverse hashes for matches. The string parameter is rather superfluous; we could have simply passed in the length of the string. However, if we wanted to eliminate the probabilistic nature of the result, we could do a verification on the string to ensure we have not encountered a false match without significant change to the running time of this algorithm.

```
1 int32_t find_palindrome(char *string,
2                          uint32_t k,
3                          MOD_VALUE *forward_hashes,
4                          MOD_VALUE *reverse_hashes) {
5
6  uint32_t n = strlen(string);
7
8  for (uint32_t start = 0; start <= (n - k); start++) {
9   uint32_t finish = start + k - 1;
10
11   MOD_VALUE forward = mod_sub(forward_hashes[finish+1],
12                               forward_hashes[start]);
13   MOD_VALUE reverse = mod_sub(reverse_hashes[start],
14                               reverse_hashes[finish+1]);
15
16   int32_t forward_exponent = (int32_t) start;
17   int32_t reverse_exponent = (int32_t) (n - finish - 1);
18
19   // adjust according to larger exponent.
20   adjust_exponents(&forward, &reverse,
21                    forward_exponent, reverse_exponent);
22
23   if (forward == reverse) {
24     return (int32_t) start;
25   }
26  }
27
28  return -1;
29 }
```

Line 1 The string parameter is rather superfluous; we could have simply passed in the length of the string. However, if we want to eliminate the probabilistic nature of the result, we actually verify that what we found is a palindrome with a character-by-character check without significant change to the running time of this algorithm.

Line 8 start points to the position in the string before the substring we are checking as a palindrome. Position 0 is before the first character and represents the hash of the string before the substring that we will subtract. Position start+finish-1 is the last position of the substring, and represents the minuend of the difference of the hashes to give us the substring hash.

Line 11–14 Calculate the forward and reverse hash for the substring.

Lines 16–21 Adjust one or the other hash based on the exponents of the substring hash's leading terms. As mentioned above, this can be as simple as a table lookup and a multiply.

Line 23 If the forward and reverse hashes are the same, we are done and can report where we found the palindrome. Otherwise, move to the next position in the string. Note that to be absolutely sure that this is a palindrome, a deterministic check can be made by checking that the *k* characters of the string at index *start* are indeed a palindrome (and if not, continue searching).

Line 28 If no palindrome is found, then return -1. In this case, we have walked through n-k pairs of hashes (with a multiplication on one of these hashes at each iteration). This is *O*(*n*).

When building an algorithm with a rolling hash, make sure to choose the modulus *p* and multiplier *a* carefully, and do your arithmetic with enough significant bits that you are not overflowing (effectively performing mod 2^{32} before mod *p*). The above routines use mod_add and mod_mul to emphasize this requirement. There are open-source packages that optimize modular arithmetic. One choice for *a* and *p* is 131 and 1,000,000,0003 when processing ASCII data on 32-bit words using 64-bit arithmetic.

Finding the Longest Palindrome by Binary Search

All of this has built up to finding the longest palindrome in a string. The key idea is to perform a binary search of the lengths of palindromes to find the longest palindrome. Each iteration requires *O*(*n*) operations (see above) and will require *log n* iterations. The result is *O*(*n log n*) time for finding the longest palindrome.

The search process is slightly different for odd palindromes and even palindromes. For even palindromes, the binary search proceeds by first looking for a palindrome of length 2. If that is found, the size is doubled and we search for a palindrome of length 4. If that is found, we double again, and look for a palindrome of length 8. If that is not found, then we look for a palindrome on length 6. If that is not found, then we know the palindrome of length 4 is the longest one available. A similar approach is used for odd palindromes with appropriate assurances that we retain the odd size when doubling or halving the expected size.

Here is an outline of the algorithm for even palindromes. Odd palindromes are handled similarly (with a slight change in the doubling). With some small modifications, the same code can handle both odd and even palindromes.

```
int32_t last_palindrome_length_found = 0;
int32_t last_palindrome_position_found = -1;
int32_t last_palindrome_length_not_found = 0;

int32_t pal_length = 2;
```

```
int32_t pal_position = -1;

while (true) {

  int32_t pal_position =
                find_palindrome(string,
                                pal_length,
                                forward_hashes,
                                reverse_hashes);

int32_t ppal_length = pal_length; // Used to check progress below.

 if (pal_position == -1) {
   if (last_palindrome_length_found == 0) {
     pal_length = -1;
     break;
   }

   last_palindrome_length_not_found = pal_length;

    // Split the difference between the size of the last palindrome found and this size
   pal_length = (last_palindrome_length_found + pal_length)/2;
   pal_length = pal_length + pal_length % 2;

   if (pal_length == ppal_length) { // No advance…we're done.
     break;
   }
  }
  else {
   // Found it.
   last_palindrome_length_found = pal_length;
   last_palindrome_position_found = pal_position;

   // If we didn't find it previously then look for a size halfway
   // between this value and that value. Otherwise double the size.
   // This is the binary search part of the algorithm.

   if (last_palindrome_length_not_found > 0) {
     pal_length = (pal_length +
                   last_palindrome_length_not_found)/2;
   }
   else {
     pal_length = pal_length * 2;
     if (pal_length > 1) {
       pal_length = 1;
     }
   }

   pal_length = pal_length + pal_length % 2;
   if (pal_length == ppal_length) {
     // Not making any progress...
     break;
  }
```

```
59 }
60 }
61
62 last_palindrome_position_found is the index of the palindrome (-
1 if not found)
63 last_palindrome_length_found is how long the palindrome is.
```

Lines 1–6 last_palindrome_length_found will eventually hold the length of the longest palindrome, and last_palindrome_position_found will be the index of the longest palindrome. Pal_length is the length of the palindrome we are currently looking for. Since we are looking for even palindromes, it is initially 2 (and you can guess that if we are looking for odd palindromes, it would be 3). Pal_position is the position of the palindrome of length pal_length.

Line 8 We loop until we can't make any progress, i.e., can't advance the length to find a longer palindrome.

Line 10 See if we can find a palindrome of length pal_length.

Line 15 If we didn't find it, there are two cases: The initial case (last_palindrome_length_found == -1) which means there are no even palindromes, or the case where we found one palindrome of size k and didn't find $2 \times k$ and we need to try between the two.

Lines 26–27 Split the difference between the two. Since we are only considering even palindromes, make sure the new length is even.

Line 29 If the new length is the same as the old, then no progress can be made and we are done.

Line 35–36 We found a palindrome. This must be the largest one we've found so far (we never search for a smaller palindrome than one we've found).

Lines 43–52 There are two cases. If we did not find a palindrome of size l in a previous iteration, and found one of size k now, there may be a palindrome between the two. Split the difference between the two: $(k + l)/2$. If, however, we only found palindromes earlier, simply double the size of the palindrome being looked for (capping it at the length of the string).

Lines 54–58 We are only finding even palindromes in this example. Round the length up to the nearest even number. If we end up with the same length as before (because we have narrowed down the search to a single length), then we know we are done.

Lines 60–61 The loop exits with last_palindrome_position_found being the index of the longest palindrome of length last_palindrome_length_found.

The algorithm can be easily changed to find odd-lengthed palindromes by changing the starting length to 3 and changing line 54 to round the new length to an odd number instead of an even number.

Since each iteration of the algorithm effectively halves the search space, the number of iterations is $O(\log n)$. Each iteration requires a call to `find_palindrome` which is $O(n)$. The result is that the algorithm is $O(n \log n)$. This is true even if you have to run it once for even palindromes, and once for odd palindromes. What changes is the constant multiplying $n \log n$ that is implicit in the $O()$ notation.

With a relatively small piece of code (around 100 lines of C code), finding the longest palindrome can be reduced from $O(n^3)$ to $O(n \log n)$. While finding palindromes is unlikely to be of frequent practical use, the use of a rolling hash and the ability to transform the problem into a binary search on simple values is a valuable lesson that has other applications. The next section shows a more practical use of these techniques.

Synchronizing Content Using Digests and Rolling Hash

There is a very practical use of cryptographic hashing and rolling hashes. Suppose we want to synchronize a large amount of content between two computers located on either side of the United States. Synchronizing the content by sending all the content from one to another could take quite a long time. If most of the content is already identical, then sending all the content would also be very inefficient.

Let's say there is a computer in Anaheim and call it ***A***. ***A*** is communicating with a computer in Boston called ***B***. One approach to reduce transmission is to take the digest of a file ***F*** in ***A*** and send that to ***B***. If ***B***'s copy of ***F*** has the same digest, then ***A*** does not need to send ***F***. The transmission has been reduced from the size of ***F*** (which could be considerable) to the size of a digest, a filename, and a response.

Now suppose ***F*** on ***A*** is 100 megabytes long and differs from ***B***'s copy by a single byte. In the current approach, the digest of ***F*** will differ from ***A*** to ***B***, and the entire file will be transmitted to simply capture the change of a single byte. One approach to improve on this is to logically chop file ***F*** into pieces and to send the digest of each piece from ***B*** to ***A***. Now only the digests of the pieces that have differing digests need to be sent. Unfortunately, this is not terribly efficacious either. If one byte is inserted at the beginning of the file then the digests of all the blocks will differ and again, the whole file will be transferred from ***B*** to ***A***.

(Tridgell 1999) proposed a way to combine rolling hash and cryptographic hash[1] (which is described more completely below) as a way around this problem. It is the basis of a popular tool called *Rsync*. In this algorithm, ***B*** breaks the content into blocks

[1] As will be discussed in a subsequent section, cryptographic hashing has stronger collision resistance behavior than the hashing so far discussed. The probability of false matches is less than a spontaneous, uncorrected memory error in the computer.

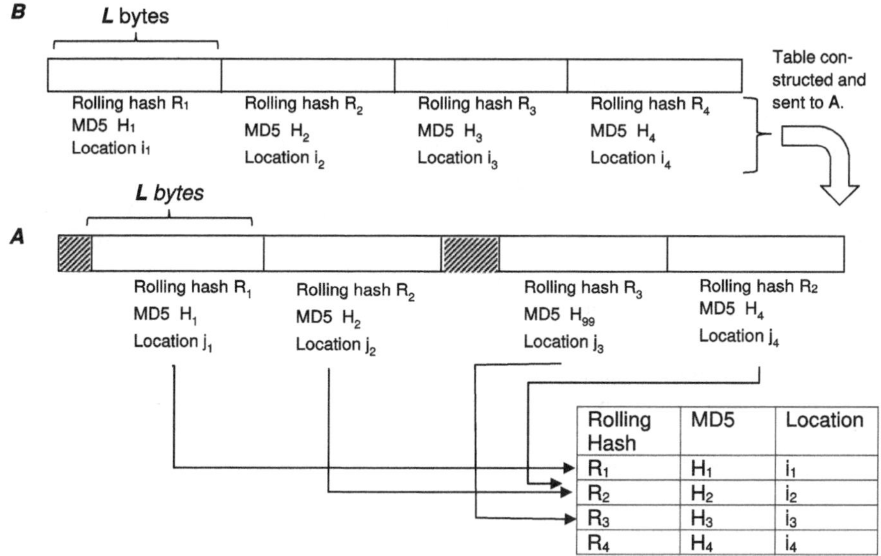

Fig. 6.5 Synchronizing content with rolling hashes—the basis of rsync

of a couple of kilobytes (we will use ***L*** for the length of the block). A cryptographic hash (say MD5) and a rolling hash[2] of the ***L*** bytes are applied to each block and sent from ***B*** to ***A*** along with a description of where the block comes from (e.g., file ABC offset 2048 for 2048 bytes).

After ***B*** completes sending the block rolling hashes, MD5 hashes, and file descriptions, ***A*** then starts processing its content by performing the same rolling hash of ***L*** bytes at each byte in the file. When the rolling hash matches a rolling hash that was received from ***B***, the matching block is checked for the same MD5, and if it matches, then those ***L*** bytes do not need to be sent to ***B***. Instead, A needs only to send a message identifying the matching block and the location it needs to be moved to. For example, B may be told that the content at file ABC offset 2,048 should be moved to offset 2049 and a new byte inserted at offset 2048. A only needs to send the one byte plus the information about the block to be moved. The content need not be transferred and it isn't necessary to limit the block comparisons to within a file. Blocks that match across files can also be handled so that if File X on ***A*** has the same block as File Y on ***B***, then ***B*** can simply copy File Y's block to File X locally without transmitting the block from ***A*** to ***B*** (Fig. 6.5).

In this example, ***B*** has broken the content into four ***L*** length chunks with corresponding rolling and MD5 hashes ($R_1..R_4$, $H_1..H_4$). These are sent to ***A***. ***A*** then proceeds to construct a rolling hash of length ***L***. When the rolling hash advances and equals a rolling hash in the table sent by ***B*** then the MD5 of the ***L*** bytes resulting

[2] (Tridgell 1999) uses a different rolling hash than shown in this section but any rolling hash that is sensitive to the order of bytes and is cheap to compute will work.

in the equal rolling hash is compared with the MD5 from ***B***. If the MD5 matches, ***B*** is told that this block at position *i* can be copied to the output at the appropriate position *j*. Only the identifier of the block and its new position need be sent over the network to ***B***; the content need not be transferred.

Also, the block at j_1 in **A** has rolling hash R_1 and MD5 of H_1. Since these match the corresponding row for R_1 in the table received from **B**, **A** does not need to send this block to **B**. Instead, only the shaded bytes prefixing this block in **A** need to be sent to **B** with instructions to move the bytes at i_1 to j_1 and to insert the new bytes.

Similarly, the block at j_2 matches **B**'s block at i_1. Instructions to relocate this block are sent to B but no content needs to be sent. In the third case, the block at j_3 matches the rolling hash R_3, but its MD5 of H_{99} does not match. **A** must send this entire block (and the shaded area before it) to **B**. Finally, the block at j_4 matches R_2, but its MD5 is not correct, and like the block at j_3, this block must be transferred in its entirety.

After **B** sends a modest amount of data (a set of hashes) to ***A***, only about half of the content needs to be sent back to ***B*** to synchronize the two systems. In practice, the amount of content needing to be synchronized between two systems that are regularly being synchronized is much less than half.

Validating Content

Suppose you have many digital documents that you want to ensure are not changed for their lifetime. This happens in many regulated industries. Stock brokers must keep their emails secure for years and prove to the Securities and Exchange Commission that they have not been tampered with. Likewise, medical records and images like X-rays, MRIs, and CT scans must be retained for a long time with a similar guarantee that they have not been modified illegally.

At one time, this sort of guarantee was provided physically: Documents and images were stored on Write-once laser disks. Companies had storerooms full of cylinders of compact disks storing content spanning years of transactions. In some cases, retrieving this content was so difficult that companies were sanctioned when they could not respond to subpoenas in a timely fashion.[3]

This state of affairs was addressed by a storage methodology called *Content Addressed Storage* (CAS) (Sheldon, 2021). CAS provides a mechanism for both finding content efficiently and verifying that the content found matches what was stored. The crux of this approach is to create a digital fingerprint of the content and then use that fingerprint as the access identifier for the content. The digital fingerprint is created with a cryptographically strong hash.

[3] Morgan Stanley was fined $10 M for failure to produce emails involving the Sunbeam fraud case. This contributed to a later judgment of $1.4B against Morgan Stanley.

Cryptographic Hashing

Chap. 1 introduced hashing as an efficient way to convert a sequence of bytes to a number based on those bytes. We did not care too much about how the hash was computed except that we wanted the hash values of a given set of byte sequences to be uniformly distributed in the hash function's range. Whether two different sequences created the same hash value occasionally was not of tremendous concern (hash collisions were handled as necessary).

Cryptographic hashing makes stronger promises than "ordinary" hashing:

1. It is virtually impossible to determine the item hashed based on the hashed value. The hash is *irreversible.*
2. Hash values are extremely well distributed
3. The probability of hash collision is very low

Three of the more popular cryptographic hash functions are MD5, SHA-1, and SHA-256. MD5 is a 128-bit hash, SHA-1 is 160 bits, and SHA-256 is 256 bits. In general, the more bits, the stronger the guarantees of the hash. MD5 and SHA-1 have been shown to have weaknesses (especially MD5) in an application where an adversary may try to create content with a matching hash without matching the content used to create the original hash. The Rsync algorithm above uses MD5 because it assumes that the two servers communicating are non-adversarial. SHA-256 is quite strong (and is used as part of the protocol for accessing secure websites) and there is a SHA-512 (which is 512 bits long) if even greater security is required.

If using SHA-256, the probability of two pieces of different content creating a hash collision is:

$$\frac{1}{2^{256}}$$

Or 1 in 10^{77}. That is an extraordinarily low probability (the Earth is comprised of approximately 10^{50} atoms to give you an idea of how big 10^{77} is). You are much more likely to have an undetected memory error than to run into this problem even with billions of pieces of content being hashed (Schroeder et al., 2009).

One of the prevalent uses of a cryptographic hash is to provide a hash of the content (also called a *digest*) that can be given as a certificate of the authenticity of the content. To use familiar cryptography characters,[4] Bob sends Alice the SHA-256 of a document followed by the document itself. Alice can verify that the document hasn't been fiddled with en route by calculating the SHA-256 of the document herself and comparing it against the separately sent SHA-256 from Bob. If there is a mismatch, then the document is definitely not the one Bob originally sent.

As we'll see later, it is important that the document and the digest for that document are not sent concurrently. At a minimum, they should be in separate messages. This

[4] Cryptography often describes exchanges between Alice and Bob and less frequently between Ted and Carol.

at least requires two messages to be intercepted and modified. Creating a chain of digests, in a manner similar to how Blockchain ledgers (Susnjara et al. 2026) work, can provide even greater authenticity. As long as the chain can be trusted (and that is a separate discussion), then the authenticity of the records recorded in the chain can be trusted.

Content Addressed Storage

In 2002, EMC introduced a concept called Content Addressed Storage (CAS) (Press, 2026). This was a storage device optimized for storing *fixed content.* Fixed content, as its name implies, rarely changes once created and, in many cases, must be shown not to have changed over its lifetime. Documents, email, seismic information, and X-rays are just a few of the types of information that fit the fixed content category.

One of the major innovations of CAS was that instead of a physical address (like a block number on a disk), or a key like a Social Security number, the digest of the content was used. An application (like an email archive system) would upload an object (like an email or an email attachment) to the system and in return, receive a digest of that content.[5] The digest would be stored in an independent system (often a database) that would be used to allow human search terms (like an email on such-and-such a date between Ted and Carol) to be associated with the digest used to access the content in the CAS system.

Why do this? There are a number of advantages.

1. It is extremely difficult to tamper with the content. If the digest of the content does not match the address used to access the content, then either the content address has been modified or the content has been tampered with.
2. Most CAS systems don't allow deletions (at least for some period of time) so even if both the referring address stored in a separate database and tampered content has been introduced into the CAS system, it is forensically possible to find the original and modified copies and detect the modification—even if the database does not maintain the previous address value.
3. If the same content is uploaded multiple times, the content address will be the same so only a single copy of the content need be saved. This provides so-called *single-instancing* of the content as a natural byproduct of content addressing.
4. Since the address is completely abstracted from the underlying physical organization of the content, the objects can be stored in virtually any fashion. The EMC device made racks of servers look like a single storage device. Requests to store and retrieve content were made over the network using a network API (Chapter 4 discusses network programming).

[5] It was a little more involved than this since arbitrary metadata could also be associated with the object including how long to require the object to remain in the system without modification.

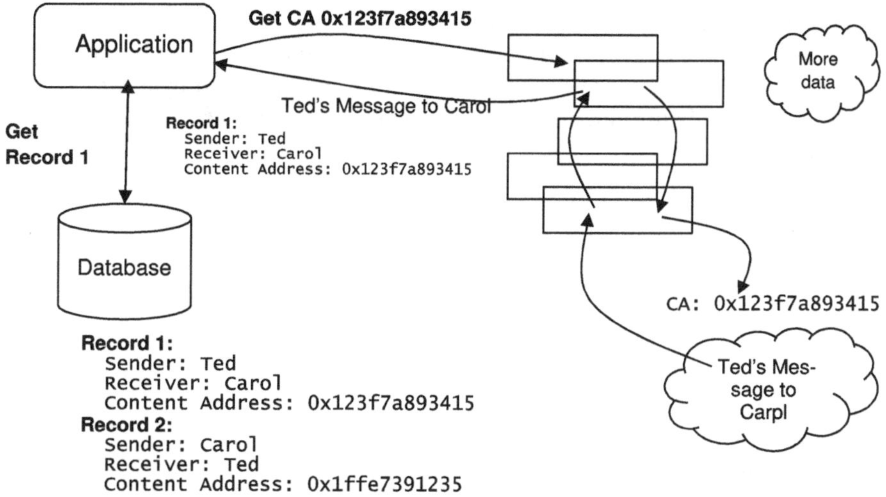

Fig. 6.6 CAS to fetch content allowing complete abstraction of the back-end store

It is important to separate the holder of the content address from the system storing the content with the content address. In most cases, this is a requirement of the application: A document indexing system would likely have a lot of structured content (indices, cross-references, etc.) that would not be stored in the CAS system but would nevertheless reference the documents stored in the CAS system. The authenticity of the content is much easier to ensure when the structured content is stored independently of the fixed content, since two independent systems need to be hacked to, for example, forge the content (Fig. 6.6).

The use of cryptographic hashes for validating content is a robust mechanism, and with the growing use of blockchains, is becoming more ubiquitous.

Remarks The goal of this chapter was to introduce powerful ways of using number theory to solve problems that don't initially appear numeric at all. While finding the longest palindrome may not be often required in practice, the technique of calculating rolling hashes to identify common pieces of content is found in very practical applications such as Rsync. A basic understanding of the approaches discussed in this chapter can lead to very elegant and efficient mechanisms for solving very non-numeric problems.

Exercises

1. Write an application that accepts the name of a file to search in, a string to search for, and then, using a rolling hash, finds the first occurrence of the search string in the file.

2. Implement the longest palindrome algorithm.
3. Synchronize file A with file B using the rsync methodology. What happens when A and B are the same, when A differs from B only in its first byte, when A has one additional byte at the beginning, and when A has one less byte than B at the end.

Chapter 7
Concurrent Programming with Threads

In this chapter, we discuss how to organize programs that do more than one thing at a time. Like network event processing, this is less about algorithms than describing patterns that help in developing correct programs that are running multiple code-streams simultaneously. Concurrent programs can take on multiple forms. Perhaps the most common way of introducing concurrency to a program is with multiple threads. Using multiple processes is also a common approach and will be covered in the next chapter. Data parallelism is yet another variant common in graphic processing unit (GPU) programming. This treatment of concurrent programming will not be exhaustive, just as our networking patterns could not possibly cover all the variations and nuances of networking. It will, however, introduce several distinct programming techniques that help in writing correct concurrent programs.

Threads

Threads can be thought of as a set of functions that are running independently at the same time and that these functions share the program data A program will contain some amount of state, such as a list of bank accounts that need to be reconciled, and functions that run concurrently processing that table (e.g., fetching balances, checking for fraud, reconciling transactions on the account and updating its balance). Programming with threads has been alluded to in earlier chapters, particularly the discussion of multiple threads accessing a hash table, or a network server processing multiple requests simultaneously (Fig. 7.1).

Supplementary Information The online version contains supplementary material available at https://doi.org/10.1007/978-981-92-0260-7_7.

M. Kilian, *Ten Software Patterns Every Student Should Know*,
https://doi.org/10.1007/978-981-92-0260-7_7

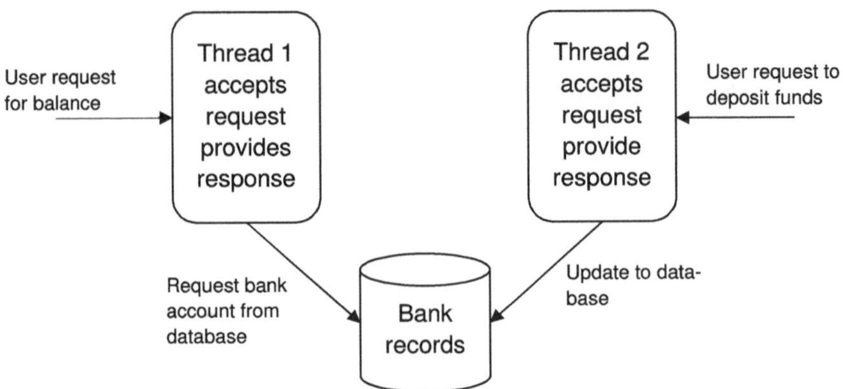

Fig. 7.1 Two threads simultaneously receiving requests and processing them against a shared database of bank records

Most programming languages have their own take on threads. In C and C++, the *pthread* API is commonly used as are various libraries such as the std::thread and Boost. Thread libraries for C++. There are also multiple programming models associated with concurrent programming. Basic threading is often layered with concepts to create more abstract models such as Actors (Agha 1986), and Linda (Cafriero et al. 1989). We will be using a simplified thread API for creating threads, taking locks, and other common functions with threads. A more detailed description of this API is presented at the end of this chapter.

Virtually every computer from tiny Raspberry Zeros to massive IBM mainframes has more than one CPU, known as a *core*. With this comes true multiprocessing: code really runs in multiple threads at the same time while sharing resources like memory, networks, and storage. This means that running code as simple as:

$$i = i + 1$$

can produce the wrong result if two threads share the variable `i` and try to increment it simultaneously. The expected behavior is that `i` will equal the number of times this statement runs. Let us suppose the value of `i` is 3 before the statement is executed. Two threads read `i` out of the memory and add one to it. Both threads have the value 4 as the result of the addition and both will store the value 4. The final value of variable `i` is 4, not the expected 5, and does not reflect the number of additions. The value will depend on when each thread is running on one or more of the cores. This is known as a *race condition* since the winner depends on who stores their value last.[1] If three threads are running simultaneously, the first two could read out the value 3, one gets the value 4 stored when the third thread reads that, increments that and stores 5 while the second thread finally writes 4 overwriting the 5.

[1] In this case, the loser of the race—the last one to execute—actually wins.

The challenge is to tame this herd of threads so that they do not trample themselves while still performing work in parallel. The following section will discuss how we govern access to state that is shared by multiple threads.

Locking Basics

One of the most common models of concurrent programs is to have multiple threads of control share a common resource.[2] One example might be a group of workers sharing a queue of work items that have arrived over a network connection (as discussed in Chap. 5: Creating a Multithreaded Server). At a high level, the thread of control managing the network connection reads a request off the network and places it on a queue. Several workers, as they become free to do work, dequeue that request and then process it. It is important that a work item is only dequeued by a single thread. Imagine a work item to add a deposit to a bank balance. While the customer may be thrilled, the bank would probably not appreciate that work item being dequeued by two workers simultaneously and applying the deposit twice!

Let's outline a basic FIFO queue with operation enqueue, dequeue, and empty functions. We will use a simple double-linked list for the implementation.

```
struct Queue_item {
 struct Item_type *item;
 struct Queue_item *next_item;
 struct Queue_item *prev_item;
};

 struct Queue {
 struct Queue_item *head;
 struct Queue_item *tail;
 };

 void enqueue(struct Queue *queue, struct Item_type *item) {
  struct Queue_item *tail = queue->tail;
  if (tail == NULL) {
  queue->tail = make_Queue_item(item);
  queue->head = queue->tail;
  }
  else {
  struct Queue_item *new_item = make_Queue_item(item);
  new_item->prev_item = tail;
  tail->next_item = new_item;
  queue->tail = new_item;
  }
 }

 struct Item_type *dequeue(struct Queue *queue) {
```

[2] It is possible to have multiple processes share a resource through shared memory. That will be discussed in Chap. 8.

```
27    if (queue->head == NULL) {
28    return NULL;
29    }
30
31    struct Queue_item *head = queue->head;
32    struct Item_type *item = head->item;
33
34    if (head->next_item == NULL) {
35    queue->head = NULL;
36    queue->tail = NULL;
37    }
38    else {
39    head->next_item->prev_item = NULL;
40    queue->head = head->next_item;
41    }
42
43    free(head);
44    return item;
45   }
46
47   bool empty(struct Queue *queue) {
48    return queue->head == NULL;
49   }
```

This is a standard queue: Items are pushed onto the tail of the queue and removed from the head (the opposite could also be implemented as well; it is a matter of taste).

A Note About Item_type

In a real application, you wouldn't use `Item_type`. In C you could most like use `void *` and let the routines managing enqueue/dequeue handle casting to the appropriate type. In C++, `Queue` would be a template type with the template parameter being the type of object in the queue (e.g., `Queue<My_Queued_Item_Type>`). We will simply use `Item_type` with the understanding that this is a proxy for a more practical type.

Now suppose two concurrent threads share this queue, both dequeuing simultaneously. It is easy to get into trouble. Imagine the following sequence of events if the two threads simultaneously dequeue items on a queue with the items 1, 2, 3 enqueued on it (1 at the head about to be dequeued and 3 at the tail) (Fig. 7.2).

One sequence of simultaneous dequeue operations might be:

	Thread 1	Thread 2
1	Line 27: The head is not NULL	Line 27: The head is not NULL
2	Lines 31–32: Point to the Queue_Item with 1	Lines 31–32: Point to the Queue_Item with 1
3	Line 40: Set the Queue_Item with 2's prev_ item to NULL and set head to this item	Line 40: Set the Queue_Item with 2's prev_ item to NULL and set head to this item

(continued)

(continued)

	Thread 1	Thread 2
4	Line 44: Free the Queue_Item with 1	Line 44: Free the Queue_Item with 1
5	Line 45: Return 1 (the item)	Line 45: Return 1 (the item)

Two fundamental errors result. At line 5 in the table, both threads return the same item. This is almost certainly not intended (assuming a worker is doing the dequeue, two workers will end up working on the same item). That can lead to logic problems. Even more fundamental is line 4 in the table: Both threads are freeing the same Queue_item. A double-free will almost certainly corrupt your heap—the memory that we used for allocating the items—and eventually the program will crash (or, worse, corrupt other data irreversibly).

What are the odds of such a coincidence happening? Maybe it's one in a million. One in a billion! But in the life of a program where these operations may be happening every 10 μs, running a billion operations requires 10,000 s or about 3 h. It will probably happen just as you start dinner and the customer support line starts ringing off the hook. In other words, it will happen. In my experience, any hole in the ordering of concurrent operations, no matter how slight, will eventually be found by the program and will be a very, very difficult problem to identify and resolve.

The standard way of preventing two threads from concurrently updating a shared data structure is to use a *lock*. There are a variety of locking mechanisms out there depending on the programming language you are using. For C and C++, there are the *pthread mutex* functions (e.g., `pthread_mutex_lock` and `pthread_mutex_unlock`). Mutexes are another term for locks. In the following discussions, a lock will be declared as `struct Mutex` with functions `lock` and `unlock`.

A thread is said to *hold* (or *acquire*) a mutex when the lock is granted with the `lock` function. The mutex is held until the holding thread releases the lock with the `unlock` function. The code executed between the acquisition of the mutex and the release is referred to as a *critical region*. The thread will only be granted the mutex if it is the exclusive holder of the mutex. If another thread holds the mutex, any other thread trying to lock the mutex will stop and wait for the mutex to be unlocked.

It is therefore very important that whenever a mutex is locked that it be unlocked as expeditiously as possible to allow another thread to access the resources. Frequent locking errors are missing the release of a mutex, or locking multiple mutexes such that a *deadlock* will occur between two threads and both are stalled waiting to acquire a mutex. Deadlocks will be discussed in the Mutex Lock Ordering section.

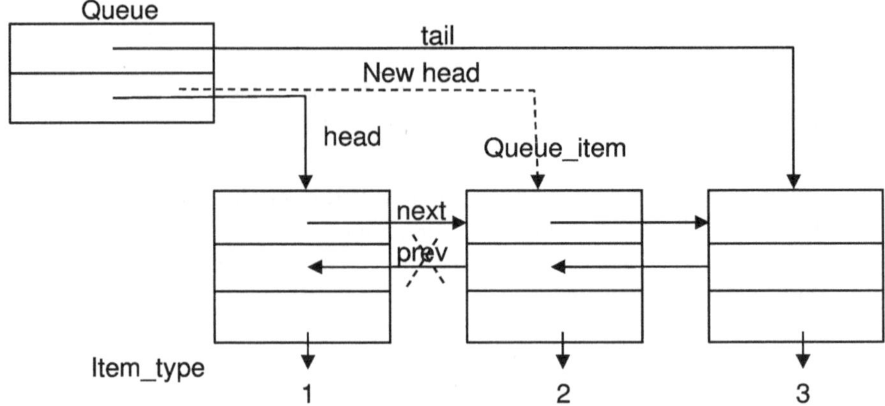

Fig. 7.2 Standard queue model showing the dequeue of item 1

For example, we might have the following change to Queue:

```
struct Queue {
 struct Mutex qlock;
 struct Queue_item *head;
 struct Queue_item *tail;
};

struct Item_type *dequeue(struct Queue *queue) {
 lock(&queue->qlock);
 if (queue->head == NULL) {
  unlock(&queue->qlock);
  return NULL;
  }

  struct Queue_item *head = queue->head;
  struct Item_type *item = head->item;

  if (head->next_item == NULL) {
  queue->head = NULL;
  queue->tail = NULL;
  }
  else {
  head->next_item->prev_item = NULL;
  queue->head = head->next_item;
  }

  free(head);
  unlock(&queue->qlock);
  return item;
 }
```

In this new code, the `dequeue` function first locks the queue's mutex (line 8). Any simultaneous dequeue will have to wait for the thread that currently holds the mutex to finish. It is important to make sure that before the dequeue function exits that the mutex is released (lines 10 and 27). The `enqueue` and `empty` functions would need equivalent locking code controlling the `qlock` mutex. In this way, only one operation (enqueue, dequeue, or empty) can work on a given queue at a time and the chance of one operation corrupting another is eliminated.

Be careful even with this simple locking. Suppose the thread holding the mutex tries to acquire that mutex again. It will block until the holder of the mutex unlocks it. If that is the same thread then it can't release the lock (since it is blocked) and the thread is stuck. This is a classic example of a *deadlock*.

Using C++ to Automatically Lock and Unlock Mutexes

The release of the lock in this example is explicit in the code. This is a requirement of C. In other languages, it is possible to use scoping rules to automatically lock and unlock a mutex. In C++ we can define a class called Scoped_mutex. The constructor of the Scoped_mutex automatically locks it. The destructor unlocks it. It is almost always the case that a Scoped_mutex is *not* heap allocated (i.e., it is not "newed"). Instead it is a scoped variable that, when it goes out of scope the destructor automatically unlocks the lock.

Here is some example code:

```
class Scoped_mutex {
private:
 pthread_mutex_t &lock;
public:
 Scoped_mutex(pthread_mutex_t &l): lock(l) {
 pthread_mutex_lock(&lock);
 cout << "Locking " << &lock << endl;
}

  ~Scoped_mutex() {
  cout << "Unlocking " << &lock << endl;
  pthread_mutex_unlock(&lock);
  }
 };
 ...
 Scoped_mutex l1(mutex_1);
  {
  Scoped_mutex l2(mutex_2);
  {
  Scoped_mutex l3(mutex_3);
  }
  }
```

Line 16 A Scoped_mutex variable is created (l1). The constructor of the Scoped_mutex (Line 5) will lock mutex_1 provided as an argument to the constructor.

Line 18 A separate Scoped_mutex is created with mutex mutex_2. L1 still holds mutex_1.

Line 20 A third lock is established with mutex mutex_3. All three mutexes are now locked.

Line 21 We end the scope of l3. The Scoped_mutex destructor (Line 10) is called for l3 which unlocks the corresponding mutex (mutex_3).

Line 22 The scope containing l2 is exited and the destructor on l2 correspondingly unlocks mutex mutex_2.

Eventually the outer scope will be exited and mutex_1 will be unlocked. When this code is run the following will be output:

```
Locking 0x5bc00e508160
Locking 0x5bc00e5081a0
Locking 0x5bc00e5081e0
Unlocking 0x5bc00e5081e0
Unlocking 0x5bc00e5081a0
Unlocking 0x5bc00e508160
```

Mutex Lock Ordering

Locking and unlocking a single mutex is not terribly error prone especially if the region of code governed by the mutex is small. As the distance between the lock and unlock calls increases, the chance that an unlock is missed increases, posing a risk of deadlock.

When multiple mutexes are used, one simple rule must be followed: The order of locking mutexes must be the same for all threads. If thread 1 locks mutex A, then mutex B, and then mutex C, then ALL threads must lock these mutexes in the same order. The reason for this can be seen with a simple example:

	Thread 1	Thread 2
1	Lock A	Lock B
2	Try to lock B: Blocked by Thread 2	Try to lock A: Blocked by Thread 1

At this point, Thread 1 and Thread 2 are deadlocked.

Releasing mutexes is not so strict. However, it is not allowed to release a mutex and then reacquire it without observing the locking order. For example, suppose a thread locks mutexes A and B in that order. Suppose this thread then unlocks A and later tries to reacquire it. This is effectively locking B (since it was previously locked) then A, which violates the order. Here's how this can cause deadlock:

	Thread 1	Thread 2
1	Lock A, B	Try to Lock A, blocked by Thread 1
2	Release A, still hold B	A is now granted. Try to lock B, but blocked by Thread 1
3	Try to lock A, blocked by Thread 2	Still blocked by lock B on Thread 1

At step 3. Thread 1 holds mutex B and is trying to get mutex A, but Thread 2, already holding mutex A, is blocked trying to get mutex B. Thread 2 won't be able to release mutex A to allow Thread 1 to proceed and eventually release mutex B. Each thread is stuck waiting on the other and cannot proceed which is a classic deadlock.

In general, it is required to unlock mutexes in the reverse order of locking them. Other strategies for managing multiple mutexes are discussed in Chap. 8.

A Word to the Wise: Wrapping Mutexes

When working on a complex system with lots of locks and not necessarily obvious locking and unlocking relationships, it is often useful to create a structure the wraps the lock with more functionality. For example, a common question when analyzing a program is "How often was this mutex used, and what was the average and maximum wait time for the lock to be granted?" It is also possible to provide simple deadlock detection by noting when the same thread is trying to lock a mutex that is already locked by that thread. There are even examples where lock ordering is monitored so that out-of-order locking can be flagged. All of these features can be added so that they are available when debugging a program but are disabled (and literally removed from the executable) when the program is shipped to a customer. We will discuss more about creating a monitoring infrastructure in Chap. 10.

For example, on Linux in C, the pthread locking system includes pthread_mutex_init, pthread_mutex_lock, and pthread_mutex_unlock. A possible wrapping might be:

```
struct Wrapped_mutex {
 pthread_mutex_t the_mutex;
 TIMER lock_hold_start;
 uint64_t num_locks;
 uint64_t wait_time;
 uint64_t hold_time;
};

void mutex_lock(struct Wrapped_mutex *m) {
   TIMER start_wait = GET_TIMER();
   pthread_mutex_lock(&m->the_mutex);
   TIMER end_wait = GET_TIMER();
```

```
13   m->wait_time += end_wait - start_wait;
14   m->num_locks++;
15   m->lock_hold_start = end_wait;
16  }
17
18  void mutex_unlock(struct Wrapped_mutex *m) {
19   pthread_mutex_unlock(&m->the_mutex);
20   TIMER lock_hold_end = GET_TIMER();
21   m->hold_time += (lock_hold_end - m->lock_hold_start);
22  }
```

Line 2 This is the actual mutex at the operating system level.

Line 3 We set this when we succeed in acquiring the lock on the mutex. It is used to determine how long the lock was held.

Lines 4–5 Statistics for the lock. How often was the lock taken, the total wait-time before the lock is granted, and the total time the lock was held.

Lines 10–13 Take the lock and record how long it took to get the lock (the wait time). GET_TIMER is a stand-in for your favorite timer, e.g., on Linux this might be clock_gettime. Chapter 10 has more discussion on timers.

Line 14 Increment how often this mutex has been locked.

Line 15 Record the start of the interval that this lock has been held.

Line 19 Unlock the underlying pthread mutex.

Lines 20–21 This completes the hold period of the mutex. Record the duration.

Note that some care must be used with this. For instance, GET_TIMER requires some time to execute so enabling this code will eat into production performance. Also note that very high-performance timers (e.g., the high-performance timestamp counter on Intel architectures) can provide different timings on different cores within the same machine. Care must be taken when using these timers when the start of a timing range is on one core and the finish of the timing is on a different core. More about how cores affect timing is in Chap. 10.

Condition Variables

Mutexes ensure exclusive access to a resource. There are times, however, when a program needs to wait for a condition to be satisfied before proceeding.

In the `Queue` example, if the queue is empty the dequeue function returns NULL. A thread waiting for work might check for a work item in a loop:

```
1  Item_type *item = NULL;
2  while ((item = dequeue(the_work_queue)) == NULL);
3   Process the work item
```

At line 2, the loop repeatedly tries to dequeue an item until it finally has one. This will work but is very wasteful of processor resources. The processor will spin, executing this loop 100's of millions of times per second waiting for a work item that might not arrive until tomorrow.

What is needed is a way to wait until a condition occurs. This is done with a *condition variable.* A condition variable is part of a pattern that allows a program to wait until some condition is satisfied. The program is not running (mostly) until the condition is met.

A condition variable has two primary operations:

1. Cause a thread to go to sleep while waiting on the condition variable.
2. Wake up another thread that is waiting on the condition variable.

The thread sleeping and the thread waking up are, almost by definition, not the same (a sleeping thread can't initiate a wake up… it is sleeping!). A condition variable is used in combination with a mutex and some type of boolean expression that decides whether a thread should wait or not. An example can illustrate the relationships of these three constructs. Let's return to the queue example and add a condition variable so that a dequeue will wait for an item if the queue is empty. In this example, the condition we are concerned about is whether the queue is not empty or not.

```
struct Queue {
 struct mutex qlock;
 struct condition_variable condition;

 struct Queue_item *head;
 struct Queue_item *tail;
};

void enqueue(struct Queue *queue, struct Item_type *item) {
  lock(&queue->qlock);
  struct Queue_item *tail = queue->tail;
  if (tail == NULL) {
  queue->tail = make_Queue_item(item);
  queue->head = queue->tail;
  }
  else {
  struct Queue_item *new_item = make_Queue_item(item);
  tail->next_item = new_item;
  queue->tail = new_item;
  }
  condition_signal(&queue->condition);
  unlock(&queue->lock);
 }

 struct Item_type *dequeue(struct Queue *queue) {

  lock(&queue->lock);

  while (queue->head == NULL) {
  condition_wait(&queue->condition, &queue->lock);
  }

  struct Queue_item *head = queue->head;
```

```
34  struct Item_type *item = head->item;
35
36  if (head->next_item == NULL) {
37  queue->head = NULL;
38  queue->tail = NULL;
39  }
40  else {
41  queue->head = head->next_item;
42  }
43
44  free(head);
45
46  unlock(&queue->lock);
47  return item;
48  }
```

Line 3 Building on the version of `Queue` with a mutex serializing access to the queue structures, a *condition variable* is added. This will be used to wait when the queue is empty, and a client wants to dequeue an item.

Line 21 When an item of work is enqueued, the condition variable is used to signal anyone who is waiting for work in the dequeue function. If nobody is waiting, then the signal goes into the ether (more about this below). The signal is sent while the queue is locked; no action can proceed in the waiting thread until the mutex is unlocked.

Lines 29–30 This is the crux of the use of the condition variable. The condition being tested is whether the queue is empty or not (`queue->head == NULL`). If it is empty, then dequeue will wait on the condition variable until it is signaled. The mutex governing the queue (specified in the second parameter of `wait`) is simultaneously unlocked (freeing the queue for enqueue). When an item is enqueued, the condition variable will be signaled by the enqueuing thread and the loop will continue in the dequeuing thread, automatically reacquiring the mutex. If the queue is still empty then the wait begins again (probably because some other thread dequeued ahead of this one). Otherwise, the mutex will be locked and we now have an item to process.

It may seem odd to wait on a condition variable and then immediately check the condition (in this case, that the queue is not empty) when the condition is signaled. If there were only one thread dequeuing, this would not be an issue and we could rest assured that, once signaled, there would be an item on the queue.

Now consider what happens if several threads are simultaneously dequeuing items (for example multiple worker threads). There is a bit of a peculiarity in the `condition_signal`: It's definition is that it will wake up *at least* one thread waiting due to `condition_wait`. That means two threads could be woken up, but only one will lock the mutex; the other will have to wait on the mutex. Let's consider the case where we have three threads: One does an enqueue, and two are going to wait for an item.

Thread 1	Thread 2	Thread 3	State of queue
	Condition-wait, unlock queue	Condition-wait, unlock queue	Empty
Enqueue locks mutex			
Enqueue item, condition-signal, and unlock mutex			1 item
	Wake, lock mutex	Wake, blocked waiting to lock mutex	1 item
	Check: queue not empty: dequeue item		Empty
	Unlock mutex	Lock mutex	Empty
		Check: queue is empty	Empty
		Condition-wait, unlock mutex	Empty

In this scenario, Thread 2 wakes up after Thread 1 enqueues the item and Thread 2 locks the mutex. Simultaneously, Thread 3 wakes up as well but cannot obtain the mutex since Thread 2 has "beat it to the punch." Thread 3 waits while Thread 2 dequeues the item which returns the queue to empty. Thread 2 unlocks the mutex allowing Thread 3 to proceed. Thread 3 returns to the top of its loop, sees the queue is still empty, and issues a new `condition_wait`, waiting for another item to be enqueued.

This pattern is very prototypical of using condition variables:

1. There is a condition that must be met to allow the thread to process some data.
2. The condition is governed by a mutex. The condition requires a mutex otherwise there is no shared state that requires any mediation. If you think you don't need a mutex when using condition variables then it is likely that a condition variable is not what you need.
3. The mutex must be locked when the thread waits. If the condition is satisfied (e.g., the queue is not empty), the thread can proceed to process the items knowing it can do so consistently.
4. If the condition is not satisfied, a `condition_wait` is executed and the mutex will be unlocked while the thread waits.
5. When the condition variable is signaled, the thread wakes up, and locks the mutex. It may have to wait to do that. Once the thread acquires the lock, it must check the condition again and we go back to #3. The condition that allowed the thread to proceed may have changed in between the condition being signaled, and the time the mutex was locked and the thread may need to wait again.

Condition variables are used frequently when doling out work through a mechanism such as a queue.

Semaphores

Another pattern, similar to condition variables, is the *semaphore*. Semaphores are used to flag that something has happened (possibly a fixed number of times) without regard to any particular state. It has two fundamental operations: `signal` (alternatively called `post`) and `wait`. The semaphore can be thought of as a counter that is set to some initial value that can be safely incremented or decremented in a multithreaded environment (this increment or decrement is said to be *atomic*). The wait operation will decrement the counter and the signal operation will increment the counter. If the counter is 0, the thread executing the wait operation will stop until the counter becomes greater than 0 by another thread signaling the semaphore. Once the counter is greater than 0, the thread waiting will resume and atomically decrement the semaphore's counter.

A semaphore can be initialized with a specific count (typically 1) instead of its default (0). Initializing to 1 is often used to ensure a section of code is running exclusively and other threads are blocked. In this case, it is almost exactly like a mutex.

```
1  struct semaphore s;
2  initialize_semaphore(&s, 1);
3  ...
4  semaphore_wait(&s);
5  ... do exclusive work here...
6  semaphore_post(&s);
```

By initializing the semaphore in line 1 to have a count of 1, the first thread to reach line 4 will be granted, but all others will need to wait until line 6 executes in the thread that just completed the exclusive work. Mutexes are almost always used in this context since they are much clearer and slightly faster.

Another common use of semaphores is to allow some number k threads to proceed but the $k + 1$ thread must wait until one of the processing threads completes. This is done exactly as above except that the count in the `initialize_semaphore` is k, not 1. This would allow, for example, k activities to be launched and no more until one of the activities completes and signals the semaphore. This pattern is simpler than a mutex and condition variable which would be required in place of the semaphore.

Concurrent Programming: The Worker Pattern

One of the more common concurrent programming patterns is the *worker pattern*. The pattern Network Event Processing alluded to the worker pattern when a network connection was made and dispatched to a worker to process.

In this section, we will create a dispatcher that uses a pool of threads. When an item of work needs to be processed, the dispatcher removes a thread from the pool and assigns it the task. When the thread completes, the dispatcher returns it to the pool to be assigned another task. The pool can be empty at first and threads added as needed until some limit is reached. If all the threads in the pool are in use the dispatcher must hold the work item until a thread becomes available. If necessary, the dispatcher can stop accepting work (creating one of the larger challenges in developing threaded applications: how to apply backpressure to avoid overwhelming the system) (Fig. 7.3).

As shown, the dispatcher dequeues work items (called *task messages*) from its work queue. Any number of threads may be enqueuing messages, and in fact, multiple dispatchers could be dequeuing messages from the same queue, though that is not a typical way this pattern is implemented. The dispatcher chooses a thread from the pool and hands it the message. While that message is being processed by the thread, the dispatcher is free to dequeue another message and assign it to a different thread from the pool. The goal is to keep a fixed number of threads (the number in the pool) busy with work arriving on the work queue.

The Work Queue needs to be thread safe since multiple threads may be enqueuing messages simultaneously (and the dispatcher will be concurrently removing messages while messages are enqueued). The message being enqueued on the work queue can be as simple as an integer identifying a specify task to do (e.g., the integer 1 means calculate the balance of an account, integer 2 means add a deposit to the balance, integer 3 means subtract a withdrawal from the balance). Alternatively, it can be as complex as a pointer to a relatively arbitrary function that will process an argument object. Simple integers are frequently used and the task dispatched will have a switch statement that will decide what to do based on the integer. The dequeued message will also have the information needed by the thread to complete its designated task.

Depending on the task, the thread may run a very short amount of time (incrementing a simple variable, for example), or process a large transaction such as querying a database. Once the thread completes the task, it is returned to the pool to be used for some other task.

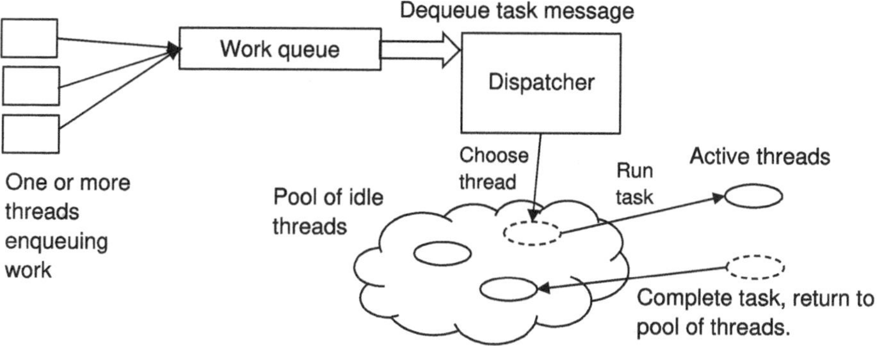

Fig. 7.3 A worker with associated worker-queue. The worker distributes tasks to worker threads

Thread Pools

One way of implementing the dispatcher would be to have it simply create a thread whenever it needed to process a message from the Work Queue and have that thread "go away" when the processing completes. A count can be kept of the number of threads active and the number of active threads can be capped based on this. One reason *not* to use this approach is that creating and launching a thread is not a trivial task in the operating system.

Instead of churning through threads, a pool of threads can be created. A fixed number of threads can be created and reused for processing the work item. The thread never really exits, it simply waits for a new work item to be handed to it. When the operation is complete, the thread is returned to the thread pool for reuse. Dispatching threads from a thread pool is at least an order of magnitude faster than creating and deleting threads for each individual work item and is encouraged if short work items are being distributed to threads rapidly.

Here is an example of simple thread pool with two operations: Get a thread and return a thread. For more information on the thread operations see the notes at the end of this chapter.

```
struct Thread_pool {
 struct Queue *pool;
 int max_threads;
 int current_running;

 struct mutex pool_mutex;
 struct condition_variable pool_cond;
};

 struct Thread *Thread_pool_get_thread(
  struct Thread_pool *pool) {
  lock(&pool->pool_mutex);
  struct Thread *thread = NULL;

  while (pool->current_running == pool->max_threads) {
  condition_wait(&pool->pool_cond, &pool->pool_mutex);
  }

  if (empty(pool->pool)) {
  thread = make_Thread();
  }
  else {
  thread = dequeue(pool->pool);
  }

  pool->current_running++;
  unlock(&pool->pool_mutex);
  return thread;
 }

 void Thread_pool_return_thread(struct Thread_pool *pool,
```

```
32    struct Thread *thread) {
33    lock(&pool->pool_mutex);
34    enqueue(pool->pool, thread);
35
36    pool->current_running--;
37    condition_signal(&pool->pool_cond);
38    unlock(&pool->pool_mutex);
39   }
```

Line 2 The container for idle threads is a queue. It could be any thread-safe collection of items. It might make sense to actually use a LILO queue in this case and this will be discussed in the section The Trouble with Threads.

Lines 3–4 `max_threads` is the maximum number of threads that can be distributed from the pool. The number that have left the pool is `current_running`. The length of the queue + `current_running` must be less than or equal to `max_threads`.

Lines 6–7 All access to the pool must be synchronous (i.e., the mutex must be locked). The pool_cond condition is used when all the pool's threads are in use and we are waiting for one to free up to satisfy the request for thread.

Line 10 There are only two operations in this simple version of a thread pool. This is the get-thread operation. The function returns a thread to the caller and will wait if the maximum number of threads for a given pool has been distributed.

Lines 15–17 If all the threads we are allowed to distribute are already running, then we must wait until one is returned to the pool. This is a classic use of a condition variable. In this implementation, the pool only has references to idle threads; once it hands out a thread it does not keep track of it until the user of the thread returns it to the pool.

Lines 19–24 If the queue of threads is empty, but the number of running threads is less than the maximum (and that must be the case at this point in the code), then we can add a new thread to the pool. We start with no threads in the pool and add them as necessary until we reach the capacity of the pool.

Line 23 Dequeue a thread from the pool. This is the case where we are reusing a thread that was previously used and was returned to the pool.

Lines 26–28 We have one more thread running, we unlock the mutex and return the thread that was either newly created or reused from the pool.

Lines 31–39 Returning a thread to the pool simply means putting it back on the queue, reducing the running count, and signaling a `Thread_pool_get_thread` that may be waiting for a thread to become available.

A dispatcher is now free to dequeue a task, get a thread from the pool, and run a function in the thread to process the task (using `Thread_run` from above). When the task is done it returns itself to the thread pool.

Here is an example of a dispatcher:

```
1  struct task_argument {
2   struct Thread *this_thread;
3   struct Thread_pool *pool;
4   struct Task *the_task;
5  };
6
7  void *run_the_task(void *void_arg) {
8   struct task_argument *arg = (struct task_argument *) void_arg;
9
10   // Do something with arg->the_task
11
12   Thread_pool_return_thread(arg->pool, a->this_thread);
13   free(arg);
14   return NULL;
15  }
16
17  void dispatcher() {
18   struct Thread_pool *pool =
19   make_Thread_Pool(max_concurrent_threads);
20   for (;;) {
21   struct Task *work = dequeue(work_queue);
22   struct Thread *thread = Thread_pool_get_thread(pool);
23   Thread_run(thread,
24   run_the_task,
25   (void *)make_work_arg(work, pool, thread));
26   }
27  }
```

Lines 1–5 We pass this structure to the thread that is actually going to perform the action. We need the thread and pool so we can return the thread to the pool when the action is over. More comments about this later. The actual action to be run depends on the function used to initialize `Task`.

Lines 7–15 This is the task that the dispatcher is launching in a separate thread (taken from the pool). The action is to be filled in at line 10. When the task is over, the thread that is running is returned to the pool, and the argument is freed since nothing is referencing it after the task completes. Note that there are some problems with this structure that we will address in the next paragraph.

Lines 18–19 A thread pool is allocated with some maximum number of threads. No threads are allocated until they are needed.

Line 20 The dispatcher just runs forever taking in work items, performing a task to service the work item, and continuing. As many work items as are in the thread pool will run simultaneously.

Line 21 The work item is received from the source.

Line 22 A thread is fetched from the pool. If there are no threads available in the pool, then the dispatcher will wait for one to become available (one of the concurrently running tasks completes and returns itself to the pool).

Lines 23–25 The function run_the_task is run in the thread retrieved from the pool. The arguments are bundled up in a structure and include the pool and thread (see comment about lines 7–15).

This is an extremely simplistic thread pool and dispatcher.

The `Thread_pool_return_thread` function has a bit of an issue. At the end of the dispatcher's `run_the_task`, the thread is returned to the pool. It is, however, technically still running, albeit briefly. This means that it would be possible for the thread to be returned to the pool and then allocated out of the pool before it is really idle. Running on such a thread would be illegal (you can't run a function on an already running thread).

Here is the sequence that illustrates as shown in Fig. 7.4.

The problem arises from the fact that the running function is returning the thread to the pool. It must be running (otherwise it couldn't execute the call). This is row 3 in the table above. There is a race condition here. If the function returns and the Thread system moves the thread from state running to idle, all is good. But it is possible that the dispatcher receives the signal that the thread is available (because the `run_the_task` function calls `Thread_pool_return_the_thread`) and the dispatcher tries to run the task function before the thread being reused moves from the running state to idle (steps 3–6). It is a small window of vulnerability but as you will find, small windows are never small enough until they are completely closed. There will be a case where something will slip through the open window and the `Thread_run` at line 23 will fail.

There are a number of ways to resolve this race condition.

1. One simple solution is for the dispatcher to check the status of the thread after fetching it from the pool. On the off chance that it is running, it can be returned to the pool and another thread can be used. The downside of this is that if this is the only thread in the pool, there will be a short period of time where the dispatcher is furiously dequeuing the thread, checking, and re-enqueuing it until it reaches a non-running state.

	Dispatcher	Pool	Thread Status	Function Being Run
1	Get thread	Has thread A to give	A is idle	Not running yet
2	Run thread	A is out of pool	A is running	Running task
3				Return to pool
4		A is back in pool	A is still running	About to return
5	Get thread	Has thread A to give	A is still running	Returning
6	Run thread: Error—thread is in running status	A is out of pool	A is running	Returning
7	We've already received an error		A is complete	Finishes. Return

Fig. 7.4 Thread transitions as it is dispatched

2. A better approach is to use the `Thread_run_with_final` API to launch the thread. The final argument would be the pool that the thread was drawn from. When the pool completes, the final function would then return it to the pool.

Here is a simple function to accomplish #2 and the modification to lines 23–25 above.

```
void standard_return_to_pool(struct Thread *thread) {
 struct Thread_pool *pool =
 (struct Thread_pool *) thread->final_parameter;
 Thread_pool_return_thread(pool, thread);
}
```

And replace the `Thread_run` above with:

```
23 Thread_run_with_final(thread,
24  run_the_task, (void *)work,
25  standard_return_to_pool, (void *) pool);
```

Now when the thread is complete, the final function `standard_return_to_pool` will be called which can then safely return the thread to the pool.

Even this relatively simple thread pool is fairly useful.

Putting It Together: Thread Pools and Dispatcher

We can combine the queue with the thread pool to write a very simple message dispatcher.

```
1  for (;;) {
2   struct Message *msg =
3   (struct Message *) dequeue(dispatcher->work_queue);
4   if (msg->message_id == SHUTDOWN) {
5   break;
6   }
7   struct Thread *thread =
8   Thread_pool_get_thread(dispatcher->thread_pool);
9
10   Thread_run_with_final(thread,
11   run_task,
12   (void *) msg,
13   standard_return_to_pool,
14   (void *) dispatcher->thread_pool);
15  }
16
17  Thread_pool_wait_to_be_idle(dispatcher->thread_pool);
```

Lines 1–3 The dispatcher repeatedly waits on the `work_queue` to get a message.

Lines 4–6	If the message is a shutdown message, break out of the loop and gracefully exit the dispatcher.
Lines 7–8	Get a thread from the thread pool. If no threads are available, the dispatcher will need to wait for a thread to become available. This is implicit in the `Thread_pool_get_thread` function.
Lines 10–14	The `run_task` function will process the message. Once it is done, the thread will automatically be returned to the pool. See the end of this chapter for details about `Thread_run_with_final`. In short, when the thread completes it will automatically be returned to the pool.
Line 17	If we get here, it is because a shutdown message was received. Wait for all the currently executing threads in the pool to complete. The dispatcher is now defunct.

The use of a message to shut down the dispatcher will be a pattern we see later when barriers are implemented using messages. "Meta-messages" like shutdown are a powerful way to control the behavior of threads using the worker pattern.

We will have more commentary about the dispatcher below.

Concurrent Programming: Barrier Pattern

Another common pattern in concurrent programming is for a program to wait until a set of tasks have completed and then continue with the result of those tasks. For example, ten threads may each sort a subset of numbers, and when they finish the subsets are merged together to a final result. The merge happens only when the ten threads are complete. The point where the program waits is called a *synchronization barrier*. It is like requiring all of the members of your reservation to arrive before sitting at a table in a restaurant.

This section will look at three ways to implement a synchronization barrier:

1. Waiting for threads to exit
2. Waiting on a condition variable
3. Using a message-passing paradigm.

The third version, while more complex, can be useful when a barrier must coordinate tasks that span multiple computers.

Using Join as a Barrier

The first mechanism works for threads within a single process. It simply runs threads and waits for them to complete. For example, here is simple way to spawn threads to sort sub-arrays so they can be merged into a final, sorted array. (`make_Argument` creates an object used by the running thread. It provides a way for the code launching the thread to pass information to the new thread).

```
1  Thread *all_threads[NUM_THREADS];
2  for (int i=0; i<NUM_THREADS;i++) {
3   all_threads[i] = make_Thread();
4  }
5  for (int i=0; i<NUM_THREADS; i++) {
6   Thread_run(all_threads[i], sort_array, make_Argument(i));
7  }
8  for (int i=0; i<NUM_THREADS; i++) {
9   Thread_wait(all_threads[i]);
10  }
11  Merge_the_arrays();
```

Lines 1–4 We will keep track of all the threads in use. The loop creates the threads but they are not running yet.

Lines 5–7 Run the threads. The `sort_array` function sorts some portion of the array communicated in the argument created by `make_Argument`.

Lines 8–10 The threads are running independent of this thread. Now we wait for them to complete. Note that `all_threads[3]` may complete while we are waiting for `all_threads[0]`. This is OK since our goal is to not proceed until all the threads complete. It may be that all the threads complete in the time it takes `all_threads[0]` to complete in which case the loop will iterate over these threads very quickly. The loop waiting for threads is the barrier. The last thread to complete essentially governs when the loop will complete.

Line 11 Once we cross the barrier, we can be assured that all the sub-arrays are sorted and can now be merged.

This works fine if the tasks are significant enough to warrant the cost of running a separate thread just for that task. If work must be distributed frequently then a thread pool can help ameliorate some of that cost.

What this technique doesn't allow for is a set of threads to perform work, each reach a barrier, and then continue doing work without exiting the thread. This can be done with a condition variable and a new way of signaling the threads waiting on that condition variable.

Using a Condition Variable for a Barrier

For simple, coarse-grained parallelism, the run-thread-and-join barrier model is fairly simple and effective. Suppose, instead, we want the threads to perform some work, reach a barrier, and then continue to the next task without exiting, and without coordinating with a central control task. The pattern would be: Work—wait at barrier until all members are done—work—wait, and repeat until the program completes.

This can be done with a condition variable. The condition will be whether the barrier is done or not. It will be protected by a mutex associated with the barrier. There are many designs available for this, but here is one where each thread receives a barrier object and they "check-in-and-wait" for all other threads to similarly check-in. The initialization includes the number of threads expected to enter the barrier. Once all the threads check-in, they all will be simultaneously "released."

Here is the basic outline of the barrier:

```
1  struct Barrier {
2   struct condition_variable condition;
3   struct Mutex lock;
4   int32_t count;
5  };
6
7  void initialize_Barrier(struct Barrier *b, int count) {
8   initialize_condition_variable(&b->condition);
9   initialize_Mutex(&b->lock)
10   b->count = count;
11  };
12
13  void Barrier_check_in_and_wait(struct Barrier *b) {
14   lock(&b->lock);
15   if (--b->count == 0) {
16   condition_broadcast(&b->condition);
17   unlock(&b->lock);
18   return;
19   }
20
21   while (b->count > 0) {
22   condition_wait(&b->condition, &b->lock);
23   }
24   unlock(&b->lock);
25  }
```

Lines 1–11 The state of the barrier is the count of threads that need to get through the barrier and is protected with a mutex. When a thread needs to wait on the barrier to complete, it waits on the condition variable. The count is initialized to how many threads must go through the barrier (including the thread instigating the barrier). All the threads share the same barrier and the barrier must be initialized before the threads enter it.

Lines 13–25 Each thread checking into the barrier decrements the count. If the count becomes 0, then the barrier is said to be *satisfied* and all waiting threads (including the thread that caused the count to be 0) may proceed. To wake up all the waiting threads, a new function is called: *condition_broadcast*. Unlike `condition_signal` which wakes up one waiter, `condition_broadcast` will wake up all the threads that are waiting.

Assume the barrier and the number of threads involved with the barrier are passed in to all the threads (e.g., through the thread argument). A program might be set up as:

```
1 num_threads = ... some value ...
2 initialize_Barrier(barrier, num_threads+1);
3 for (int i=0; i<num_threads; i++) {
4  Thread_run(thread[i], do_something, (void *) barrier);
5 }
6 Barrier_check_in_and_wait(barrier);
7 // We know that all the threads are complete.
```

`Num_threads` will be launched and will perform a `Barrier_check_in_and_wait`. When all threads are accounted for (including the thread that initiated the barrier hence the count of `num_threads+1` in line 2), the threads can proceed to other tasks. As long as the number of threads that will participate in the barrier is known, this is a straightforward and reasonably efficient barrier construction.

Using Message-Passing for Barriers

The final approach to barriers we will present uses messages passed between threads to participate in a barrier. It is not only applicable for multiple threads, but it is useful for multiple processes, including processes that span machines, which will be discussed in more detail in Chap. 8.

In this chapter, each thread is implementing the worker pattern[3] described above except it will immediately run actions, not dispatch them to threads from a thread pool (though this would work also). The worker repeatedly dequeues the work item, performs some action, and then fetches the next item. The queues are globally known, i.e., each worker can send a message to any other worker and that message contains the sender of that message. This global knowledge of the other workers is a simplification to allow any-to-any communication and isn't strictly required.

A barrier can now be implemented as a series of messages. The barrier is instigated by any of the workers, and that thread becomes the *coordinator* of the barrier. This is similar to the creator of the barrier in the counted condition variable approach above. The messages involved are:

- Launch a barrier operation. The thread that receives this message will instigate and coordinate the barrier.
- Run a task operation within a barrier. Each worker participating in the barrier will receive this message to run a task.
- Signal that the operation on a thread is done. When a thread completes a task, it signals back to the coordinator of the barrier that it has finished.
- Signal that the barrier has been met. When the coordinator determines that all the tasks are complete, it sends out a message that the barrier is done and "normal" processing can resume.

---

[3] For the purposes of this section, a *worker* is equivalent to a *thread*. All threads in this model are running the worker code to dequeue and dispatch messages.

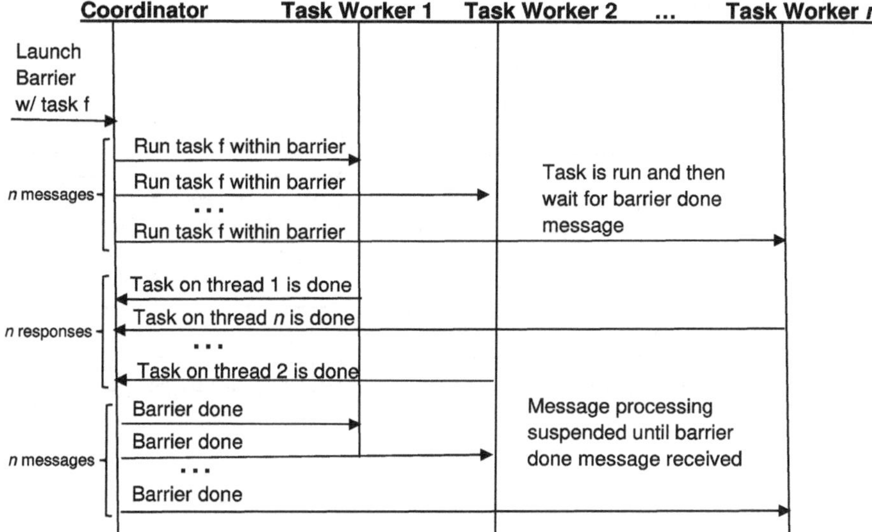

Fig. 7.5 Implementing a barrier with messages

Diagrammatically, the message passing for barrier synchronization looks like as shown in Fig. 7.5.

Note that a task may finish on one worker before another worker even starts its task. Once the coordinator receives the specified number of "task done" messages, it sends out barrier done messages to the barrier participants and the workers resume normal processing.

While the coordinator is marked as separate from the other workers, it can be any worker in the system and may receive `run-task` messages itself. That illustrates an important point: The coordinator need not simply wait for the task workers to report back. It can run a task as a member of the barrier too.

The workers need to keep a little extra state as well. For example, the coordinator needs to know how many workers it included in the barrier and counts that down. When the count reaches zero, then the barrier is complete. It also needs to remember which workers are participating in the barrier so it can send the barrier done message to them upon completion.

Each worker also needs an extra queue. Normally, messages are delivered to a worker's queue and the worker reads from the queue and dispatches the message to an appropriate action function. When the barrier is running, messages arriving at a worker participating in the barrier that don't concern the barrier (e.g., messages to execute an ordinary task) must be postponed until the barrier is complete. A message will be dequeued from the primary queue. If it is not one of the barrier messages listed above, then it is saved on a separate queue (called the *deferred queue*). Once the barrier is complete, any messages on the deferred queue will be processed before the primary queue. This ensures that messages retain their order at the worker.

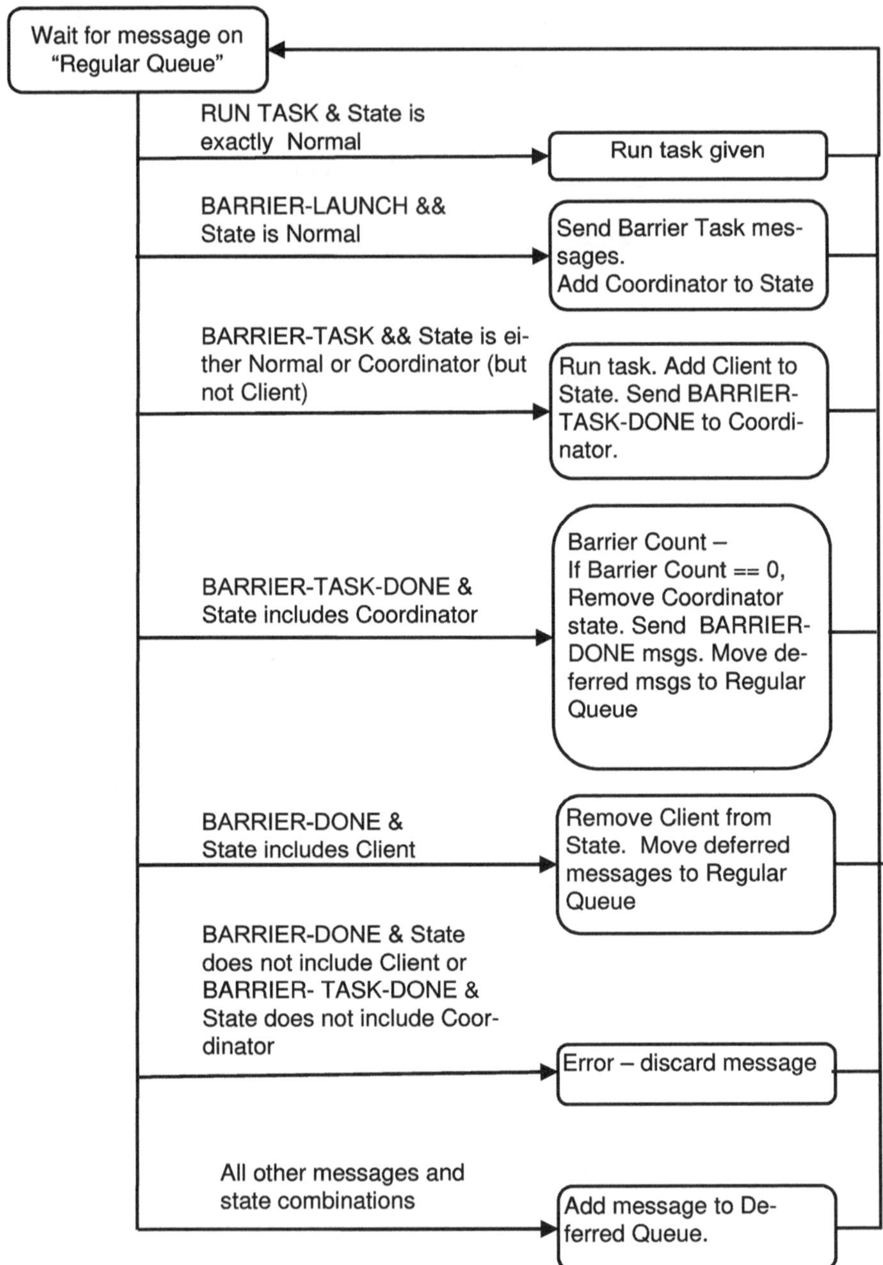

Fig. 7.6 State transitions for barrier messaging

To manage the two queues, a separate piece of state in the worker designates whether the worker is running normally or running inside a barrier as a coordinator or as a client of the barrier. As mentioned above, a worker can be both a coordinator and a client of a barrier.

Here is a quasi-finite state machine of a worker supporting barrier operations. State transitions are based on the message received and the state the thread is in. A TASK message is an ordinary task that is executed, a BARRIER_LAUNCH message starts a coordinator that then sends BARRIER_TASK messages to the participating workers to run a task in a barrier. Those workers will send BARRIER_TASK_DONE messages to the coordinator when the task is completed. When all the tasks are done, the coordinator will broadcast a BARRIER_DONE message to the participants and processing will resume in normal fashion.

Here is one way of implementing the state machine in Fig. 7.6. It assumes that we have a worker with the deferred queue and thread status, and messages that carry information specifying a task to be executed and the return-address information that allows a thread to return a message to the sender.

```
SET_STATE(worker, WORKER_NORMAL);
struct Message *msg = NULL;

while (!(IS_SHUTTING_DOWN(worker))) {
 msg = (struct Message *) dequeue(worker->msg_queue);
 if (IS_EXACTLY_NORMAL(worker) &&
 (MESSAGE_ID(msg) == MSG_SHUTDOWN)) {
 ADD_STATE(worker, WORKER_SHUTTING_DOWN);
 free(msg);
  continue;
 }

 if (IS_EXACTLY_NORMAL(worker) &&
  (MESSAGE_ID(msg) == MSG_TASK)) {
  Worker_run_task(worker, msg);
  free(msg);
  continue;
 }

 if (IS_EXACTLY_NORMAL(worker) &&
  (MESSAGE_ID(msg) == MSG_BARRIER_LAUNCH)) {
  ADD_STATE(worker, WORKER_BARRIER_COORDINATOR);
  struct Message_task *barrier_msg =
  (struct Message_task *) msg;
  worker->barrier_count = num_workers;
  worker_broadcast_message(worker,
  (struct Message *)make_Message_task(
  MSG_BARRIER_TASK,
  worker,
  barrier_msg->function));
  free(msg);
  continue;
 }

```

```
35 if ((IS_NORMAL(worker) || IS_COORDINATOR(worker)) &&
36  (!IS_BARRIER_CLIENT(worker)) &&
37  (MESSAGE_ID(msg) == MSG_BARRIER_TASK)) {
38  ADD_STATE(worker, WORKER_BARRIER_CLIENT);
39  Worker_run_task(worker, msg);
40  Worker_send_message(msg->header.sending_thread,
41  make_Message(MSG_BARRIER_TASK_DONE, worker));
42  free(msg);
43  continue;
44 }
45
46 if (IS_COORDINATOR(worker) &&
47  (MESSAGE_ID(msg) == MSG_BARRIER_TASK_DONE)) {
48  worker->barrier_count--;
49  if (worker->barrier_count == 0) {
50  REMOVE_STATE(worker, WORKER_BARRIER_COORDINATOR);
51  merge(worker->msg_queue,
52  worker->deferred_msg_queue);
53  Worker_broadcast_message(worker,
54  (struct Message *) make_Message(MSG_BARRIER_DONE,
55  worker));
56  }
57  free(msg);
58  continue;
59 }
60
61 if (IS_BARRIER_CLIENT(worker) &&
62  (MESSAGE_ID(msg) == MSG_BARRIER_DONE)) {
63  REMOVE_STATE(worker, WORKER_BARRIER_CLIENT);
64  merge(worker->msg_queue,
65  worker->deferred_msg_queue);
66  free(msg);
67  continue;
68 }
69
70 if (((MESSAGE_ID(msg) == MSG_BARRIER_DONE) &&
71  !IS_BARRIER_CLIENT(worker)) ||
72  (MESSAGE_ID(msg) == MSG_BARRIER_TASK_DONE) &&
73  (!IS_COORDINATOR(worker))) {
74  // This is a message we can't handle in the state we are in.
75  // How this is handled is unspecified.
76  }
77  enqueue(worker->deferred_msg_queue, msg);
78 }
```

Line 1 Each worker in the system starts in the NORMAL state. It is ready to take messages and process them. We will have COORDINATOR and CLIENT states for threads working within a barrier.

Line 4 The thread loops until it shuts down. Shutdown is instigated by a message.

Line 5 Dequeue a message. How the message is queued is left unspecified (it might be a network handler, or another thread queuing it).

Lines 6–11 If we are running normally (i.e., not in a barrier) and receive a shutdown, then put the thread into the shutdown state. If we are executing a barrier, the barrier will complete before the shutdown (the shutdown message will be queued to the deferred message queue below).

Lines 13–18 If we are not in a barrier then we can execute the task message. In this model, tasks are run synchronously so we expect them to run quickly. When the task completes we are done with the message and free it and return to the top of the loop to dequeue the next message to process.

Lines 20–33 If this is a launch of a barrier then add COORDINATOR to our state. Note that we can be in multiple states simultaneously. For example, this worker can be a coordinator and a client at the same time. Set the barrier count to the number of workers we are sending to (in this case, we are not specifying what this is; how the barrier worker set is chosen is open ended). Broadcast to the participants the task to execute within the barrier. That completes processing this part of the barrier and we free the message and wait for another message, now in the COORDINATOR state.

Lines 35–44 If we are in either the NORMAL or COORDINATOR state but not in the CLIENT state, and we receive a BARRIER_TASK message, then execute that task in the barrier. Add the CLIENT status to the thread state, which prevents us from processing another BARRIER_TASK message until we complete the current barrier. Run the task and when it is complete, reply to the barrier that we have completed the task. It is not allowed to be a barrier client in multiple barriers in this implementation.

Lines 46–59 If we are the coordinator and receive a TASK_DONE message from one of our clients, then decrement the expected number of responses. If we need more responses (line 49's condition is false) then simply wait for more TASK_DONE messages to arrive. Once the barrier is complete (lines 50–55) remove the COORDINATOR status. Any messages that were deferred while we were in the barrier are transferred to the primary message queue, and all the members of the barrier are notified that the barrier conditions have been met.

Lines 61–69 If we are a client and receive the BARRIER-DONE then all the deferred messages are transferred to the regular queue and we can resume normal processing.

Lines 70–78 There are some illegal combinations of state and messages. Receiving a BARRIER_DONE message on a thread that is not a CLIENT would be inconsistent (why would a non-client thread receive such a message). Likewise, receiving a BARRIER_TASK_DONE and not being a coordinator would also be wrong. How these errors are handled is unspecified.

Line 77 If all the other conditions haven't handled the message and continued the loop, then we must be inside the barrier and should not process the message yet. Enqueue it on the deferred message queue. These messages will be picked up when the barrier is completed.

All of this may seem awfully complicated for something that was handled with 25 lines of code using condition variables and mutexes. But there are a number of advantages here.

1. As mentioned earlier, this model is not restricted to threads. The messages can be transported by TCP/IP, so this model generalizes to clusters of machines, not just groups of threads.
2. The threads are *mostly* blocked (Goldman 1986). Just as messages that control the barrier are allowed to run in deferred mode, other messages can also be given that privilege. For example, the system can be shutdown cleanly by sending a SHUTDOWN message that is exempt from being deferred (we chose to defer shutdown in this example). Likewise, various debugging messages can also be exempt. This is much more difficult to do with condition variables (though not impossible).
3. It is pretty easy to implement looser barriers within this infrastructure. We might want to have only the coordinator waiting for the completion of the workers, and the workers immediately go into the catchup state when they send their BARRIER-END messages.
4. Deferred messages can be considered even when in a barrier. For example, if the barrier takes a long time, and a deferred message is time sensitive, it can be allowed to run even before the barrier completes, or it might be deleted from the deferred message queue with an alert raised that the message could not be processed before its deadline expired.

Despite looking very complex, the code above has been simplified. For example, a more functional system might allow a single worker to coordinate multiple barriers on disjoint sets of other workers. Enumerating the workers that participate in the barrier when launched is left as an exercise.

More Concurrent Programming with Messages

Building barriers with messages was a brief introduction to writing concurrent programs using message-passing as a primary organization. A number of other programming concurrent programming patterns arise from this model.

The Dispatch Loop

When building barrier synchronization using message passing, there is one loop dequeuing messages and then calling the action function that implements the semantics of the message. For example, `Worker_run_task` carries out the actions of the TASK message. A multithreaded program using this pattern will have many workers working at once. Often there is a worker for each CPU core in the system. Algorithms are sometimes expressed as *protocols* that describe the pattern and actions of the messages (like the description of the message-based barrier in section Using Message-Passing for Barriers).

A protocol is basically a set of messages with known meanings. Protocols can be request-response based or unidirectional. HTTP is a well-known request-response protocol. A web client will issue a GET message with a bunch of other information, and the web server will reply with the data requested (a web page, a photo, a database query result), and other information describing the response. The protocol for HTTP is described in a set of standard documents labeled RFC-7230 through RFC-7235.

Protocols can then be layered on top of protocols. A Remote Procedure Call (RPC) protocol called Representational State Transfer (REST) is expressed in HTTP but provides an additional layer of semantics. It is used for a web client to invoke an operation on a web server (like a database query) and receive the answer in some other format (Javascript Object Notation (JSON) is a popular format).

Protocols can be completely bespoke. The key is that the protocol must precisely define what the messages contain and what should happen when a given message is received.

The worker can have a lot of flexibility in how it processes messages. It is possible, for example, to have higher priority messages placed on a separate queue that are processed before lower priority messages. Messages to diagnose problems in the worker might be placed on the high-priority queue. Shutting down the system might also be a high-priority message.

The worker is the primary model of threading, often with one worker per core performing actions dictated by the messages it receives. However, it need not be the exclusive model. Hybrid models are possible. If an action is extremely long-lived, perhaps involving some kind of I/O, it is not unreasonable to place this in a separate thread (from a thread pool) and then return from the action. Short-term actions continue to be done synchronously from the dispatch-loop while this long term action occurs in the background. This works as long as:

1. The number of threads can be capped. If message DO-LONG-TASK requires a thread, then receiving 10,000 of these messages might not work so well if the dispatch loop tries to create 10,000 threads. A thread pool that caps the number of threads in the pool is useful.
2. The independent thread is not dependent on future actions of the dispatch-loop. Such a dependence can create a deadlock (see section Locking Basics above). For example, suppose a thread operating on a long-running task issues a message to the same dispatch-loop that owns the thread. If that dispatcher is waiting on that thread to complete (because it is waiting for a thread to free up from the thread pool), then the long-running task's message may be waiting for the thread that is waiting for the message to be processed to complete. In general, a long-running task should not be dependent on another computation to be handled outside of that task's thread.

One-Way Messages

Though it may look like there is a send-reply going on in the barrier example, in fact, all messages are one-way (though they carry a reference to the sender). The sender never waits for a reply. The response to an action (e.g., I have run a task in the barrier) is simply a message that is received like any other message.

When working with one-way messages that are mimicking send-response, the sender must establish some sort of state that can be correlated with the response. In the case of the barrier messages, the state established was that a barrier had been established and the number of workers participating in that barrier. Messages were deferred based on this state and BARRIER_TASK_DONE messages act as replies to the BARRIER_TASK messages. Any number of other messages can be received between the time a message is sent and when a message corresponding to a response is received. The messages are correlated by protocol design, not intrinsically as reply to a specific request in the message system.

This is often called *continuation-based* programming (Friedman et al. 1984). Messages carry state (or references to state) that allow a computation to progress. Once sent, the sender is done with the message. For example, once the launch-barrier function sends out the start-barrier messages it is done, and the main loop simply processes the next message according to the state it is in (which may have changed as part of the barrier launch).

This illustrates why *reliable message passing* is highly desirable in this model. Suppose a BARRIER-TASK-DONE message was lost on its way from the worker to the coordinator. The barrier would never be complete (the count of expected responses would never decrement to 0) and all the threads in the barrier would hang waiting for the coordinator to send the BARRIER-DONE message that would never be sent. Fortunately, most message-passing systems are reliable (for example TCP/IP works very hard to ensure a message makes its way from sender to recipient). For even greater reliability, systems like Kafka (Confluent 2026) can be used.

Consuming Messages

Messages dequeued must be freed at some point. As the number of types of messages increase and the functionality they implement becomes more complex, it can become easy to “forget” to free the message, or to squirrel away a message for later use only to never free it, causing a memory leak (Chap. 9 will deal with memory management in more detail).

A useful approach is to assume that all messages are consumed after being processed. Often the body of a dispatch loop is a switch statement that chooses what action function to execute based on the type of message being processed. Following the switch, the message will be automatically deleted. If an action function needs a copy of the message, it is responsible for creating that copy and for ultimately freeing the copy of the message. A common example of this is when a message is forwarded to another dispatcher. In this case, a copy of the message is sent to that dispatcher which will then take care of freeing the message when it is processed.

Another challenge with the dispatch loop model is that state, like the barrier count above, must be preserved between messages. Again, this needs to be handled thoughtfully. Attaching state information to the `Worker` as shown above is a simple way of capturing state. If the system becomes more complex, for example, requiring multiple versions of state (like managing multiple barrier contexts), a dictionary associating a key in the message to the state object might be appropriate.

Throttling

Regardless of whether auxiliary threads are being used in the dispatcher or not, it is possible that dispatch loops can get behind the work being queued for them. This is one of the dangers of the message-passing system. Tasks can effortlessly queue messages and it is not hard to imagine that if the queueing happens faster than the processing of the messages, queues can get very long and the time between queuing the message and actually executing it grows unbounded.

One approach to this is to simply cap the size of the queue. The queue can keep count of the pending entries and when it reaches a certain high-water mark, it can decline to accept any more entries. When the dispatcher dequeues below a low-water mark, the queue can be re-enabled. This is easier said than done. If an action function being called by the dispatcher is unable to complete its task because it cannot enqueue a message, what should happen? If all the action threads in the pool end up in this state, it is possible to deadlock. Suppose the action X is running from dispatcher A’s pool and all the threads from the pool have been deployed and A’s dispatch queue is full. X needs to send a message to A but is blocked because A’s dispatch queue is full. X must wait until A processes more messages, but because the actions are blocked at A, trying to enqueue to A will also be blocked. No progress can be made to reduce the queue length and so the system locks up.

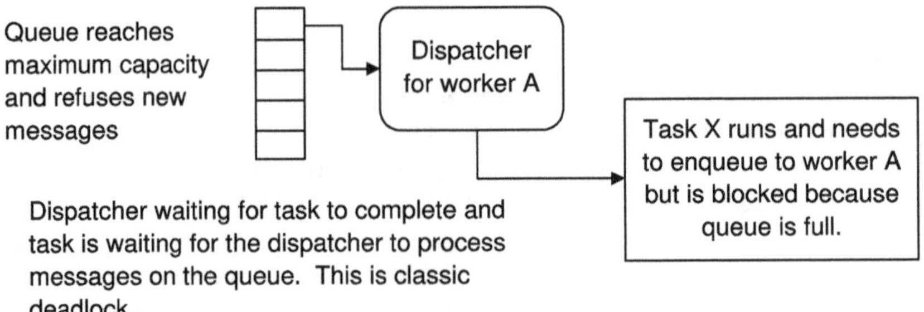

Fig. 7.7 Classic deadlock if dispatcher queue isn't allowed to grow past a certain point

How does one remediate this? Does X's failure to enqueue a message cause it to fail (releasing it back to the thread pool)? If so, how does that ripple through the system to either retry or abandon the task that could not be completed? Alternatively, the sender could wait until the queue reaches its low-water threshold using a condition variable. The trouble is that if that queue is associated with the same dispatcher that is running the sender task (as in the above example), it will deadlock (Fig. 7.7).

What if the messages are not sent by directly adding a message to a queue, but instead with a TCP/IP message between dispatchers? In this case, the TCP/IP buffers will eventually fill up if the messages are not being read fast enough. Like the case with the enqueue failing, the message will ultimately fail to send (or the sender will be blocked). This is exactly analogous to the failed enqueue and suffers from the same potential deadlock.

There is no simple solution to this since it very much depends on how sensitive the application is to delays or failed operations. Blocking operations can lead to deadlocks. Giving up on a task could lead to inconsistencies (the deposit went through, but the withdrawal failed!).

This is one of the principal drawbacks of a message-based system. The loose coupling of the sender and receiver makes managing load much more difficult. Chapter 8 will further address this.

Lock-Free Concurrent Data Structures

This section is more of a cautionary tale than really instructive. It has two major goals: Introduce the concept of atomic instructions, and to show how difficult writing truly multithreaded code can be. In the latter case, how we describe a flow of control across multiple threads demonstrating failures is useful when reasoning about complex thread interactions.

While locking and releasing mutexes is certainly the most prevalent way of protecting shared data, it is not the only way. In particular, most processors have a set of instructions that can perform operations that can manipulate memory atomically, i.e., no interleaving of thread operations is allowed. The number and type of instructions will depend on the processor the program is running on, so it is necessary to be aware of the availability of these instructions when writing code that might execute on multiple processor types.

Two common atomic instructions are:

`fetch_and_add`—fetch the current value of a variable and atomically increment it by some other value. For example, if 100 threads are simultaneously executing `fetch_and_add` with an increment of 1 on the variable `a`, that value will be 100 greater than the value it started with. This is not true if 100 threads execute `a++`. Without synchronization, it is likely that a thread X will retrieve say the value of 5 for `a`, several other threads will increment `a` to 9 and then the thread X will store 5+1 in `a` thereby canceling out the other increments. `Fetch_and_add` does not suffer this problem. The return value of `fetch_and_add` is the value of the variable passed in the first parameter *before* it is incremented.
`compare_and_swap`—This primitive takes three parameters: A variable, a value to compare the variable against, and if the value of the variable and the comparison value are the same, a value to store in the variable. Again, this is all done atomically. An example of its use might be if you want to store a pointer in a variable `ptr` only if the value of `ptr` is NULL. This would look something like `compare_and_swap(&ptr, NULL, new_value);` The return value of `compare_and_swap` is true if the swap occurs (the contents of ptr is NULL), and false otherwise. Attempting the same function with a statement like

```
ptr = (ptr == NULL) ? new_value: ptr;
```

would not end well if executed by multiple threads sharing the variable `ptr`. Suppose this is to set the next pointer in a list. It would be very simple for thread X to see `ptr == NULL` simultaneously with thread Y also seeing `ptr == NULL`. Thread Y gets in first and sets `ptr` to a pointer to some object (a new element in the list). Thread X does exactly the same thing with a different destination object. Thread Y's update of `ptr` is overwritten by X, most likely corrupting the list or, at a minimum, losing Y's entry in the list. Using `compare_and_swap(&ptr, NULL, new_value)` eliminates this problem.

The names will vary depending on what language you are using. In C++ using the Gnu compiler, `fetch_and_add` is `__atomic_fetch_add`. In Java it is the AtomicInteger class with methods like getAndIncrement().

Incrementing a counter is much simpler and faster using the atomic primitives. For example, using gcc, here are the two techniques:

`__atomic_fetch_add(&the_counter, 1);`	`pthread_mutex_lock(&the_lock);`
	`the_counter++;`
	`pthread_mutex_unlock(&the_lock);`

As always, your mileage will vary but the fetch_and_add is in the ballpark of three times faster than the mutex model (and the fact that it is only three times faster is a testament to the optimizations by the implementers of the pthread locking facility[4]).

It may well be faster to establish a mutex, increment half a dozen variables "normally", and then release the mutex. This is especially true if the variables reside on the same cache line.

`__atomic_fetch_add(&counter1, 1);`
`__atomic_fetch_add(&counter2, 1);`
`__atomic_fetch_add(&counter3, 1);`
`__atomic_fetch_add(&counter4, 1);`
	`pthread_mutex_lock(&the_lock);`
	`counter1++;`
	`counter2++;`
	`counter3++;`
	`counter4++;`
	`pthread_mutex_unlock(&the_lock);`

In this case, the cost of the lock is amortized over multiple increments each of which are much faster. The likely reason for the difference between and __atomic_fetch_add and the postfix increment ++ is that fetch_and_add flushes the instruction pipeline and the number of instructions executed per second is reduced. It is rarely the case, however, that a significant number of counters are updated at one time, so atomic increments are quite useful.

A Lock-Free Multithreaded Circular Buffer

Given that atomic operations can perform some of the roles of mutexes, it is reasonable to wonder about developing multithreaded algorithms using only atomic operations. We've already seen a trivial one: consistently increment a counter by many simultaneous threads. Lock-free multithreaded patterns are quite tricky but offer the advantage that a thread rarely (if ever) needs to wait for a lock (though sometimes it needs to retry an operation multiple times).

In this section, we will implement a lock-free circular buffer. Even this relatively simple data structure will show the difficulty of writing lock-free data structures. The goal is not to provide an efficient circular buffer but to satisfy the curiosity one might have for using atomic operations for more sophisticated functions. It will also illustrate how multithreading can lead to subtle and difficult to diagnose errors.

In this simplified example, we will assume that fixed-size objects are written into the buffer and that the buffer is exactly a multiple of these fixed-size objects that sit

[4] For more information about mutex implementation see Arpaci-Desseau et al. (2013).

end to end with no left-over bytes in the buffer. Let's assume that N objects fit into the buffer. When N objects have been written, the next object written will overwrite the first object in the buffer and then the next object and so forth. Call the position where the next item is to be written the *write-index*. The items in the buffer will be in roughly time order. Assuming that the buffer is full, we will traverse all the items by beginning at the write-index (the oldest item), wrapping around at the buffer boundary, and continuing to just before the write-index (the most recently written object). Uses for this sort of data structure include keeping the last n records for some process (see Chap. 10 where a circular buffer is used for keeping analytical information).

If the buffer were infinitely long, then lock-free multithreaded writing would be simple. Let's say each entry in the buffer is n bytes. We want to have multiple threads writing simultaneously. What can be done is to have each thread atomically return the current write-index and advance that index by n. Adding an object is simple:

```
int index_to_write_to = fetch_and_add(&write_index,
size_of_object);
memcpy(&buffer[index_to_write_to], object, size_of_object);
```

The `fetch_and_add` returns the previous value of the `write_index` and simultaneously advances it for the next write. The memory copy can proceed knowing that nothing else will occupy that buffer location.

Unfortunately, infinite buffers are very difficult to implement. Instead, we take the strategy that when N records are written, `write_index` is reset to 0 and older records are overwritten. The goal is that we preserve the basic ordering of storing in the buffer such that if records are stored at indices x, y, and z and the record at index y is overwritten, so must the record at x (i.e., we should never have entries stored at indices x and z without also storing an object at index y).

One approach is to simply set write-index to 0 if its current value is N, i.e., the size of the buffer.

```
if (write_index == N) {
write_index = 0;
}
```

This introduces an interesting problem. Suppose thread 1 has determined the position for record q in the buffer is at index $a < N$ but has not yet written q to the buffer. Thread 1 reaches the end of its time quantum and is suspended before it writes q. Thread 2 now runs with the index at $a + 1$ (since thread 1 did advance the index). It writes $N + 1$ records, wrapping the index so that it manages to write records x, y, z to indices $a - 1$, a, $a + 1$. Thread 1 is then given time to execute and proceeds to write its record q at index a which it established before losing its quantum. This leads to an unexpected sequence of records: x, q, z. Record y is effectively removed from the sequence violating our ordering requirement (Fig. 7.8).

There are a number of strategies that can be used for managing the wrapping and subsequent overwriting of the entries. In this case, we are going to count the number of accessors of the buffer. Only a single thread will be allowed to wrap the

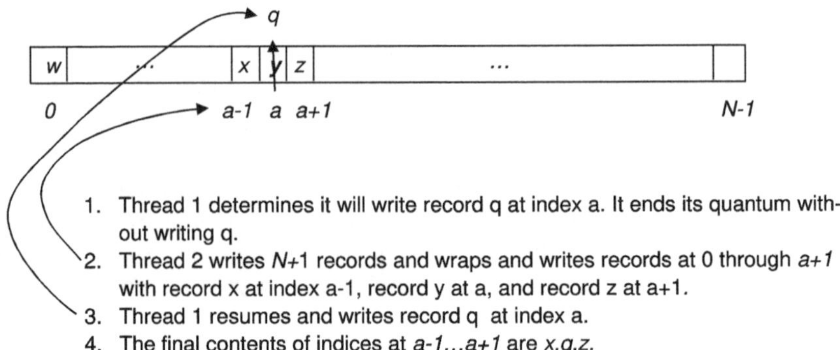

Fig. 7.8 Thread 2 wraps and runs ahead of thread 1 which then clobbers an entry

write-index. If the index must be wrapped, the reference-count must be 1, i.e., the thread doing the wrapping is the only thread accessing the buffer. This thread will wait for the reference-count to decrement to 1 before proceeding with the wrap. It is possible that multiple threads may reach a point where the index is to wrap but only one will succeed to wrap it and all others will serialize behind it. Here is the basic code:

```
struct Circular_Buffer {
 uint8_t *buffer;
 int32_t reference_count;
 uint32_t write_index;
 uint32_t size_of_element;
 uint32_t total_buffer_size;
};

void Circular_Buffer_append(struct Circular_Buffer *buffer,
  uint8_t *item) {
  do {
  fetch_and_add(&buffer->reference_count, 1);
  uint32_t reserved_index =
  fetch_and_add(&buffer->write_index,
  buffer->size_of_element);
  if (reserved_index == buffer->total_buffer_size) {
  while (buffer->reference_count != 1) {
  delay(yield);
  }
  buffer->write_index = 0;
  refcnt = fetch_and_add(&buffer->reference_count, -1);
  continue;
  }
  if (reserved_index > buffer->total_buffer_size) {
  fetch_and_add(&buffer->reference_count, -1);
  delay(sleep);
  continue;
  }
  memcpy(&buffer->buffer[reserved_index *
```

```
30  buffer->size_of_element],
31  item,
32  buffer->size_of_element);
33  fetch_and_add(&buffer->reference_count, -1);
34  return;
35  } while (true);
36  }
```

Lines 1–7 We point to a buffer (line 2). In this example, we assume all the entries in the buffer are of the same size (line 5) and the buffer is of a fixed size once it is created (line 6). Our reference-count is at line 3 and the write-index in the buffer is at line 4. Write-index is in byte units and increments in `size_of_element` bytes at a time.

Line 11 Like many non-locking patterns, we may need to repeat an action until a consistent state is achieved. We'll see that happen several times in this routine.

Line 12 Mark that we are accessing the buffer by incrementing its reference-count.

Lines 13–15 Get the next place to put the item. There are three cases:

1. The index is less than the buffer length. We can simply store the element at the index.
2. The index is exactly the buffer length. This thread will handle the wrap.
3. The index is greater than the buffer length. Someone else will handle the wrap and this thread will restart the operation once that happens.

Lines 16–19 Handle the wrapping case (2 above). We must ensure that this is the only thread accessing the buffer. We wait until the reference-count indicates this thread is the sole accessor (reference-count is 1). Note the delay. This yields the current threads quantum to other threads to ensure they have a chance of finishing and decrementing the reference-count. We discuss why this delay is required below.

Line 20 Once we have exclusive access to the buffer, we can reset the write-index. Threads can resume inserting into the buffer.

Lines 21–22 We reduce our reference-count and try the append again with the new write-index by returning to the top of the outer loop at line 11.

Lines 24–28 If the write-index is greater than the buffer length then we know that some other thread is in the process of wrapping write-index. We delay a small amount (for example, a few 10s of nanoseconds) to give time for the write-index to be reset and try again.

Lines 29–33 At this point the write-index is less than the size of the buffer and reference-count reflects that this thread is processing the buffer. Copy the item into the buffer and decrement the reference-count. The append is complete.

This implementation avoids locking the whole buffer to append items until the index needs to be wrapped at the expense of incrementing and decrementing a reference-count. This can be faster than a locked-buffer approach. The tricky part is when the write-index needs to be wrapped. In this case, one thread "wins" and other threads must wait until the winning thread completes (a very short amount of time). The need to wait for the winning thread only happens when two threads are adding simultaneously at the end of the buffer. Depending on the use case this waiting may rarely be invoked.

When waiting, it is important to include the delays for the algorithm to work efficiently. The first delay (line 18) gives other threads a chance to finish their work and decrement the reference-count to allow the thread exclusive access to proceed with wrapping the write-index to the beginning of the buffer. Without this, the thread might spin uselessly until its execution quantum is over, effectively blocking a thread that might be needed to complete an append and reduce the reference-count. The append operation is very fast (nanoseconds depending on the size of the object being stored), so the number of iterations waiting for the current operations to complete is relatively small (all depending on the number of threads there are).

The second delay (line 26) is important for a different reason. In this case, an append has been started after another thread has started to wrap. It is important that the wrap completes before this new append proceeds. Also note that at this point, reference-count is at least 2 (this thread and the thread doing the wrapping). It may be the case that the wrapping thread is waiting for this reference-count to go to 1 (as discussed in the previous paragraph). If this thread were to decrement the reference-count and then immediately increment it again (i.e., by returning to the top of the loop with the `continue` statement), the time that the reference-count is 1 is exceedingly small (a fraction of a nanosecond), which makes it difficult for the thread doing the wrapping to "catch" the reference-count at exactly 1. This can lead to each of the threads waiting for the wrap to complete postponing the thread that is wrapping. The delay in this case provides the thread performing the wrap time to detect that it is the only thread accessing the queue.

Here is a picture illustrating the effect of the sleep (Fig. 7.9).

While the `sleep` does not guarantee the indefinite postponement will not occur, it makes the probability of such an event extremely low. The amount of sleep will depend partly on the maximum number of threads. More delay will be required if more threads are involved.

> A word to the wise: System level mutexes (like `pthread_mutex_lock` in Linux) are very efficient and in almost all cases, any time you are doing something more complex that simply incrementing a counter, it is usually as fast or faster, and certainly clearer to use a mutex instead of a complex set of atomic instructions.

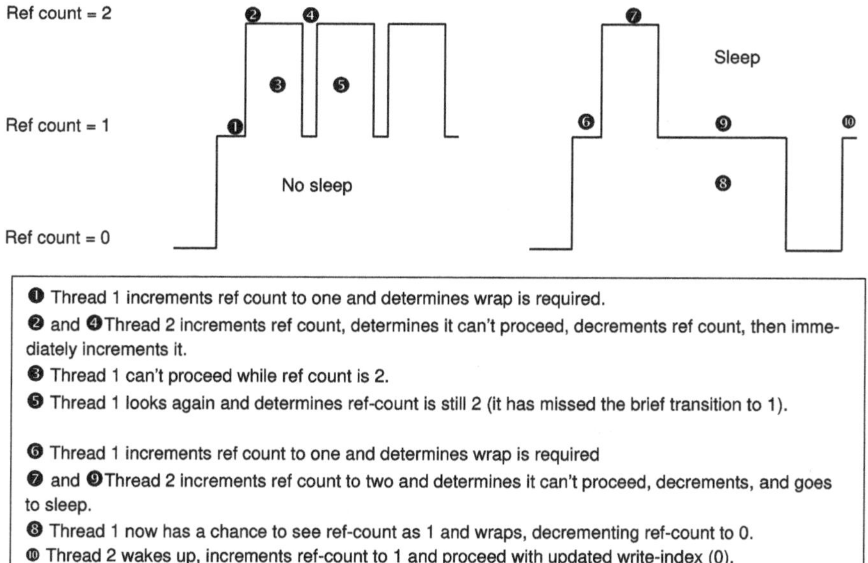

Fig. 7.9 Sleeping, even very briefly, nearly eliminates indefinite postponement

A Lock-Free Multithreaded Queue

Queues have shown up in a couple of contexts in the previous sections (handling multiple TCP/IP connections, and the more general dispatch-loop pattern). To make these thread-safe, a lock is used to ensure that the head and tail pointers are not modified inconsistently.

It is possible to create a lock-free version of a queue. In some ways, it is extremely elegant, but as will be shown, also frustratingly difficult. This section is less about creating a usable lock-free thread-safe queue than to show the challenges with relying on atomic operations to avoid mutexes. The goal is to demonstrate a more sophisticated use of atomic operations (in particular, using the `compare_and_swap` operation) rather than a practical pattern for lock-free queues.

> Note: This section demonstrates the necessity of carefully analyzing multithreaded programs. In fact, the lock-free queue is not practical and a conventional mutex guarded queue is almost certainly not only going to outperform this approach but be much simpler to understand and be bug-free. Feel free to skip this section if you have no interest in the analysis of this particular lock-free pattern.

The queue is implemented as a linked list in a manner similar to the queue implementation shown at the beginning of this chapter. There are head and tail pointers,

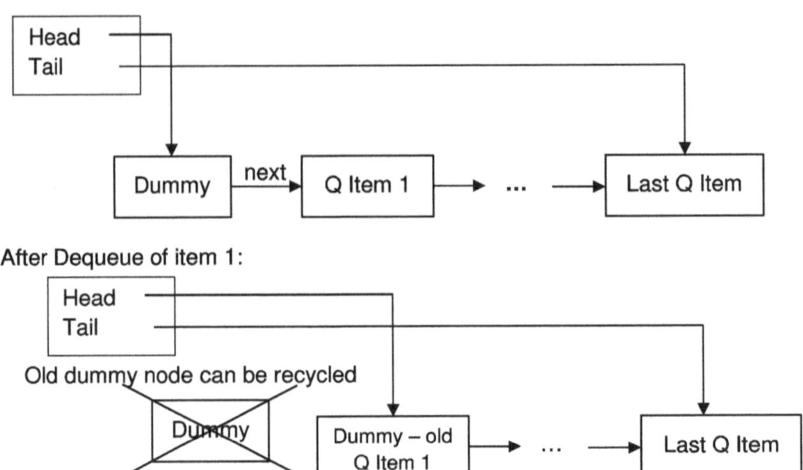

Fig. 7.10 Dequeuing item with dummy node on front of queue

and, as above, items are dequeued from the head of the queue and queued to the tail. For enqueue, instead of locking the queue, we will attempt to atomically add an element to the end of the list. Most of the times this will just work. There are cases however (described below) where it is necessary to iterate to find the tail (because someone else has "snuck" in and replaced the tail after we thought we had it). Dequeue is somewhat similar: We pop the front of the list off and update the queue's head pointer in such a way that concurrent dequeues do not interfere with one another.

There is one change to the linked list structure from that used above. In this implementation, there is always a single dummy Queue_item at the head of the queue. The head pointer points to this and the first usable item on the queue is at `head->next`. The reason for this will be explained later. A queue now looks like as shown in Fig. 7.10.

The challenge is to ensure that two simultaneous threads do not corrupt the links such that two enqueues are properly serialized, and similarly that two dequeues do not, for example, return the same element. We will use the compare-and-swap function extensively in this approach. It will be used to verify that an assumption (for example, that the item we are adding is being linked to the last item of the queue) before completing an operation.

Here is enqueue. The gist of this approach is to atomically add the queued item to the tail unless some other thread adds to the tail between the time we arrive at the enqueue function and the time we set the new tail pointer.

```
void enqueue(struct Queue *queue, void *item) {
 struct Queue_item *qitem = make_Queue_item(item);
 struct Queue_item *orig_tail = NULL;
 bool swapped = false;

 do {
 orig_tail = queue->tail;
```

```
8
9   swapped = compare_and_swap(&orig_tail->next_item,
10   NULL, qitem);
11   } while(!swapped);
12   compare_and_swap(&queue->tail, orig_tail, qitem);
13  }
```

Line 2 This is the item wrapped in the Queue_item object to be enqueued.

Line 6 Similar to the circular buffer, we may have to retry an operation multiple times because other threads are "sneaking" in ahead of us. In this case, we loop until we know that we have actually added an item to the tail.

Line 7 We start with the tail of the queue. We want to add the item from line 2 to the tail.

Line 9 This is the crux of the approach. The compare and swap will set the next-item of the current tail to the new item if the current tail's next item is NULL (and return true). If another thread has already updated the tail, then compare_and_swap will return false and the swap does not occur.

Line 11 If we weren't able to swap, it's because someone beat us to updating the tail. Keep iterating until we succeed in adding our item to the tail. The number of times we perform this will depend on how many concurrent threads are enqueuing simultaneously.

Line 12 Once the item has been added to the end of the list, this swap updates the tail. If the tail has been reset by someone else (because another thread did an enqueue between line 9 and 12) then the tail will not match the orig_tail set above. If that is true, the tail has already been updated. Otherwise the compare-and-swap will succeed and point to the item just added.

Here is an example where two threads are simultaneously enqueuing and having their executions interleaved. The queue has X on it. Thread 1 will enqueue Y and thread 2 will enqueue Z. Each row is a step in time where both threads are running and the columns are showing the state of the queue and variables in the thread (Fig. 7.11).

In this ordering, thread 1 succeeds in adding its item Z to the queue (row 3 in table) but it fails to set the tail pointer. This is because thread 2 has managed to execute rows 3–6 before thread 1 executes line 12 (row 7). Thread 2 fails to update the next pointer of the tail because thread 1 did manage to do this (row 3). Thread 2 returns to the top of the loop at row 4. It is now able to set the tail's next pointer to Z at row 6. Finally at row 7, thread 2 updates the tail to point to the newly added entry.

It is a useful exercise to try out different interleavings to demonstrate that tail always ends up at the end of the list and no items are missed.

Dequeue is similar. In this case, we must ensure we do not dequeue an item twice. The compare-and-swap in this case makes sure that we only remove the head if some other thread hasn't dequeued it ahead of us.

	Thread 1	Thread 2	Queue Tail	Thread 1: orig_tail	Thread 2:orig_tail
1	qitem = Y	qitem = Z	X		
2	Line 7 set orig-tail	Line 7 set orig-tail	X	X	X
3	Line 9 swap OK set next pointer of tail element	Line 9 swap fails	X with X->next == NULL	X->next == Y	X w/ X->next == Y (because thread 1 swap succeeded)
4		Line 7 set orig-tail	--	--	Y w/ Y->next == NULL
5		Line 9 swap OK			Y->next == Z
6		Line 12 swap OK Thread 2 done	Tail is now set to Z		Y->next == Z
7	Line 12: swap fails. Thread 1 done.		Z		

Fig. 7.11 Interleaving threads adding entries to the queue

```
1  void *dequeue(struct Queue *queue) {
2   struct Queue_item *orig_head = NULL;
3
4   do {
5   orig_head = queue->head;
6
7   if (orig_head->next_item == NULL) {
8   return NULL;
9   }
10
11   } while(!compare_and_swap(&queue->head, orig_head,
12   orig_head->next_item));
13
14   void *item = orig_head->next_item->item;
15   // We have a problem with freeing orig_head. See below.
16   return item;
17  }
```

Line 5 Establish the head.

Lines 7–9 The head is never null; it always points to a dummy item. If the next_item is NULL then in fact the queue is empty. Enqueue and dequeue can be wrapped with condition variable signal and wait versions so that an empty queue will cause dequeue to wait.

Line 11 The crux of the dequeue. The head is advanced to the next item (which will become the next dummy item) as long as nobody has popped off an item from the time orig_head was set (line 5) and the time the compare-and-swap is executed. Once the compare-and-swap finishes, the queue head will point to the item we have dequeued which is the new “dummy” entry.

Line 14 The item to be returned is set from the queue item that was dequeued in line 11. Note that orig_item pointed to the dummy item, the next_item is the item that has been dequeued (and head now points to it) and we have set head to point to the next_item so that is now the dummy item (which has the item to return). This may seem confusing. It is important to realize that once line 11 completes, nothing will reference orig_item->next_item except the thread executing this dequeue.

Line 15 At this point, orig_head points to a useless Queue_item. The queue head points one beyond it. Ideally we would free orig_head at this point. Unfortunately this cannot be done. There is a race condition between freeing orig_head and accessing next_item to get the value to return. See below.

The inability to free the Queue_item at line 15 is a real thorn in our side. Here's what can happen. Let's assume the queue is X → A → B → C (X is the dummy head) (Fig. 7.12).

	Thread 1	Thread 2	Queue Head	Thread 1: orig_head	Thread 2:orig_head
1			`X->A->B->C`		
2	Line 5		`X->A->B->C`	X	
3	Line 11 swap OK		`X'->B->C (X' is new dummy head, formerly A)`	X	
4		Line 5	`X'->B->C`	X	`X' (which was A)`
5		Line 11 swap OK	`X''->C (B is new dummy X'')`	X	`X' and X'->next_item = B`
6		Line 14: retrieve item from `X'->next_item.item (B)`	`X''`	X	`X'`
7		**Line 15 Assume orig_head (which pointed to A) is freed.**	`C`	X	`X' (A) is freed`
8	Line 14: Retrieve item from `X→next_item.item`. But `X→next_item` is A, which was freed above!			`X and X→next_item is A!`	

Fig. 7.12 The problem with freeing an item

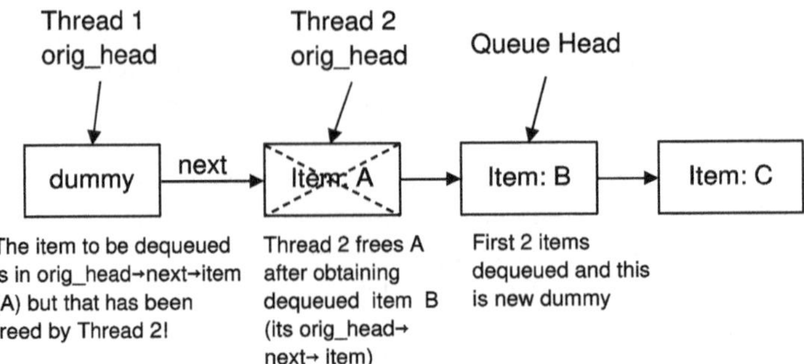

Fig. 7.13 Thread 2's free corrupts thread 1

If at row 7 in the table, thread 2 frees orig_head (which points to A and is no longer referenced by the queue since we reset the `queue->head` to `orig_head->next_item`, i.e., `B`) then thread 1 will try to reference this freed item (`X->next_item`) at line 14. Accessing a freed item is clearly not allowed.

The state of affairs after row 7 is shown in Fig. 7.13.

Not freeing the Queue_item is also unacceptable. Suppose there are billions of dequeues (and since this is very fast code that might be measures in seconds). A billion dequeues would consume tens of gigabytes of memory. That's clearly not going to hold up. It is non-trivial to fix this problem; most approaches involve some form of *ref-counting*. Ref-counting will be discussed in Chap. 9.

One of the motivations for presenting this example is to stress the care one must take when writing code to run in a multithreaded environment. It is an illustration of how the interleaving of unsynchronized code can be very arbitrary and if there is a way for code to interleave improperly it almost certainly will.

We should also point out that in the dequeue function above if the queue is empty, a NULL is returned. If we want to wait for an element in dequeue (as we did in the earlier queue examples), a condition variable would need to be set up. If the lock-free dequeue returns null, then wait on a condition variable. Likewise, enqueue would signal the condition variable to indicate that an element is ready. Depending on how often the dequeue outpaces the enqueue, many of the condition signals would be for nothing, wasting a handful of nanoseconds.

You may wonder if all this is worth it and that is a very reasonable question. In fact, once you add in the condition variable and some kind of mechanism to clean up the queue items that have been dequeued, it is quite likely that this code is actually *slower* than the code where a mutex is locked and unlocked in the enqueue and dequeue functions. It also requires that any other thread-safe actions (incrementing statistics for example) must exercise the same lock-free techniques to ensure consistency (for example, using `fetch_and_add`).

To sum up, using atomic operations like `fetch_and_add` or `compare_and_swap` can be very powerful but typically for narrow, well bounded memory accesses. Using them to implement more complex data structures (like a queue) can be extremely difficult and ultimately it may not be any faster than simply locking the structure with conventional mutexes. Even simple increments and decrements may be faster with mutexes if several are occurring consecutively.

Clearly there are a lot of factors in deciding whether and how to use atomic instructions. A rule of thumb might be: If you are manipulating a single value, use an atomic instruction. If you are updating multiple items (be they counters or pointers in a queue), the mutex may make your code not only perform better, but is also easier to understand.

Cautions About Threads

Concurrent programming with threads is not terribly difficult to get started with: Threads are created and coordinated with mutexes and condition variables and all the program state is equally accessible to all threads. Queues and similar structures can provide higher level synchronization models.

In some ways, threads are almost too easy to use. There are some important considerations to consider when designing a multithreaded concurrent program.

Context Switches and Thread Migrations

Suppose you have 8 cores in your processor and 16 threads. Clearly, not all the threads can run at the same time. Each thread is assigned a time interval to run (a *quantum*) and after the time interval is up, another thread can run on the core. Unless otherwise stipulated, any thread that is available to run can run on that core. Time-slicing like this has been around since the 1960s (then called *time sharing* (Corbato 1963)).

When a thread reaches the end of its quantum it stops processing and a *context switch* happens. The context of the thread is all the state needed to run the thread and includes the machine's registers (like the program counter, stack pointer, arithmetic registers), memory mapping, and other information. When a context switch occurs, this information is saved for the running thread and a new thread's context is loaded and that code then begins running at the point where it left off when its context was saved. In this way, multiple tasks can be interleaved on a single CPU.

Now suppose thread 1 is running on core A and thread 2's context has been saved by core B. A context switch occurs on core A, thread 1's context is saved and thread 2's context is loaded. This is called a *thread migration*. The thread has migrated from core B to core A. Functionally this will work fine; registers are correct, memory can be accessed properly, but there is an important difference. All of core B's L1 and L2 cache populated when running thread 2 on core B is now useless because thread

2 is now running on core A. Oversubscribing the cores of a computer can reduce the probability that a thread will be reassigned to its previous core and will pay an accompanying penalty.

There are approaches to help mitigate this. Threads can be *pinned* to processors which prevents them from being migrated to other processors. The program decides which threads go where and locks them to those cores. Now the threads should have at least some of its cache entries available across a context switch. The downside is that if a core is lightly loaded, and another core is heavily oversubscribed, the system cannot migrate a thread from the overloaded core to the underutilized core. The net effect of pinning may be worse performance than if threads had been allowed to migrate.

A better approach is to simply limit the number of threads to roughly the number of cores and design those threads to be busy as much as possible (the dispatch-loop pattern is a good example of this). Having other threads that are occasionally needed is fine, as long it is more the exception than the rule.

Sharding Data

Just as threads are almost too easy to deploy, the fact that virtually anything allocated in the process hosting the thread is equally accessible is another potential problem. Consider threads sharing a common hash table. We've already seen that it is extremely difficult to make the table multithreaded and relatively simple to make it thread-safe. Threads sharing the hash table will end up serialized. As long as the work outside of the hash table access is large enough, this overhead shouldn't be too great. But if the accesses are fast enough, the parallelization enabled by multithreading could be severely degraded by sharing the common hash table.

One way of solving this problem is to *shard* the hash table. Sharding means dividing the aggregate data structure into pieces (shards) that act independently. This is often done for parallelizing databases (both relational and non-relational) as well as in-memory representations of collections of objects.

Building on the hash table idea, Fig. 7.14 is an example of how sharding can work.

In this example, three threads are accessing a hash table that has been sharded into three pieces. Each thread wants to retrieve the value for a different key. The function F maps the Key to one of the sub-tables (a number from 0 to 2 inclusive in this case). Since in this case the table shards chosen are disjoint, the three threads can each take the lock on the shard without any of them being blocked and access the table without interference.

The choice of the sharding function F needs to be coordinated with the Hash function used in the table. It shouldn't be the same. For example, consider F for 2 sub-tables. If F is defined as *H(key) mod 2* and the hash table uses *H(key) mod N* (where N is the number of buckets), then sub-table 0 will only use half of its buckets (the even buckets), and sub-table 1 will use half of its buckets (the odd buckets). F

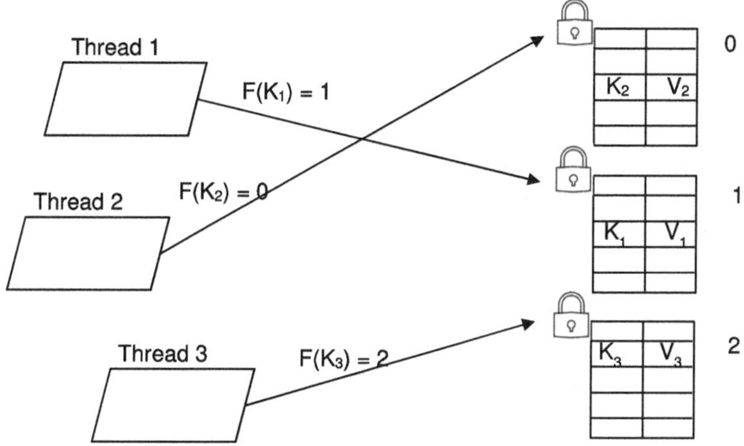

Fig. 7.14 Sharding the hash table to enable multiple concurrent access

should be a different Hash function or use different bits within the Hash value to determine the sub-table.

Sharding the hash table is one of the easiest ways of providing multithreaded access to the table.

Thread Failure

No program is ever perfect. It will crash at times. Unfortunately, if one thread crashes (for example, by accessing a NULL pointer), all the threads sharing the process with that thread will also crash. Concurrent programming with threads makes this problem unavoidable; programming with processes can help firewall failures. Concurrent Programming with Processes shows how to use messages to coordinate processes in much the same way messages were used to manage threads above.

A Simple Thread API

In the discussion above, a simplified thread API was used that contains just a handful of functions. It is a slight abstraction beyond the pthread library. Here are more details about this API.

```
struct Thread *make_Thread()
```

Creates a thread but is not running anything yet.

```
Thread_status Thread_run(struct Thread *thread,
```

```
Function_ptr function, void *argument)
```

Run the function inside the thread. `Function_ptr` is a pointer to a function of type `void *function(void *)` (i.e., takes an arbitrary pointer as the argument, and returns an arbitrary pointer as the result). The argument to the function is the third parameter. This function immediately returns while the function runs in the other thread.

It is illegal to try to make a thread run a function while it is already currently running a function.

`Thread_status` may be one of four values:

`IDLE`: The thread has been created but is not running a function.
`RUNNING`: The function is running. This is the status that Thread_run should return.
`COMPLETE`: The function has completed and a result (if any) is available.
`STOPPED`: The function was stopped while it was running. No result is available. The function cannot be resumed.

Threads should go through states `IDLE`→`RUNNING`→`COMPLETE`→`RUNNING`...

```
Thread_status Thread_run_with_final(struct Thread *thread,
Function_ptr function, void *argument,
Final_function_ptr final,
void *argument)
```

Identical to Thread_run except that when the function completes the final function is called. The final function receives a thread pointer as its argument and can access the final argument from that structure. The final function may be called even if the thread is stopped and can be used to perform a "cleanup" especially when the thread is running completely independently (i.e., the thread was created, and the function run, but the Thread object is "forgotten" by the thread initiating the run). As we will see below, this is particularly useful for cleaning up after a thread completes.

```
Thread_status Thread_wait(struct Thread *thread)
```

Wait for the function being run in the thread to complete. The return value of the function being run will be available through the Thread_result function.

```
void *Thread_result(struct Thread *thread)
```

If the thread has completed running the function, the result will be returned. If the function is still running or was stopped, then NULL will be returned. Note that a function is free to return NULL so this cannot necessarily be used to know if the function is complete; use `Thread_status` instead.

```
Thread_status Thread_stop(struct Thread *thread)
```

Stop the function. The result value will always be NULL in this case. If the thread status is not RUNNING, then that status will be returned, otherwise the status STOPPED will be returned.

```
Thread_status Thread_status(struct Thread *thread)
```

A thread can be in one of four statuses: IDLE, RUNNING, COMPLETE, STOPPED. A thread is only IDLE when it has been created but has not run a function yet.

Exercises

1. Write a thread-safe queue. Thread A should enqueue items as fast as it can, and thread B dequeue as fast as it can, waiting if there are no elements on the queue. Run for a total of 10,000,000 enqueues/dequeues. How often does thread B need to wait? What is the maximum length the queue grows to?
2. Implement thread pool with a counted semaphore instead of the mutex and condition variable shown in section Thread Pools.
3. Take an array of N items and divide it into k equal groups each of N/k items. Have k threads each sort one of the groups. When the k groups are sorted, merge them into a final result. Compare the performance with simply sorting all N items in a single thread. Compare various values of N and k.
4. Build a multithreaded hash table by sharding the table into k shards. Use 20 threads to access it. Compare the performance with 20 threads accessing a single hash table with a single lock to hash tables with 2 shards, 4 shards, and 8 shards.

Chapter 8
Concurrent Programming with Processes and Messages

Threads, when used properly, provide a convenient way of writing concurrent programs. By sharing the address space of the process they are running in, it is simple to share information while coordinating access. As mentioned above, they are not without problems. If one thread crashes, they all crash. Similarly, if one thread runs off the rails and begins gobbling up resources such as CPU, memory, or network bandwidth, that thread can starve the other threads causing the whole system to degrade.

Threads are also limited to a single computer though that computer may have many processors. If the application fits on a single (perhaps large) computer, this can be a simple way of leveraging the multiple processors as long as the risk of crashing the system is low. The use of very large monolithic computers with lots of cores has become less popular (at least as of 2025). This is for two reasons:

1. Increasingly companies want the option of running large-scale applications on cloud infrastructures such as Amazon AWS, Microsoft Azure, and Google Cloud. While the providers have very large servers available, they are not inexpensive. Furthermore, if the application has a mixture of busy periods and lower use periods, the ability to dynamically change the amount of compute power allocated to the application can dramatically improve the economics of using the cloud.
2. Building applications using *containerization* like Docker and Kubernetes offers further flexibility. The applications being managed are placed in containers with a group of containers called a *pod* (in Kubernetes vernacular). Container management systems can automatically restart containers if they fail and add containers if the load on the system increases. For example, if the application units accessing the sharded table in Fig. 7.14 are getting overwhelmed, additional application units can be deployed.

Processes can allow more flexible scaling and better fault isolation but introduce some other problems as well. Launching a process is more expensive than launching a thread. Sharing of state is limited so communication between processes might need

M. Kilian, *Ten Software Patterns Every Student Should Know*,
https://doi.org/10.1007/978-981-92-0260-7_8

to be more structured to ensure enough state is passed along without transferring megabytes between processes.

In this pattern, we will explore how to organize process-based concurrent programs using a mostly shared-nothing approach (Stonebraker, 1986). Instead of sharing tables and large-scale data structures, the processes will pass messages back and forth to retrieve information and initiate actions. Some information will be shared among all of the processes (like where data is located in the network), but otherwise the data in different processes is isolated from one another.

Tables and similar structures will be split into shards (see section Sharding Data for a discussion of shards) when necessary. The set of shard boundaries is part of the information shared among the processes (e.g., hashes in the range [0,X) go to shard 0, range [X,Y) go to shard 1 and so forth).[1] This is a relatively small amount of information that needs to be shared. There are other approaches that are possible for sharing state (e.g., putting large tables in shared memory that multiple processes can access), but the goal of this pattern is to support processes that may be distributed over a network of computers where memory cannot be shared.

Note: We do not address reliable messaging or reliable distributed computation. Those are much more difficult topics and while a student should be aware of the requirements for these, the algorithms and implementation of these types of systems is non-trivial. Areas to explore for this are reliable computation environments such as *Paxos* (Pease, et al.,1980), RAFT (Ongaro,et al., 2014), and reliable message passing such as Kafka (Confluent, 2026) and RabbitMQ (RabbitMQ, 2026).

Message-Based Interprocess Communication

Messages were used earlier in the barrier synchronization example (see Using Message Passing for Barriers in Chap. 7). We are going to further generalize this model for passing messages from process to process.

As an example, let's implement the sharded hash table example in Fig. 7.14 as processes, using messages to communicate between the processes. The table will be part of a simple banking application. Each record in the table will contain an account number (the key), the name of the account holder, and the current balance. The application has only one job: Keep an accurate balance by posting deposits and withdrawals.

Processes will be divided into application processes and table processes. The application processes interact with users to gather data, etc., and each table process

[1] The notation [X,Y) means the range from X (including X) to Y (not including Y). [X,Y] is the range including X and Y, and (X,Y) is the range from X to Y not including X and Y (the endpoints).

will manage one shard of the hash table and accept messages directing how to update the table, get values, etc.

Figure 8.1 is very similar to the shard example shown in Fig. 7.14 except that instead of directly accessing the shard in memory, the application processes send messages to the table processes to perform some action. Which shard receives a message is governed by the function *F* (see section Sharding Data for more discussion about choosing an appropriate function *F*). Also different from the threaded model is that since the messages are naturally serialized (i.e., the shard only processes one message at a time), no locking needs to be provided at the shard level.

In general, the shard processes will perform application-specific actions. A shard performing just hash table operations is unlikely in practice; it is more likely that functions on records stored in the hash table will be the fundamental operations provided by a shard.

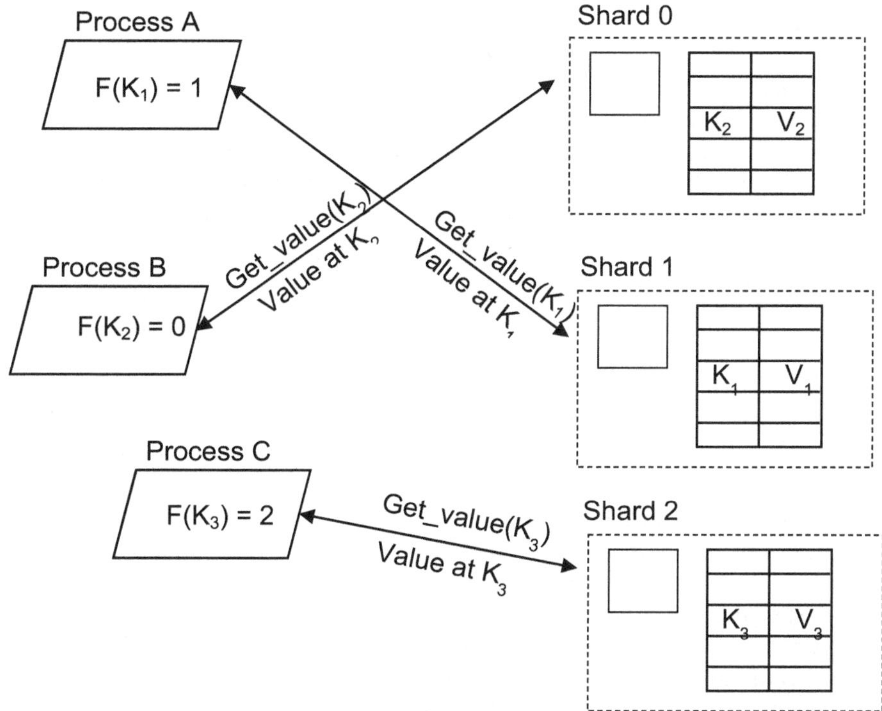

Fig. 8.1 Implementing shards as processes with message-passing

What Are Messages

Up to now, messages have been used in a number of contexts without fully describing what a message is. At a high level, messages are like the slips of paper passed between students in grade school. They typically carry a small amount of information about a narrow topic. We've seen examples such as "Task is done" and "Barrier done." Some more concrete characteristics of messages are:

- Messages will travel on byte streams such as network connections that don't have implicit record boundaries.
- The receiver of the message must be able to distinguish the boundaries between messages. Multiple messages may be transmitted at one time on a single connection and the receiver must be able to figure out where one message begins and another ends.
- The contents of the message must be identifiable, e.g., a Get_value message needs to be distinct from a Put_value message.
- The messages cannot contain pointers. Structures must be *serialized* (or *marshaled*) into the message.
- If the message is going between heterogenous hosts where byte-ordering may differ (for example, between a Linux system and an AIX system) then integers should be encoded by the sender and decoded by the receiver in a single "endianness" (see the section on reading and writing to a socket in Chap. 4 for more details on the byte ordering of numeric types).

When a process receives a message, it will appear as a stream of bytes. Multiple messages may appear on whatever the conduit is for the messages (e.g., a socket or a shared memory buffer) and the process must be able to quickly parcel out the messages. A simple way is to encode the length of the message in the first couple of bytes of the message (sometimes referred to as a *counted-bytes* message). The process reading the message simply reads, for example, 4 bytes, and knows immediately how many bytes constitute the message. This was described in the section Reading and Writing on a Socket in Chap. 4.

Another possibility is to encode the message with an end-marker. The process reads bytes until it receives the end-marker. This is useful when the sender doesn't know the length of the message beforehand and can simply stream the bytes until the message is done. One challenge is to make sure the body of the message is encoded so that part of the object within the message is not misinterpreted as the end-marker. URL-encoding (used for encoding URLs to replace certain characters with a hex encoding for the character) or base64 encoding (where each 6 bits is replaced with one ASCII byte so that only printable ASCII characters are in the output) are two mechanisms commonly used for encoding data into a limited character set.

Another common way of encoding is to use a textual format. For example, Javascript Object Notation (JSON) encodes Javascript objects in a specific and easily parsed format [JSON]. Structures are enclosed in braces ({ }), arrays in square braces ([]) and fields are explicitly given by name value pairs ("field-name": value). For example, a record containing the name of a person and an array of favorite food would be written as:

```
{ "name": "Emeril Lagasse",
  "favorite-foods": [ "Salmon",
                      "Calde Verde Soup",
                      "Roast Pork and Clams",
                      "Pho",
                      "Banh Mi"
                    ]
}
```

Yet another mechanism is how HTTP encodes its requests and responses as a combination of name/value pairs delimited by line feeds and a section that is encoded as counted-bytes (Fig. 8.2).

Here are some examples of encoding:

The binary-encoded counted message is the simplest format and very compact. In this example of base64 encoding, the fields are individually encoded. The 4-byte message type of 1 encodes to AQAAAA = = . In this case, each field is encoded separately. Encoding piecemeal allows fields to be decoded independently, which is important when a single field might be large and rarely accessed. It also allows a string to be separately allocated apart from the fixed sized fields when decoding the base64. The `account_holder` field in this example can be separately decoded, placed into a dynamically allocated piece of memory, and the pointer to it stored in

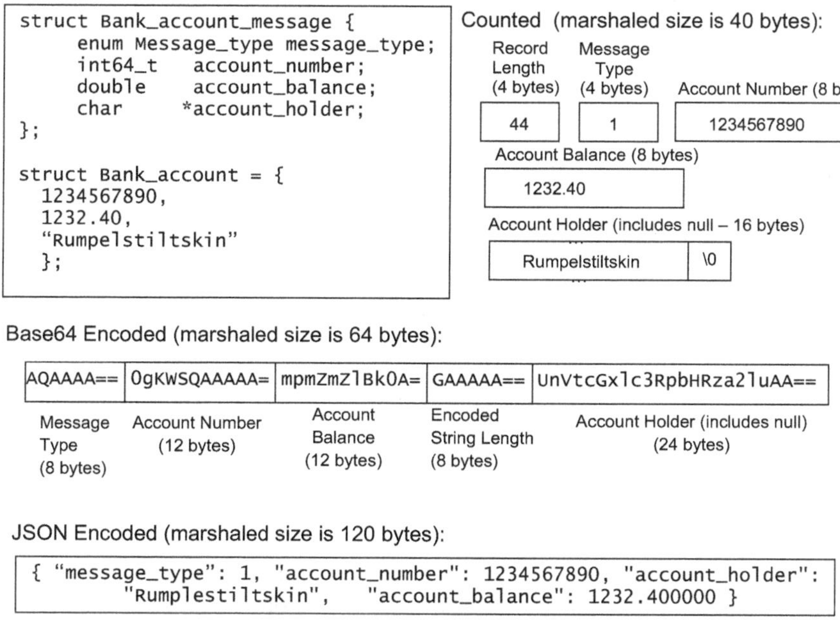

```
struct Bank_account_message {
     enum Message_type message_type;
     int64_t    account_number;
     double     account_balance;
     char      *account_holder;
};

struct Bank_account = {
   1234567890,
   1232.40,
   "Rumpelstiltskin"
   };
```

Counted (marshaled size is 40 bytes):

Record Length (4 bytes)	Message Type (4 bytes)	Account Number (8 bytes)
44	1	1234567890

Account Balance (8 bytes)
1232.40

Account Holder (includes null – 16 bytes)	
Rumpelstiltskin	\0

Base64 Encoded (marshaled size is 64 bytes):

Message Type (8 bytes)	Account Number (12 bytes)	Account Balance (12 bytes)	Encoded String Length (8 bytes)	Account Holder (includes null) (24 bytes)
AQAAAA==	OgKWSQAAAAA=	mpmZmZlBkOA=	GAAAAA==	UnVtcGxlc3RpbHRza2luAA==

JSON Encoded (marshaled size is 120 bytes):

```
{ "message_type": 1, "account_number": 1234567890, "account_holder":
        "Rumplestiltskin",   "account_balance": 1232.400000 }
```

Fig. 8.2 Examples of serializing a message

the Bank_Account_message struct. The JSON encoding is very readable and is suitable for passing to a variety of systems (like Javascript) which can translate them into native objects quickly. It is frequently used between browser applications and webservers. However, for most applications, it is inefficient in both space and the processing time to parse it.

Here is a simplistic example of the routines to marshal and unmarshal the Bank_account struct above using a counted representation for the marshaled representation.

```
1  int Marshal_counted(struct Bank_account *acct,
2                           unsigned char *buffer) {
3    int cursor = 4;
4    * (int32_t *) (&buffer[cursor]) =
5                                  (int32_t) acct->message_type;
6    cursor += 4;
7    * (int64_t *) (&buffer[cursor]) = acct->account_number;
8    cursor += 8;
9    * (double *) (&buffer[cursor]) = acct->account_balance;
10   cursor += 8;
11   size_t l = strlen(acct->account_holder)+1;
12   memcpy((char *)&buffer[cursor], acct->account_holder, l);
13   cursor += l;
14   *(int32_t *) (&buffer[0]) = cursor;
15   return cursor;
16 }
17
18 int Unmarshal_counted(unsigned char *buffer,
19                             struct Bank_account *acct) {
20   int cursor = 4;
21   acct->message_type =
22              * (enum Message_type_enum *) (&buffer[cursor]);
23   cursor += 4;
24   acct->account_number = * (int64_t *) (&buffer[cursor]);
25   cursor += 8;
26     acct->account_balance = * (double *) (&buffer[cursor]);
27   cursor += 8;
28   int32_t l = strlen(&buffer[cursor])+1;
29   char *s = (char *)malloc(l);
30   memcpy(s, (char *)&buffer[cursor], l);
31   cursor += l;
32   acct->account_holder = s;
33   return cursor;
34 }
35
36 int Marshaled_size_counted(struct Bank_account *acct) {
37   return 24+strlen(acct->account_holder)+1;
38 }
```

Line 1 Marshaling takes a Bank_account structure and creates a representation of it in the buffer. The representation is position-independent, which means that it is valid wherever it is located in memory (there are no pointers in for example).

Line 3 The cursor is where the next byte is to be written; 4 bytes are reserved for the size of the marshaled object which will be filled in at line 13.

Lines 4–6 The message type is stored in the buffer and the cursor advanced. If this marshaled object is to be transported among heterogeneous systems, it may be necessary to convert integer values to a network-ordered number.

Lines 7–8 The account number is encoded.

Lines 9–10 The account balance is stored in much the same way as the account number is.

Lines 11–13 The Bank_account structure contains a pointer to the name of the account holder. Pointers are not allowed in a marshaled object (since it clearly wouldn't make sense in another process let alone another host). The string is copied to the output buffer. If efficiency is of the essence, then the length of the string can be encoded in front of the string. This avoids an extra `strlen` call when unmarshaling.

Line 14 The final size of the object is stored in the first four bytes of the marshaled representation.

Line 18 Unmarshaling converts the buffer in marshaled form to the native representation. In this case, it is fairly straightforward.

Lines 21–27 We reverse the marshaling by extracting out the fixed size fields.

Lines 28–32 The only tricky part of this is extracting the account holder. We figure out the length of the account holder, allocate that (making sure to leave space for the trailing null), and copy from the buffer into the new string. This is then assigned to the `account_holder` field in the `Bank_account` object.

Lines 36–38 Care must be taken that if the marshaling routine changes, that the marshaled size is also updated.

As you can imagine, as the number of messages increases and the structures that need to be passed from process to process get more complex, a tool for generating these routines becomes essential. The input to the tool is a description of the structure and the output is the routines required to marshal, unmarshal, and, depending on the tool, the marshaled size of that struct. For example, Google has a marshaling system called *protocol buffers* [Proto]. A file describing the messages is compiled using a tool called `protoc` into functions can be used to marshal and unmarshal the fields of the messages. There are a number of other message definition systems as well (e.g., Apache Avro).

A Word to the Wise: It is worth thinking about how messages can be versioned to allow applications at different revisions to still exchange messages. Long-living systems rarely have versions of the distributed software perfectly in sync. Simply deploying an upgrade will usually require that a process of one vintage exchanges messages with a process of another vintage, especially if the application must remain running during the upgrade process. If you are building your own message representation (as opposed to using an off-the-shelf tool like protocol buffers) then give some thought to how message versioning might be represented and handled by the message system.

Using Messages in the Banking Example

Let's continue with our simple banking example. It is relatively simple to use one-way messages to communicate with the shard processes. As discussed, this continuation model will want to carry some state along so that if process A sends a message requesting the balance of account 123, then the response message, which will be received asynchronously by the application process, must identify the returned value as belonging to account 123. The response can then be matched with the request and the appropriate action can be taken in the application process (like updating a field on the screen of the user).

Choosing the messages to implement is important. For example, suppose the choice is Get_value(account_number) and Set_value(account_number, new_balance). Updating the account balance might be written as (Fig. 8.3):

The application sends a message to get the value of a specific account. That amount is returned to the application (as a separate message), and the application adds $27.50 to the balance to get the new balance. This is then sent back to the shard to update the account with the new balance.

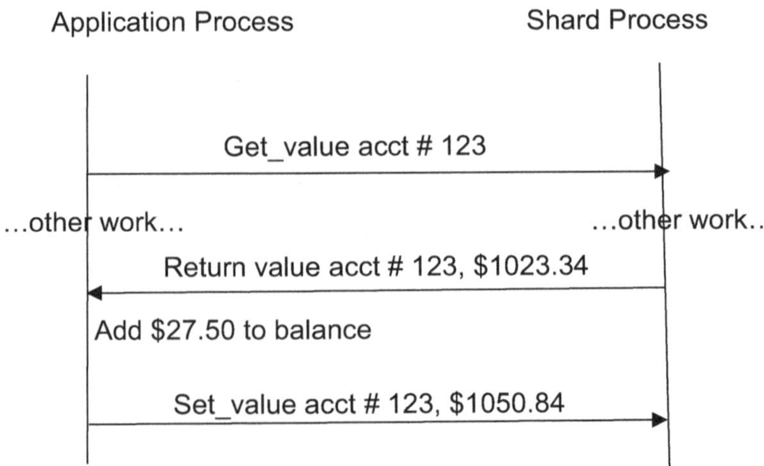

Fig. 8.3 Exchanging messages to update a balance

Unfortunately, the moment two application processes try to update the same account at the same time, the balance is likely to come out wrong. Both processes could request and receive the same value $1023.34. The first process might add $27.50 and set the balance to $1050.84 while the second process might deduct $10.00 and set the balance to $1013.34. Regardless of which `Set_value` "wins," the balance will be wrong since one process is overwriting the effect of the other.

A simple way to solve this problem is to introduce a message that updates the balance atomically. Instead of sending the new balance, the amount to change the balance is sent to the shard process. It then retrieves the old balance and adds the update (a negative number for withdrawals) and stores the updated balance as a single operation in the table, i.e., the value is retrieved, updated, and stored. This has the added advantage that a single message can update the object rather than two and only the deposit/withdrawal needs to be included with the message. For high transaction-rate applications this can be a considerable savings.

This is an example of why it is important to work out what messages will be used in the protocol, and how they interact with one another.

A more complex way of solving the consistency problem is to allow the application process to lock the account. This is useful when the action on the account is complex and is the responsibility of the application process, rather than the shard process. For example, an application may want to lock one or more accounts and perform some algorithm to detect if fraud is occurring and only when the algorithm is complete, to update the account and release the locks. The shard could have a lock field in the record that would be set for a given access and released by the holder of the lock. The exact mechanism depends on how complex the locking needs to be (for example, are deadlocks detected?).

Another reason for this more complex model is that it allows multiple locks to be established across multiple objects. This can be important but also can be extremely dangerous: without some care, a deadlock is easy to stumble into. If process A needs to lock objects 1 and 2, and process B needs to lock objects 2 and 3, and process C needs to lock objects 3 and 1, then we can get into a situation where each process locks the first object but none can lock the second and each process is waiting for a mutex that another process holds.

There are multiple strategies to avoid this deadlock that generally apply to concurrent programming (introduced in Chap. 7). The first is to ensure that there is a defined order for locking objects. In this case, we may require that objects are locked in the order of their "ID" (i.e., 1, 2, and 3 in the example above). In this case, thread A will acquire locks in order of 1 followed by 2, thread B locks 2 followed by 3, and C must lock 1 before 3. Now if thread A succeeds in getting 1 and 2, then B will be blocked and so will C. When A completes, B and C may both proceed (B locking 2 and C locking 1), but only one will succeed in locking 3. Assume that C obtains the lock and B must wait. Once C completes using 1 and 3 and releases the locks, B may proceed. Here's a diagram of this sequence:

Object 1	Object 2	Object 3
A acquires, C waits	A acquires, B waits	
A releases, C acquires	A releases, B acquires	C acquires, B waits
C releases	B acquires	C releases, B acquires
–	B releases	B releases
–	–	–

If lock ordering can't be determined from the objects doing the locking, a "give-up-and-try-again" strategy can be used. In our example, A might acquire locks for both 1 and 2. B would be immediately blocked because it cannot even acquire the lock for 2. C might acquire lock 3 but when it cannot acquire the lock on 1, it must give up the lock on 3 and retry getting the locks. This is a challenging approach since a naïve implementation may have C looping on locking and retrying burning CPU for what may be a long time.

Synchronous Messages

For some systems, it is also perfectly reasonable to use synchronous request-response messages instead of one-way messages. A request is made and the thread making the request waits until the response arrives from the server. This avoids having to carry context in the messages; the context is implicit in the send-response transaction. Instead of having to carry around which account is being operated on in the response, the thread issuing the request clearly knows which account the response is for.

If using sockets, then each application process would persistently connect to each shard. A shard would listen for requests, quickly answer the request and then process the next request (using an event-based networking scheme as presented in Chap. 5). This is similar to a web server and in fact the requests could be HTTP requests (as discussed in the Requests and Responses section of Chap. 4). However, if each process is waiting for a response on a connection it could be the case that most of them are waiting for responses rather than processing some other task in parallel.

Scaling Connections

Up to now, each process connected to the other processes it needed to exchange messages with. If there are 60 shard processes and 30 application processes, then a total of 1,800 connections would be made. That is manageable. What about 2,000 servers, each with 100 processes all talking with one another? Each process would need to theoretically connect to 200,000 processes and a single host with 100 processes would need to manage 20,000,000 connections.

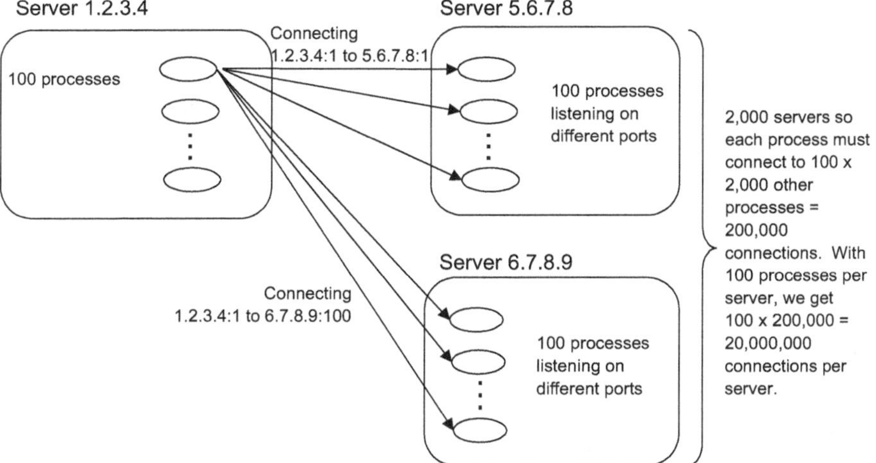

Fig. 8.4 Complete connectivity between lots of servers creates lots of connections!

TCP/IP is designed for up to 65,535 connections between one host and some other host. For example, host A with IP address 1.2.3.4 connecting to host B with address 5.6.7.8 and advertising port 80 could connect as 1.2.3.4 port 1 to 5.6.7.8 port 80. It could also connection with 1.2.3.4 port 2 to 5.6.7.8 port 80, and so forth for the 65,535 ports available for that connection. The process repeats for 1.2.3.4 port 1 to another host, say 6.7.8.9 on its port 80. As long as the combination of host address, host port, destination address, destination port is unique, TCP/IP technically allows the connection. The connectivity model for TCP/IP would actually support our 2000 server × 100 processes example (Fig. 8.4):

Since each destination host has a unique IP address and each process its own port, the TCP/IP model would theoretically be able to establish all of the connections to completely connect all the processes. However, a single host supporting 20,000,000 simultaneous connections would require huge amounts of memory in the OS dedicated to the TCP/IP buffers for those connections.

UDP

There are multiple ways of solving this problem. One is to reject TCP/IP and use UDP: User Datagram Protocol. UDP is a connectionless model: Each packet is independently addressed to its destination. A packet is sent and more or less forgotten about. Messages can address any number of destinations and a server can receive messages from any number of senders. However, unlike TCP/IP, UDP makes almost no guarantees about the packets sent:

- A packet is not guaranteed to be delivered to the destination and there is no built-in mechanism to indicate that a packet has been dropped. UDP is an *unreliable* transport.
- Packets may be delivered out of order. Packets 1,2,3 sent in that order may be received as 1,3,2.
- There is no flow control. If buffers can't accommodate a packet, the packet will be silently dropped (see #1).

The advantage of UDP is that since there are no connections, there are no limitations on the number of destinations for packets. However, to achieve reliable message transport, especially of information that spans multiple packets, requires a lot of information to be kept at each host. Packets may need to be retained so they can be retransmitted if lost. Even figuring out whether a packet is lost or not can be difficult. Reducing transmit rates to avoid congestion and buffer overflows can be challenging. In other words, creating TCP/IP-like features on your own over UDP may be quite challenging (considering that TCP/IP has thousands of man-years of development).

Creating Connection Hubs

Connecting each process to every other process, while simple, is unnecessary. Instead of every process contacting every other process, each host can contact every other host. In the above example of 2000 servers there would be 2000 connections per host (1 bidirectional connection per host) instead of 10 s of millions. This is quite a manageable number of connections. Each host would create a *hub*. The hub would distribute messages to and from processes on that host and when the destination of a message is to a process on another server, would forward that message to the hub on that server which would relay it to the destination process (Fig. 8.5).

Each hub would have an identity (a key into a table of the connections, e.g., "HubA"). Likewise, each hub would know about its processes and would have a table of these as well (with a key such as "process 1"). A message contains the destination (Hub B: process 2) and a return address (who is sending the message, e.g.,Hub A: process 1). The hub is responsible for routing these messages to the hub on the appropriate host, which will then route to the designated process.

This technique has a number of advantages and disadvantages. One disadvantage, besides the extra complexity of introducing hubs and tables of connections, is that it does incur an extra hop between the process and the hub. The cost of this hop depends on the mechanism used to send a message between the process and hub. Since the process and hub are on the same host, there are a number of options for implementing their communication path that will be discussed below.

You might wonder if routing all the traffic through one TCP/IP connection would be fundamentally less performant than having each process send traffic through its own connection. Assume there is a single physical ethernet cable between the servers. The traffic between the servers is going to be more likely limited by the wire than

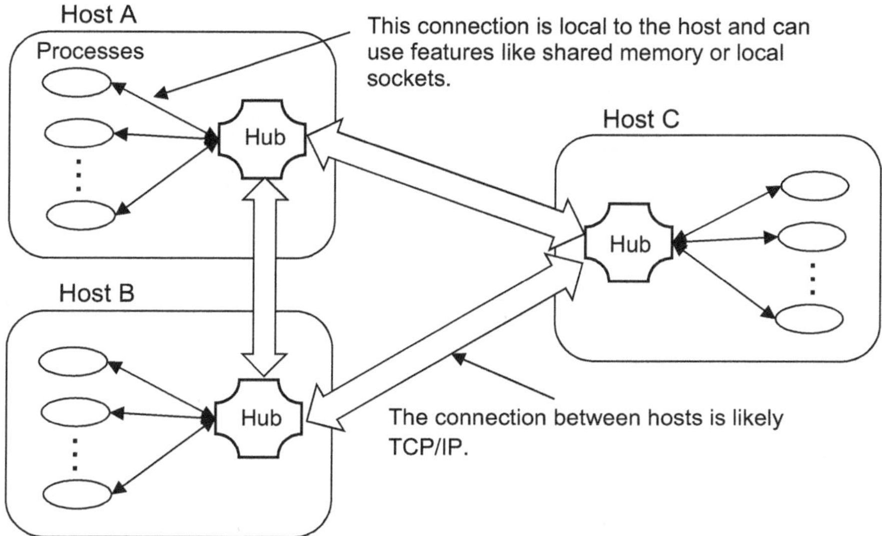

Fig. 8.5 Hubs on each host route traffic to peers

the CPU available to the sender. The hub should be able to push at least as much traffic as the multiple processes over the wire. If for some reason the hub becomes a bottleneck, it is possible to use multiple hubs to increase the bandwidth while still significantly reducing the overall connection count between hosts.

The extra hop between the process and the hub can introduce increased *latency* (the time it takes a message to get from one place to another). A message directly sent from process A to process C will often get to process C more quickly than a message that goes from process A to hub X which then forwards the message to hub Y which delivers the message to process C. This isn't always the case though. Generating more traffic over fewer links may have benefits in packet utilization between the hosts as well as driving the Nagle algorithms more efficiently (see Reading and Writing on a Socket in Chap. 4). Prototyping and performance measurement are almost always required when writing high performance hub-based networking.

This hub pattern as shown also presumes that a significant number of processes are on each server (in our example, we presumed 100 processes per host) so that the hub on that host significantly reduces the overall number of host-to-host network connections. Clearly if only one process is running on a host, then placing a hub on that host serves no purpose. As mentioned earlier, many factors are pushing the number of processes per server (or container) to smaller numbers. In this case, the hub may need to be hosted externally to the processes. The same basic model holds, but the choice of communication between processes and hubs is reduced to TCP/IP instead of other mechanisms available when the hub and process are on the same server (discussed in section Hub Implementation Techniques below) (Fig. 8.6).

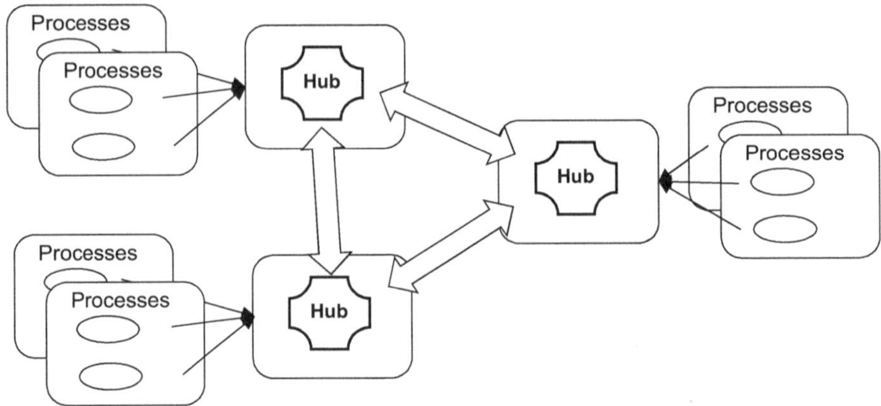

Fig. 8.6 Hubs have their own hosts

Other Hub Advantages

Hubs also have some unique advantages. Suppose the services of Host C:process 1 can also be provided by Host D: process 3. Host D: process 3 might be the failover for Host C: process 1 so that if host C: process 1 fails, Host D: process 3 can pick up its tasks. Hubs can encapsulate that knowledge. In this case, a hub can recognize a failed connection to Host C, and knowing that Host C: process 1 is backed up by Host D: process 3, automatically reroute Host C's messages to the alternate host (Fig. 8.7).

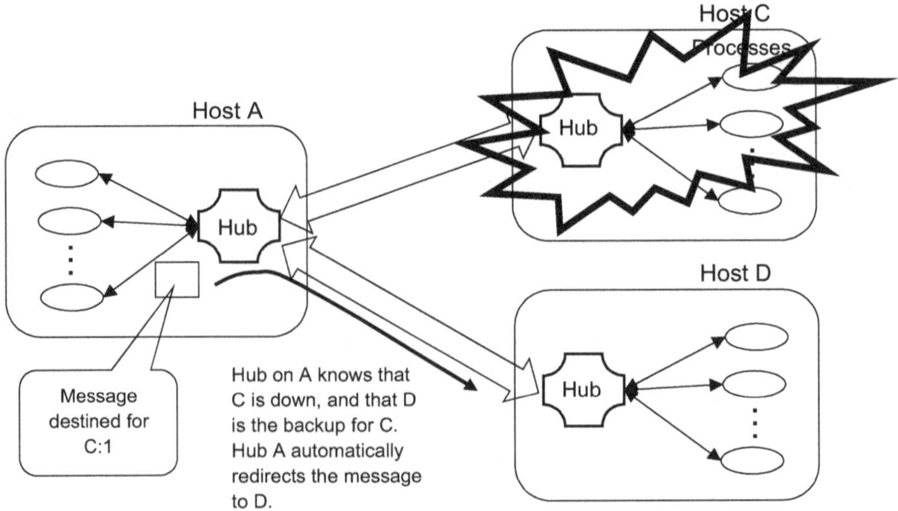

Fig. 8.7 Hubs can transparently manage failover if backup services are available

Hubs can also have multiple connections between themselves. Suppose we have two servers with two ethernet cables between them and we want to leverage both to increase the bandwidth between the two servers. One choice is to tell the operating system to treat the two cables as if they were one. This is called *bonding*. It simplifies the application (it only has to consider a single logical connection which will have the performance of two separate cables). Unfortunately, configuring bonding is a non-trivial exercise and requires cooperation with the switch the server is connected to.

Instead, a hub can simply manage multiple links itself. Suppose there are two physical connections between Hub A and Hub B (connection-1 and connection-2). When Hub A decides that a message needs to go to Hub B, it can consult its connection table, see that two connections are available, and then choose one to use (possibly by round-robin, possibly using the next available leveraging an event mechanism).

Using multiple connections can, however, make message-ordering difficult. One of our requirements for messages is that if a process X sends message A and then message B to process Y that Y will receive them in that order (or be able to order them so that it sees A then B). Consider our banking application that issues two messages: Deposit $100 into account X and withdraw $50 from account X. If the messages are processed in that order, we know that account X will have the necessary funds for the withdrawal to succeed. What if a Hub sends the deposit message by connection-1 and the withdrawal message by connection-2 and connection-1 is backlogged such that the withdrawal message arrives at the destination before the deposit message. The withdrawal fails (from insufficient funds), while the later deposit message will succeed. The application's intended order is lost, leading to an incorrect result.

One solution is to require that a given process's messages must always go over the same connection. This could reduce the throughput of a single process but the overall throughput of the hub across the multiple processes should still reflect the multiple paths available. Only if its assigned connection failed would a process be assigned another connection (e.g., connection-1 fails so process X is assigned connection-2).

We have not addressed the reliability of these connections. If a connection fails, one or more messages on that connection may be lost. This leads us to *reliable messaging* which is outside the scope of this chapter. Numerous packages exist that provide reliable messaging including Kafka (Confluent, 2026) and RabbitMQ (RabbitMQ, 2026).

Another approach to ensuring correct ordering is to issue sequence numbers to the messages. All messages from Hub A:process 1 will have a sequence number 1, 2, 3, 4, 5.... Message 2 can't be processed until message 1 is received. If we receive messages 2..100 without receiving message 1, then it might be reasonable to assume message 1 has been lost and some remediation has to take place. This is on the path to a reliable message system mentioned above. It requires more state to be kept by the connection (for example, what sequence numbers have been received) and requires actions to take to recover messages if a process fails and restarts.

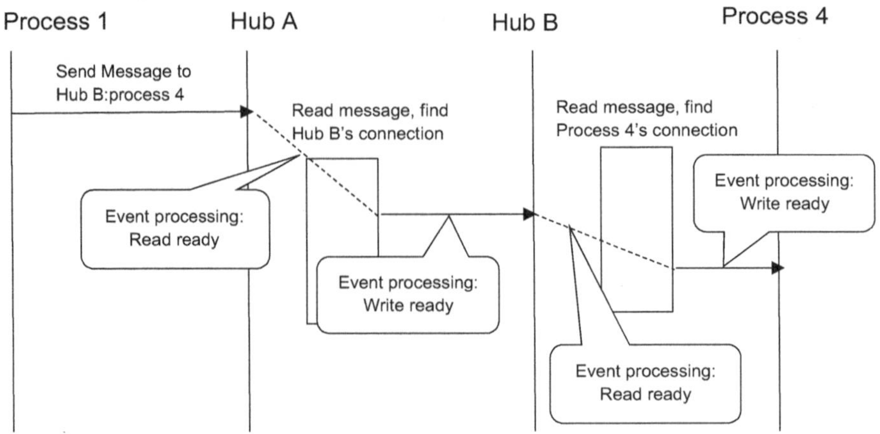

Fig. 8.8 Message forwarding across hosts using event processing

Hub Implementation Techniques

The hub architecture is similar regardless whether the hub is co-resident with processes or on its own host. When the hub is a separate host, it accepts connections from processes, it connects to other hubs, a message arrives from a process, the destination is read from the message, and the message is sent out an outgoing connection. Likewise, a message arrives from an incoming connection, the process it is destined for is parsed from the message, and the message is forwarded to the appropriate process. All of this will be done with "normal" TCP/IP (AF_INET) socket connections and read/writes and event processing (see Event Based Networking in Chap. 5) (Fig. 8.8).

When the hub is on the same host as a set of processes, there are other choices available for connecting the processes to the hubs (hub-to-hub connections remain TCP/IP based as above). Two popular mechanisms for intrahost connections are *local sockets* and *shared memory*.

Local Socket Hubs

One approach to intrahost communication is very similar to what is shown for the interhost communication between hubs except a new type of socket is used. In Chap. 4, the sockets created were AF_INET (TCP/IP) sockets. In this approach to hubs, the interhub communication remains on TCP/IP sockets but the local traffic (process to hub) traffic will be on AF_UNIX sockets. AF_UNIX sockets can only connect between endpoints that are on the same host.

The setup of the socket is slightly different. On Linux, an AF_UNIX socket listening for local process connections is established with a filename instead of an IP address or qualified name[2]:

```
#define SOCKET_NAME "/tmp/local-socket"
int socket = socket(AF_UNIX, SOCK_STREAM, 0);
struct sockaddr_un addr;
strcpy(addr.sun_path, SOCKET_NAME);
addr.sun_family = AF_UNIX;
bind(socket,
     (struct sockaddr *) &addr,
    strlen(addr.sun_path) + 1 + sizeof(addr.sun_family));
listen(socket, 10);
```

The only significant difference in establishing the socket is that `addr` is not `sockaddr_in` but `sockaddr_un` and instead of an address/port combination being used to address the socket, a filename is used.

This socket can be used like any other socket. The primary advantage to using an AF_UNIX socket is that it avoids a number of network layers (and hardware) that a "regular" AF_INET socket incurs and so it is much faster. It is largely a shared memory buffer that is being written into (with a `write`) by one process and read from (using `read`) by another on the same host. Otherwise, it behaves like a socket: if the buffer is full then writes will fail. Reads and writes still trigger events. One difference is that since AF_UNIX sockets do not have packet boundaries the Nagle algorithm doesn't apply, and there are no inefficiencies in writing small items.

Shared Memory Hubs

Most of the time, a process accesses its own memory and isn't allowed to touch another process's memory. *Shared memory* provides a region of memory that one or more processes can access simultaneously. The shared memory is a contiguous, bounded range of bytes that is not necessarily at the same memory address in each process. The first byte might be at address X for process 1 and at address Y, $X \neq Y$ for process 2. It is possible to try to get the same address for processes 1 and 2, but it is not guaranteed to be possible. Here is a simplified picture of memory shared between two processes (Fig. 8.9):

Because shared memory can have multiple addresses in multiple processes, some care must be exercised as to how it is used. For example, pointers from one location in the shared memory to another location in the memory can be dangerous. Suppose we have the two processes sharing a linked list. Let's assume that process 1 maps the shared memory to 0×100 and places two items on the list. Process 2, which has mapped the shared memory to $0 \times 100{,}000$, tries to visit each item (Fig. 8.10).

In this case, process 2 will process the first record fine (assuming `first` is set of 0x100,000). On the next iteration, the address in `p` is 0x120. That is not in the

[2] A qualified name is the "ordinary" name of a host on a network, e.g., cnn.com.

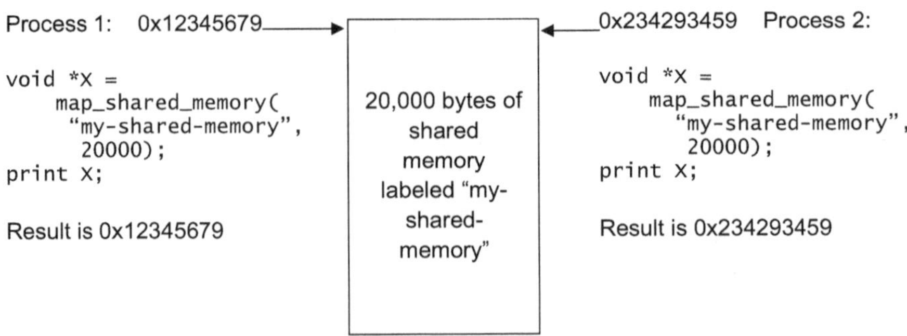

Fig. 8.9 Shared memory doesn't necessarily reside at the same address in separate processes

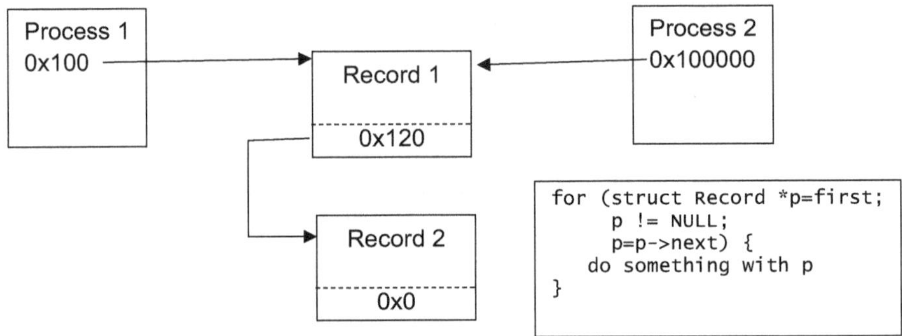

Fig. 8.10 Process 2 will exhibit bad behavior because the records are at different addresses in the two processes

shared memory mapped by process 2. It may be program instruction memory, or some other data, or memory that has not been allocated to process 2. If you are lucky, this will result in a segmentation fault and a clear signal that something is wrong. Worse would be that it simply accesses some random data in the program resulting in baffling results. If the "do something with p" in the body of the loop updates some value, it could be scribbling over some other valuable data leading to corruption.

When using shared memory that requires references from one location to another, the simplest way to avoid problems is to not store pointers, but to store offsets from the beginning of the shared memory buffer.[3] Since the offset 0 is a legitimate "pointer," a NULL pointer is represented by a -1. In this case, the linked list might appear as the following (with `shared` being the pointer to the beginning of the shared memory) (Fig. 8.11).

Clearly pointers to unshared memory from shared memory would have to be used only by the process owning the unshared memory. It is possible to have this sort of construction but it is not recommended.

---

[3] A marginal benefit of this is that pointers can typically be represented as 31-bit offsets and as long as the shared memory is not more than 2 GB this reduces the size of the pointer from 8 to 4 bytes.

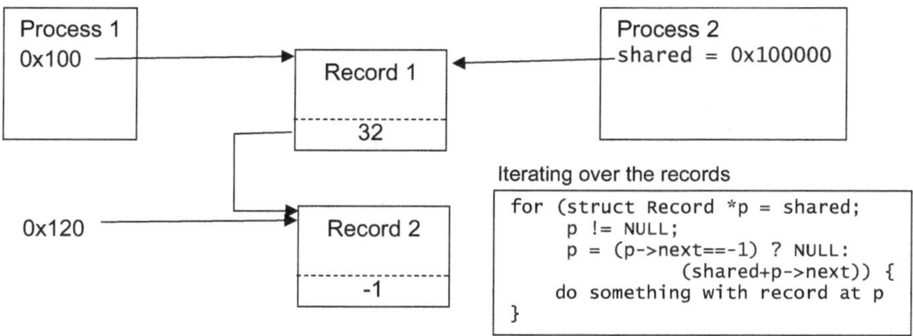

Fig. 8.11 Using offsets instead of pointers allows references to be shared between processes

A shared memory buffer can act as a conduit between two processes. Unlike the socket, items are placed in it just like "regular memory" as opposed to reading and writing to the socket. For example, instead of writing a message to the socket:

```
write(fd, message, message_length);
```

the message is copied to wherever the bytes need to go (e.g., a queue entry):

```
memcpy(p, message, message_length);
```

This may seem equivalent, but a `write` is considered a system call (in most operating systems). It transfers control from the user's program to the underlying system (the OS kernel) which then transfers the user's buffer to an internal buffer. The corresponding `read` also transfers control to the kernel to copy from the internal buffer to the user buffer. The transition between user and kernel is not inexpensive. Parameters are checked to ensure the kernel constraints are met, parameters are copied to registers, contexts are saved, and then the function is called using a special instruction that does more than a typical call-function instruction. The `memcpy` on the other hand does not invoke any of that mechanism (and in some cases can be compiled directly into a handful of CPU instructions).

Using shared memory is not entirely a free ride; however, if two processes are simultaneously storing and removing messages from a shared memory buffer, they must be synchronized in a way that is quite similar to the queue example in Chap. 7. Locks and condition variables may be needed to synchronize access to shared memory.

The strategy to lock a mutex, store a message, signal a consumer that the message is available, and unlock the mutex may not be the most efficient communication mechanism. If this is done for every message being queued, especially if messages are being queued at a high rate, the overhead may come to dominate the runtime. It may make sense to store several messages before signaling the consumer as long as the messages arrive within some amount of time (for example, 1 microsecond). Gathering messages by delaying the signal to the consumer is the equivalent of TCP/IP's Nagel algorithm.

The use of the condition variable can be avoided by having each consumer poll the shared memory to see if one or more messages are available. There are several strategies that can be used to manage the polling.

1. The consumer simply checks for work, processes any, and then loops back up to check again. The challenge with this approach is that if there is relatively little work, the consumer thread is spinning its wheels performing the check and burning CPU time for little effect. You can reasonably argue that you are simply burning CPU allocated to that thread anyway, but there is a cost for that in energy (the chip will literally warm up some). In comparison, the socket model notified the process when items were on the queue (i.e., a socket could be read) greatly reducing wasted CPU cycles. Instantly checking for work also does not really allow any batching, and, since some locking will still be required to populate the shared memory, can cause significant lock contention on busy systems.
2. Rather than immediately polling to determine if work is available, each poll can be delayed by some configurable amount of time. After the delay, the process checks to see if anything is present in the queue (and processing whatever is there). The process sleeps before checking again. This sleep can be relatively small (for example a microsecond). This will increase the latency of the messages (which may or may not be critical), but should not impact the throughput as long as the queue doesn't fill up (i.e., no more entries are allowed to be placed on it). The CPU time, however, will be dramatically lowered compared to option 1.
3. Yet another way to manage this is to check for items on the queue, process any that are there, and then *yield* the thread to allow other threads to run. A yield tells the thread scheduler to halt this thread and activate another thread. This is similar to strategy 1 except that when there is no work to be done other threads have more opportunity to run (and possibly generate work for the thread that is yielding). This approach looks like this:

```
for (;;) {
    if (Queue_empty(shared_queue)) {
        yield();
        continue;
    }
    struct Message *message = Queue_dequeue(shared_queue);
    Process message
}
```

Strategy 1 will be the fastest and the most expensive. Strategy 2 is the slowest but has the lowest impact, especially during idle times. Strategy 3 falls in between in performance but yielding is not cheap so if there is significant idle time, it can be almost as expensive as strategy 1 but with lower throughput and higher latency. The choice will depend on the load experienced by the hub.

Locking can also be avoided to some degree. A lockless list is possible (Harris, 2001) similar to the lock-free circular buffer that was discussed in Chap. 7. Care must be taken to remain in the shared memory segment (the list is bounded by how much shared memory was allocated).

Hubs and Flow Control

Hubs have numerous advantages. They reduce network resources, can improve bandwidth, and improve resiliency. There is one area that must be carefully managed and that is flow control.

In a connection not involving a hub, process A sends directly to process C over TCP/IP. If C gets very busy it may read the messages more slowly than A can write them. In this case, TCP/IP will initiate flow control and A will not be able to write any more (its network buffers will be filled). A is throttled and the system remains stable.[4]

Now consider the case where process A sends messages to hub H which forwards messages to C. The hub H reads the message from A, determines it needs to be routed to C, and, when C is ready, writes the message to C's connection. Now it is the case that A can send to lots of places (C, D, E…). The hub H must look at the message from A to determine where to route it. If the hub simply reads the message, it will grab messages as fast as it can, queuing them to their destination, and no TCP/IP back-pressure will be applied to A. So that's a problem. There is no feedback to A that C may be congested since only hub H will receive back-pressure from C and A does not experience it.

A strategy to control the flow is to stipulate that if H must wait to write to C, then it should not read messages destined for C. The connection to C should be marked as "busy." But how does hub H know if a message from A is destined for C through H? A might be sending to D or E. If H reads the message to identify the destination then it has cleared the TCP/IP buffer and more traffic from A is enabled.

One way of handling this situation is to access the data being received from A without actually reading it (and removing it from the network buffer). This is called *peeking* at the data. Different platforms support this to various degrees. On Linux platforms, there is a function called `recv` that is very similar to `read` except that it takes a fourth parameter which is one or more flags on how to receive the data (`recv` only works on sockets, not files which is a major difference between it and the function `read`). One flag to `recv` is MSG_PEEK which instructs the system to receive the data but not advance the internal read cursor. Now we can look at the message header, see what the destination is, and if the destination has been marked as busy then don't read the data from the socket. This will leave it in the network buffer and back pressure will be applied to the sender.

Once the connection to C frees up (e.g., `Event_write_ready` is true), then the connections waiting on C can be "opened up" and normal reading and forwarding can proceed.

The downside of this approach is that if A is sending to C, D, and E, and C is backed up, then not only will A's message to C be suspended by hub H, but any other messages following this message will also be blocked by the hub. Without some

[4] Assuming that A takes some action to slow down. If A simply queues data waiting for the connection to be available again it can run out of memory if the write rate exceeds the read rate for too long. If A writes to the socket synchronously, then it will automatically slow down.

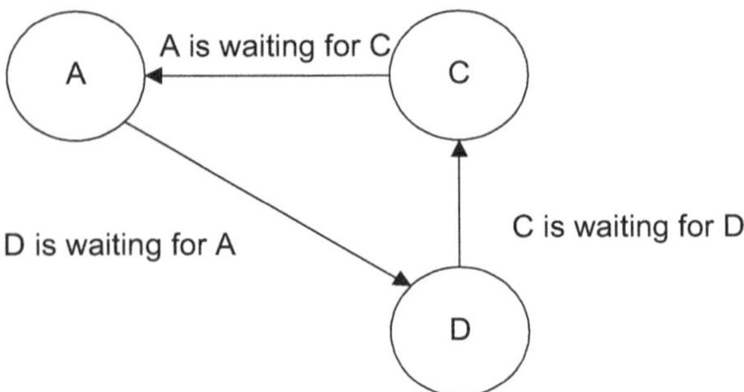

Fig. 8.12 Classic deadlock

care, it is possible to get into deadlock. Suppose A is sending a message to C and D through its hub and the connection to C is suspended. It could be the case that C is not processing messages because it is expecting a message from D, and D is waiting for a message from A. We have a classic deadlock (Fig. 8.12):

It is very difficult to resolve this at the hub level, particularly with sockets and "peeking." The simplest solution is to redesign the algorithm so that circular dependencies don't exist. This is not necessarily a trivial problem, though in most cases, the locking loop used in the example above is not a common problem.

As in the socket case, shared memory also requires flow control. If the link to a destination cannot accept writes, then incoming messages destined for that link should not be processed. The shared memory queues will fill up and some mechanism must exist at the client sending messages to handle "queue full."

Shared memory offers some advantages over sockets in this respect. In the AF_UNIX case, reading without clearing the socket buffer was cumbersome and reading messages out of sequence not possible (i.e., if we've received messages for A, B, and C, in that order, we cannot read A and C but not B). Shared memory buffers don't suffer from this difficulty. A list of messages can be traversed and those that can proceed can be extracted while leaving the stalled messages.

Hubs and Message Broadcasting

In Chap. 7, barrier synchronization with message passing was introduced. In this case, a controlling thread would send messages to a group of threads, each performing a given task and only when all of the tasks were complete would the controlling thread proceed. As described in Chap. 7, the controlling thread sent individual messages to each of the participating threads.

This can be made more efficient by using a hub to distribute the messages. The controlling thread sends a single message to a hub with all the destinations included in the single message. The hub then iterates over the destinations in the message and takes care of sending copies of the message to each of the destinations.

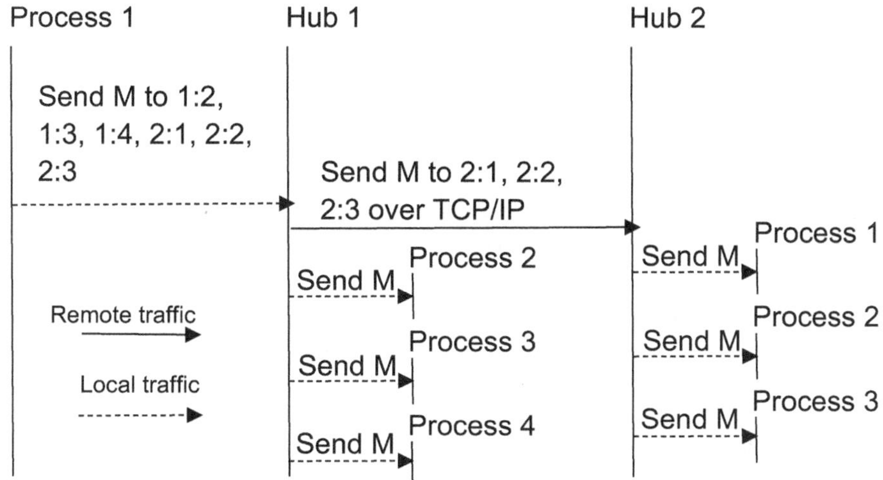

Fig. 8.13 Using hubs to manage message broadcast

Using hubs to broadcast can be made even more efficient by first grouping the messages by destination hubs. A hub can then broadcast to its own local processes, and then forward the broadcasted message with its specific destinations to each hub which then distributes the message to the appropriate processes. Now the traffic between hubs is a single message per destination hub rather than a message per destination process (Fig. 8.13).

While this can reduce traffic, flow control is still required. Now we must peek to see if any of the message destinations are blocked to know if a message should be held up. Care also must be taken not to create endless loops of messages. Hub 1 connects to hub 2, but it is symmetric and hub 2 also connects to hub 1. We don't want messages endlessly bouncing back and forth between hubs. There are a number of ways of avoiding this. In a single tier system where every hub is connected to every other hub, then it is as simple as broadcasting to hubs and the hubs only broadcast to their local processes. In a more complex hub arrangement where multiple hops may be required to get to all the hubs, a *spanning tree* (Perlman, 1985) can be followed that guarantees all hubs are only accessed once.

Summary

This pattern has been an overview of using message passing to implement concurrent programs across multiple processes on multiple hosts. There are several advantages to this pattern:

1. A common model can be used regardless of whether the processes are co-resident on a host or distributed over a network.

2. It can enable heterogeneous systems to work together uniformly.
3. Failures are localized. With proper error recovery a failed process can be avoided by the surviving members of the compute cluster, recovered, and reintroduced to the system.
4. Reasoning about what is happening in parallel can be simplified by looking at the routes messages take. This can be more difficult in "plain old" multithreaded programs where cause and effect are not necessarily obvious.
5. With the introduction of hubs, parallel programs can scale very large without exhausting network resources.

Small-scale parallel systems can use simple point-to-point connections (each process connects to every other process in the cluster of processes). However, as the number of processes scales, hubs provide a convenient way to concentrate communication and reduce the total number of connections required.

There are multiple strategies for implementing how hubs communicate with local processes. Two choices are to use AF_UNIX sockets or shared memory. The choice ultimately will depend on the application and how critical throughput is. With AF_UNIX sockets, the code is uniform for local and remote communication and event-based processing can apply to both. Shared memory has the advantage that it avoids the overhead of kernel transitions for reads and writes. It has the disadvantage that notification of events needs to be built using one of the strategies listed in the implementation section above. And unlike sockets, a process doesn't receive notification when another process sharing the memory fails.[5]

A reasonable question is: "If this is such a good way of parallelizing a program, why aren't there standard packages to setup message passing and hubs?" In fact, there are some packages such as MPI (Message Passing Interface) (OpenMPI, 2026) that provide this functionality. To date, MPI has predominantly been used in the High Performance Computing (HPC) arena (e.g., National Labs like Argonne and Sandia) and, more recently, some artificial intelligence has found use for it. However, its use in more generic, non-numeric applications has been more limited.

Exercises

1. Build a program that accepts a connection and receives messages that are processed. The messages are either: STORE < *key-string* > *integer* or `FETCH` < *key-string* > . The messages are synchronous, i.e., they expect a response. Responses are:

```
STORED <key-string> integer to indicate the value has been stored
FETCHED <key-string> integer in response to the FETCH message.
```

[5] In some systems, the two processes establish a socket between the two in parallel with the shared memory for the explicit purpose of receiving an error on the socket to detect that the peer process has failed.

2. Using the messages in Exercise 1, create a client and client that use asynchronous messages. Multiple requests can be made by a client before the response is received, and responses may be out of order. You will need some way to associate responses to a particular request and may change the message format to accommodate that.
3. Build a very simple hub that will relay from one host to another hub that will relay to its local host. You will need to add a destination address to the message format. Use local sockets for communication to and from client processes to their hub, TCP/IP sockets for the interhub traffic.
    a. Compare the performance of the solution for Exercise 2 with the same setup with the relay inserted between the client and server.

Chapter 9
Memory Management

One of the greatest challenges of programming a large, complex system is managing dynamically allocated memory. We've implicitly used dynamically allocated memory in most of our examples (for example `make_Queue`). There are several challenges found with memory management:

1. Efficiently allocating and deallocating smaller objects that rapidly appear and disappear. Queue elements are a good example of this: entries are often rapidly enqueued and dequeued.
2. Deallocating objects that are shared by multiple data structure such that there are no pointers left referencing an object that has been freed. Likewise, making sure that an object is not freed twice. For example, suppose thread A and thread B both have pointers to a single object X. If A frees X, then B had better not! Referencing freed memory and double-freeing memory are some of the most common memory related errors in programming.
3. Another common memory related error is removing all references to an object but not freeing it. This is called a memory leak and often occurs when trying to avoid double-frees in a multithreaded program.

Different languages have different exposures to these programming challenges. Java and Python take over memory management: Objects are freed only when they are no longer referenced which takes care of items 2 and 3 (and as will be seen, techniques for 1 can be employed by these languages as well). C, C++, and Rust (to a lesser extent) suffer from all three of these challenges and require a certain discipline to avoid the common traps.

The following sections will look at approaches to managing dynamically allocated memory.

M. Kilian, *Ten Software Patterns Every Student Should Know*,
https://doi.org/10.1007/978-981-92-0260-7_9

Specialized Allocators

It used to be that anyone building a large program, especially a multithreaded program, felt compelled to write their own memory allocator. Specialized memory allocators were sold as a replacement for malloc.[1] The main reasons for this was that the system provided memory allocator's (e.g., malloc) performed poorly in multithreaded applications. Often problems arose when small and large objects were allocated and freed causing fragmentation (see the earlier discussion on memory fragmentation in Chap. 1—Hash Tables). These sorts of problems have largely been addressed in modern allocators. Memory allocators are not only thread-safe, they are multithreaded, i.e., multiple threads can simultaneously allocate memory without conflicting with one another, and will group like-sized objects together in *pools* to reduce memory fragmentation.

Given the current state of the art, when does it make sense to write a specialized allocator? The cases are pretty limited but typically are for:

- When all the objects are of the same size.
- When objects have very short lifetimes.

Free-Lists

Queue entries are a prototypical example where a specialized allocator can be useful. Entries on the queue come into being, and almost as quickly, are discarded (if the create and discard rate were not nearly equal, the queue would grow in an unbounded way, creating yet another memory problem: *memory exhaustion).*

For example, the queue could have the following modification to reuse entries whenever possible:

```
struct Queue {
  pthread_mutex_t lock;
  pthread_cond_t condition;

  struct Queue_item *free_list;

  struct Queue_item *head;
  struct Queue_item *tail;
};

struct Queue_item *get_Queue_item(struct Queue *queue,
                                  void *item) {
  if (queue->free_list == NULL) {
    return make_Queue_item(item);
  }
  struct Queue_item *qitem = queue->free_list;
  queue->free_list = qitem->next_item;
```

[1] I worked on a product in the late 1990s called Memory Tuning System that replaced malloc and improved performance in memory intensive programs by as much as 30%. Most of the techniques used in that product are now features of malloc, or tcmalloc (Google's version of malloc).

```
18     initialize_Queue_item(qitem, item);
19     return qitem;
20   }
21
22   void return_Queue_item(struct Queue *queue,
23                               struct Queue_item *item) {
24     item->next_item = queue->free_list;
25     queue->free_list = item;
26   }
27
28   void enqueue(struct Queue *queue, void *item) {
29     lock(&queue->mutex);
30
31     struct Queue_item *qitem = get_Queue_item(queue, item);
32
33         ... the code as it appears in Condition Variables
34            in Pattern 7.
35   }
36
37   void *dequeue(struct Queue *queue) {
38         ...the code as it appears in Condition Variables
39            In Pattern 7 where head and item are set.
40
41     return_Queue_item(queue, head);
42
43     unlock(&queue->mutex);
44     return item;
45   }
```

Line 5 — We declare a free-list per queue. This means that multiple queues can proceed in parallel without having to synchronize access to the free-list. This list will have items added to its head and removed from the head (LIFO). The goal is to improve cache hits by reusing memory as much as possible.

Lines 11–20 — Instead of simply calling `make_Queue_item`, we will see if there are any items on the free-list. If not, then make a new item. Otherwise grab an item off the free-list and reinitialize it. `Get_Queue_item` must only be called when the queue's mutex is locked.

Line 22–27 — Instead of freeing a `Queue_item`, we return it to the free-list. See the comments below about the downside of this approach. In this case, we don't touch the item before adding it to the free-list. There are cases where this is insufficient and we will point this out when we discuss reference counting. As with `get_Queue_item`, `return_Queue_item` must only be invoked when the queue's mutex is locked.

Line 31 — Instead of just making a `Queue_item` out of thin-air, we use the routine to retrieve from the free-list.

Line 41 — Likewise, instead of just freeing the `Queue_item`, we return it to the free-list.

Using a free-list has its disadvantages. If items are enqueued much faster than dequeued then the free-list will be empty much of the time and more entries will be created than actually recycled. Ultimately these will be dequeued and placed on the free-list, but this can lead to keeping around a long free-list instead of releasing items back to system memory (i.e., using free). Of course some policy could be instituted that trims a free-list when it grows too long. This requires more bookkeeping and the cost of a "bulk-free" may interfere with response time guarantees.

A word to the wise: It is relatively cheap to keep a couple of statistics with the free-list. For example, keeping the current length, the maximum length it has grown to, and how many items have been reused is useful information to see if the free-list is providing the expected benefit. We will discuss this in more detail in Chap. 10.

Object Pools

Another case when a specialized allocator can be useful is when the dynamic objects are small (less than 16 bytes). Every system allocator adds some overhead per object, typically at least space to store the size of the object (malloc on Linux always allocates at least 8 extra bytes). This information allows objects to be freed. For larger objects, this overhead is small. However, for small objects it can exceed the size of the object. If huge numbers of small objects must be managed, the overhead may become untenable.

As an example, consider this little program:

```
uint8_t *p1 = (uint8_t *) malloc(1);
uint8_t *p2 = (uint8_t *) malloc(1);
int64_t diff = p2 - p1;
printf("Difference = %ld\n", diff);
```

In at least one case, the difference is 32 bytes suggesting that to represent the dynamically allocated 1 byte requires 32 bytes. This is common for malloc.

One approach to eliminate the allocation overhead is to pool like-sized objects together. A single chunk of identically sized objects can be allocated and parceled out with almost no overhead per object. Each allocation simply returns a pointer to one of these objects. If we never had to free the object the job would be done. In fact, much of the overhead with any allocator is to enable freeing and reusing that object. There are many ways of managing this and the following is an (incomplete) example.

Let's assume that the object size is fixed and is greater than 2 bytes. One simple approach is to allocate a single chunk of memory that is divided into the fixed sized objects. When an allocation request is made, a pointer to one of these objects will be returned. But which object? How do we know which objects are in use and which are free?

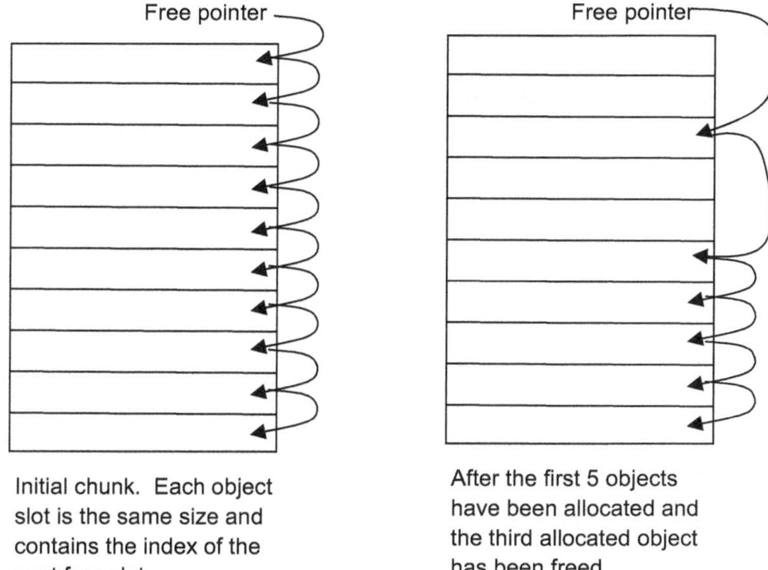

Fig. 9.1 Initial arrangement of objects in an object pool, and after allocation/deallocation

To keep track of the objects that are allocated versus free, the chunk of memory is initialized such that each slot for an object has the index of the next free entry. The first object in the chain of free objects is pointed to by a *free pointer* Fig. 9.1.

Each pointer in this figure is the offset to the next object in the chunk. If the offset is 6, then the pointer to the object in the chunk is the free pointer + 6 * size-of-object. It is possible to make objects as small as 2 bytes (the size of our offset) and accommodate up to 65,535 objects in the chunk with minimal overhead. The offset N (where N is the number of objects in the chunk) can be used to indicate the NULL pointer (since offset N is outside of the chunk). All the free entries are initially linked together and as they are allocated, they are removed from this linked list. When object at index 0 is allocated, the free pointer is advanced to the object that object 0 links to. When the object is freed, it sets its next point to the free pointer and the free pointer now references the freed object.

The object can be any size greater or equal to the 2 bytes required to store the offset of the next free object.

Here are simplified routines for a pool allocator. There are many points missing. Errors need to be handled for cases like freeing an object that wasn't allocated from this chunk, or trying to allocate from a chunk that has no more free objects.

```
1  struct Chunk *make_Chunk(int obj_size) {
2    size_t size_of_chunk =
3                sizeof(struct Chunk) +
4                   (objects_per_chunk * obj_size);
5   struct Chunk *chunk = (struct Chunk *) malloc(size_of_chunk);
6    chunk->free_index = 0;
7    chunk->num_allocated = 0;
8    chunk->object_size = obj_size;
9    for (uint16_t i=0; i<objects_per_chunk; i++) {
10     uint16_t *chunk_object_ptr = index_to_pointer(chunk, i);
11     *chunk_object_ptr = i+1;
12   }
13   return chunk;
14 }
15
16 void *allocate_object(struct Chunk *chunk) {
17   if (chunk->free_index >= objects_per_chunk) {
18     return NULL;
19   }
20   uint16_t *free_pointer = index_to_pointer(chunk,
21   chunk->free_index);
22   chunk->free_index = *free_pointer;
23   *free_pointer = objects_per_chunk + 1;
24   chunk->num_allocated++;
25   return (void *) free_pointer;
26 }
27
28 void free_object(struct Chunk *chunk, void *object) {
29   uint16_t *object_as_index_pointer = (uint16_t *) object;
30   *object_as_index_pointer = chunk->free_index;
31   uint16_t object_index = pointer_to_index(chunk, object);
32   chunk->free_index = object_index;
33   chunk->num_allocated--;
34 }
```

Lines 1–7 We make a chunk. The size of the chunk is the size of the chunk information (the free pointer, number of objects allocated, and the object size), and room for the objects stored in the chunk.

Lines 9–12 Each slot in the chunk for an object is initialized with the index of the next slot. The last slot has one more than the number of objects allowed in a chunk and indicates the end of the list. `Index_to_pointer` returns the address of an item in the chunk given its index.

Lines 17–19 There are no free objects if the free index is greater than the number of objects in a chunk. If this is the case, then simply return NULL.

Line 20–21 We establish a pointer to the object at the free index. This is the object we will return to the caller. We cast this pointer to point to a 16-bit integer and dereference it to get the next free object in the chain.

Line 22 The free chain is updated to the next free object. The need to initialize the whole chain of free objects when the chunk was created is now clear: it is trivial to allocate and remove an item from the free-list.

Line 23 The next free object index in the allocated object is set to a value that would make it unusable in a free-list to show this item has been allocated. This is a safety measure and is not strictly required.

Line 24 Keep track of what is allocated. This could be derived from the free chain but it is handy to have. As such, keeping track of this is optional.

Lines 28–34 Freeing an object is quite simple (with a caveat below). We treat the object being freed as a pointer to a 16-bit integer. We set that pointer to the current free index for the chunk and then set the free index to this object. It is basically a standard linked list addition.

A chunk can only be manipulated serially. Like the free-lists, chunks should be associated with a particular thread-safe or multithreaded data structure and accessed while that data structure is locked or otherwise serialized. As mentioned before, another layer needs to manage multiple chunks. It will ensure that when a chunk is full and an allocation is requested, a new chunk can be allocated. When an object is freed, the correct chunk needs to be identified (or, as the code is shown above, "Bad Things Will Happen"). It also goes without saying that this approach only works when the objects being allocated and freed are all of the same size (at least for a given chunk).

Summary

It is difficult to say whether a special allocator provides a huge improvement in performance over simply using malloc/free types of memory management (partly because a huge amount of work has been put into making system level memory management very efficient). When space is a premium and very small objects are being allocated, creating an object pool can be very useful. As in many cases, there will be a space/time tradeoff: less space will be required but the bookkeeping, especially for managing multiple chunks, will likely exceed a standard approach. Allocation and deallocation of objects should be encapsulated so that different approaches can be experimented with to determine what is the most effective.

Reference Counting

The implementation of a queue using atomic operations illustrated the difficulty when the freeing an item that was concurrently being accessed by another thread. This is one of the most common bugs in a multithreaded program (as well as single-threaded programs for that matter).

This section will use the term *object* to refer to any discrete piece of memory (like a dynamically allocated struct). We are not talking about a specific object model (like Java or C++) or object-oriented programming, though we will touch upon that at the end of this section.

Languages like Java relieve the programmer of memory management by cleaning up abandoned objects in memory itself with a process called *garbage collection.*[2] Periodically Java will sweep through memory (or portions of memory) and identify objects that are no longer *accessible* (or *reachable).* Consider the scenario where object A references object B. We say that object B is accessible through object A. Some objects are *root* objects; they are always accessible by definition (global variables are root objects). When an object is not accessible it is considered garbage. Since it cannot be reached, it cannot be used to do meaningful work. If A stops referencing B (and instead references C), B is *orphaned* by A and can be removed from the system.

It isn't always simple to determine if an object can be removed. Suppose A references B and D also references B and F references D:

A and F are root objects. Let's suppose that A removes its reference from B. B is still accessible from D and so it cannot be removed yet. Now remove the reference from F to D. D is not accessible and can be removed. As a result of it being removed, its reference to B is also removed and so B, now separated from both A and B, is inaccessible and can be removed.

In languages like Java, one form of garbage collection starts at roots and follows all the references until all accessible objects have been visited [this is a *mark-sweep* algorithm (Schorr et al.,1967)]. Any objects that haven't been visited are then removed from memory (*collected*). Another form of garbage collection is to copy objects that are referenced into a new *generation* of objects and throw away the older generation. It is easy to imagine how this process of tracing out objects in memory to find the inaccessible ones can be very time-consuming. Couple that with the fact that if the program is multithreaded, the garbage collector must be thread-safe. This can result in a programming pausing while garbage collection occurs and makes maintaining uniform performance hard to guaranteet. Note that some languages like Python simply stop all threads until garbage collection is complete.

Scanning and sweeping out garbage is just one way of automatically managing memory. Other approaches include languages like Rust, which has a model of handing off *ownership* of memory and then requiring limits on how the memory is referenced after the handoff. The goal is to minimize concurrent updates to memory and to avoid a thread changing objects out from under another thread.

This section will describe another pattern to manage memory safely called *reference counting*. Using the C programming language, reference counting can be onerous. Other languages like C++ and Rust have constructs that simplify the use of

---

[2] Garbage collection has been a topic of interest for software designers since the mid-60 s.

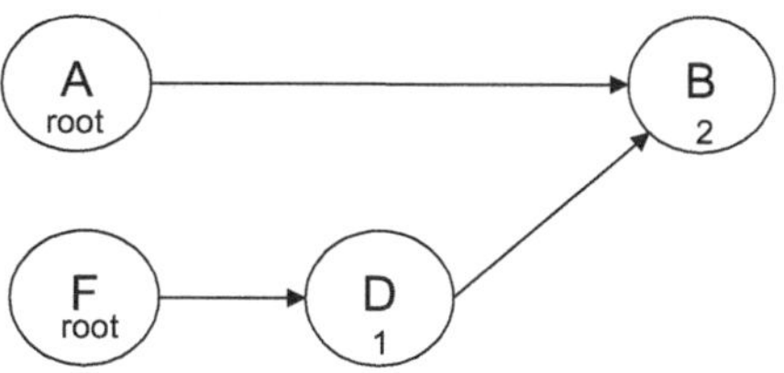

Fig. 9.2 Object B is accessible through A and D

reference counting. Reference counting requires the program to either automatically (through the programming language) or through disciplined coding style keep a count of how many references are made to an object. An object with a 0 reference-count can be considered unreachable and subject to garbage collection.

What Is Reference Counting?

In Fig. 9.2, D has one reference to it, and B has two. These are the reference counts of these objects. When an object has no references, it can be reclaimed. To accomplish this, every object contains a reference-count and every time an object establishes a pointer to an object, that object's reference-count is incremented. Likewise, when an object removes a pointer from some object (for example, by changing a pointer from one object to a different object) the previously referenced object's reference-count is decremented.

When in the course of decrementing a reference-count it becomes 0, the object is eligible for garbage collection, e.g., it can be freed. For simplicity, we will assume two functions:

```
int add_ref(struct Counted_object *object);
```

and

```
int rem_ref(struct Counted_object *object);
```

`Add_ref`'s parameter is the object that is about to be referenced. It will atomically increment the reference-count of the object and return the new reference-count. `Rem_ref` correspondingly decrements the reference-count of the object given as a parameter. If rem-ref decrements the object's reference-count to 0, it will reclaim it. Reclamation depends on the programming language—it may be `free` in C, `delete` in C++, or an application specific mechanism.

Here is an example of how it can be implemented and used in a simple linked list. There is a (dangerous!) assumption that the first field in any reference counted object is the reference-count. A pointer can therefore be cast to a `(struct Ref_count *)` to access its reference-count regardless of the overall structure being referenced. In C, we can't inherit this property as could be done in C++ or other languages that feature inheritance (reference counted objects would simply inherit from a class Ref_count).

```
struct Ref_count {
  int ref_count;
};

int add_ref(void *p) {
  if (p == NULL) {
    return -1;
  }
  return fetch_and_add(&(REF_COUNT(p)->ref_count), 1)+1;
}

int rem_ref(void *p) {
  if (p == NULL) {
    return -1;
  }
  int x = fetch_and_add(&(REF_COUNT(p)->ref_count), -1);
  if (x == 1) {
    free(p);
  }
  return x-1;
}

int get_ref(void *p) {
  if (p == NULL) {
    return 0;
  }
  return REF_COUNT(p)->ref_count;
}

struct Simple_List_element {
  struct Ref_count ref_count; // MUST BE FIRST
  int item;
  struct Simple_List_element *next;
};

struct Simple_List {
  struct Simple_List_element *head;
  struct Simple_List_element *tail;
};

void Simple_List_push_item(struct Simple_List *l, int v) {
  struct Simple_List_element *e = make_Simple_List_element(v);
  if (l->tail == NULL) {
    add_ref(e);
    add_ref(e);
    l->head = e;
    l->tail = e;
    return;
  }
  add_ref(e);
  l->tail->next = e;
  rem_ref(l->tail);
  add_ref(e);
```

```
54     l->tail = e;
55   }
56
57   int Simple_List_pop_item(struct Simple_List *l) {
58     if (l->head == NULL) {
59       return -1;
60     }
61     int v = l->head->item;
62     struct Simple_List_element *next = l->head->next;
63     rem_ref(l->head);
64     // See below for why ref counts are not manipulated here.
65     l->head = next;
66     if (l->head == NULL) {
67       rem_ref(l->tail);
68       l->tail = NULL;
69     }
70     return v;
71   }
```

Lines 1–3 This is a hack. A reference-count is simply an integer. We assume that the objects that are going to be counted have a `Ref_count` struct as the first attribute.

Lines 5–10 Adding a ref is just incrementing the counter. The check for a null prevents failure on null pointer and perhaps warrants an error message. This is deferred to the caller who can check the reference-count returned, see it is negative, and take some action. The `REF_COUNT` function simply casts the void pointer passed to the function to a `Ref_count pointer`. `Fetch_and_add` is used so reference counting is multithreaded, *but this doesn't mean the data structures that are reference counted are multithreaded.* The count *after* the increment is returned (which is why 1 is added to the result of the `fetch_and_add`).

Lines 12–16 Removing a ref is similar to adding a ref except now the count is decremented.

Lines 17–21 If the count returns to 0 (x in this case is the count before the decrement so when it is 1 the final count will be 0), then the reference counted object is freed. As we will see, the order of adding and removing references is important since as soon as a reference-count is decremented to 0, the object can no longer be legally accessed.

Lines 23–26 A convenience function. In a multithreaded program, the value returned can almost immediately become stale. Extreme care must be used with this function. If the value returned is 0 then the pointer passed in is either a newly allocated object with no other object pointing to it, or freed memory.

Line 30–38 Now we build a `Simple_List` of `Simple_List_elements`. We will push items onto the tail and pop them off the head. The `Simple_List_elements` will be reference counted.

Lines 42 This is the element to be added to the list. Its reference-count is initially 0. Note from above that it is only when we *transition* to 0 that a reference counted object is freed.

Lines 43–49 If the list is initially empty, then the head and tail will both point to the newly added element (lines 46–47). Therefore, the reference-count needs to be incremented twice (once for the head reference, and once for the tail reference (lines 44–45)). In general, it makes sense to set a reference counter before a change to the actual reference is made (see the discussion for lines 61–69).

Lines 50–54 If we are adding to the end of the list, then we set the tail element's next pointer to the new element. This represents a new reference to the new element so we add a reference (line 50). The element the list's tail pointer referenced is no longer going to be pointed to by the tail so we decrement its reference-count. The list's tail pointer is set to the new element so the new element's reference-count is again incremented (line 53). This means that the last element in the list will have a reference-count of 2: the reference from the previous element in the chain and the tail pointer in the Simple_List.

Lines 61–63 In the pop routine, we remove the item at the head. This is simple: Get the value of the element at the head and the head's next pointer and decrement the reference counter to the head. Since it is likely that the head element is going to be freed, we must make sure to get the item and next pointer from it *before* decrementing the reference-count.

Lines 64–65 Technically the reference-count should be incremented on the next item since we are about to set head to it, and then decremented because we have removed the element whose next pointer referenced it. Since these reference operations cancel out, they are skipped.

Lines 66–69 If the head is now NULL then tail will be set to NULL and whatever it previously referenced will need its reference-count decremented. This is the situation when the last element on the list is removed.

It is important to realize that two threads simultaneously adding and removing items from this list, will almost certainly fail. The reference counted `Simple_List_element` is not providing thread-safety to the overall `Simple_List`. For example, it would be possible to interleave operations such that the head pointer is NULL and the tail pointer is still pointing to a `Simple_List_element`. Some form of locking or atomic operations are required to make the list thread-safe as discussed in Locking Basics in Chap. 7.

Reference Counting Drawbacks

Reference counting seems like a magic bullet for our memory management woes. Of course there are many caveats.

Space Overhead

A reference-count adds at least four bytes to every object (any object with more than a couple billion references can be considered "uncollectable" so 4 bytes is usually more than enough). However, if we require the 4 bytes to be the first field in a struct, and follow that with an 8 byte pointer (which is the size of a pointer on most processors these days), then the struct will not be 12 bytes (4 byte reference-count + 8 byte pointer), but 16 bytes. This is because languages like C often align structure members on the boundary corresponding to the size of the member. An 8-byte pointer will be aligned on an eight byte boundary. This can lead to "holes" in the struct. For example (Fig. 9.3):

The final padding is again language specific but in many cases, the structure is rounded up to a multiple of 8 bytes so that if we have an array of these structures, the structures can follow one after the other and remain properly aligned.

There are ways around this even for C. One simple approach is to always list fields in descending size, i.e., all pointers and 64-bit fields first, then 32-bit integers, etc. The difficulty is that for reference counting in C, we pretty much are limited to putting the reference-count at the front and so 8 bytes will likely be used for this count if any following field requires more than 4 bytes.

There are compiler directives that can tell the compiler to pack the structure and ignore alignment. How this is represented depends on the compiler. For example, in the popular GNU C compiler, the struct is annotated with:

```
struct  badly_aligned {
  int    field1;
  char *field2;
  char field3;
  int64_t field4;
  char field5;
};
```

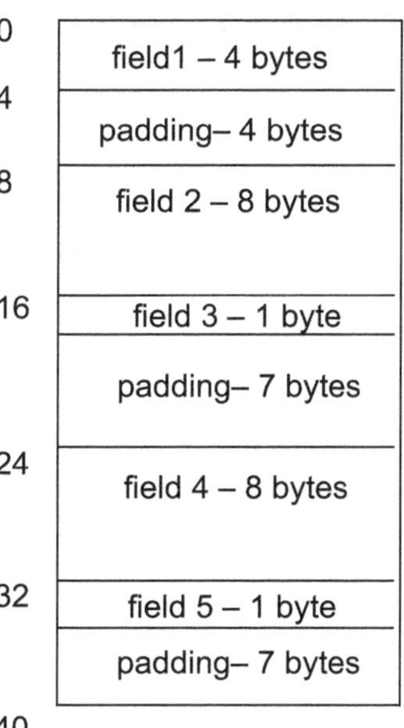

Fig. 9.3 Alignment in memory of structure members

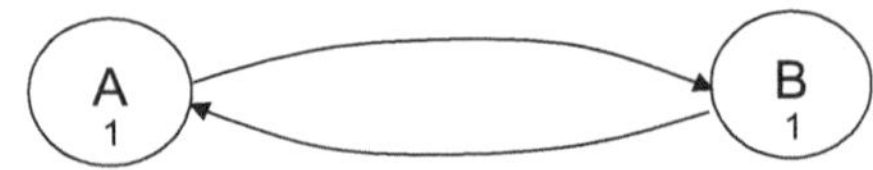

Fig. 9.4 Circular references

```
struct __attribute__((packed)) badly_aligned {
  int field1;
  char *field2;
  char field3;
  int64_t field4;
  char field5;
};
```

Some machines don't support this and for machines that do support it, unaligned access is slightly more expensive than aligned access, though packing may help improve cache utilization so the access cost may be outweighed by increasing cache hits. Your mileage may vary and in general organizing structures in descending size as much as possible is a good approach to "naturally" pack a structure.

Increment and Decrement Cost

There is also a slight cost to incrementing and decrementing the counters with fetch-and-add. Unless changing pointers dominate the runtime of the application, this should be insignificant.

Circular References

Another issue with reference counting are *circular references*. Circular references occur when a chain of pointers between objects end up referencing an object already in the chain and must be treated with a little care. Suppose we have the following:Fig. 9.4

Let's assume that before we delete an object, we must decrement the reference-counts on all objects that it references. In this case, we are decrementing the reference-count to A to 0, so we must decrement the reference-count on B. B's reference-count is now 0 so it must decrement the count on A. A's count is already 0 at this point so B is done, and can be deleted. This case is handled simply by recognizing a reference-count is 0, assuming a deletion is in progress and short-circuiting the process there Fig. 9.5.

Now consider this:

Now let's assume the incoming reference to A is removed, and A's reference-count is reduced to 1. A will not be removed (and neither will B) but there are no other references in this picture other than between A and B. A and B are stranded and become *memory leaks*. To fix this, more work has to be done within the application to explicitly walk the chain and delete entries.

Fig. 9.5 Circular references with an external reference from outside

Simplify When Possible

Situations like circular references illustrate a general problem with reference counting: It can be very difficult to always add references and remove references when necessary (the simple linked list required some careful thought about where to increment and decrement reference counts). Updates to reference counts should be in as few places as possible and wise data encapsulation (Meyer, 1991) can help enormously with this. Some of the complexity can also be simplified with more advanced languages.

Reference Count Implementation in C++

> Unlike previous discussions which used C to communicate algorithms and patterns in a general way, this section is how to program reference counting specifically in C++. It is strictly an example of using specific features in C++to simplify implementing reference counting. As such, it only introduces a language pattern, not a particular design pattern, and can be easily skipped if the reader is uninterested in C++.

Explicitly incrementing and decrementing reference counts is an error-prone task. If explicit reference counting is required (e.g., programming in C), it is important to strongly limit the access patterns of the pointers to the reference counted objects to ensure that objects aren't yanked out from under a pointer (a *dangling* reference).

If you are programming in C++ (or Rust), reference counting can be greatly simplified. In these cases, a class of object can be a *subclass* of an abstract class (for example the class `Ref_counted`) that defines the reference counted field and operations to add and remove references. Ref_counted objects are referenced not directly with a pointer but with a *template class* called a *smart pointer*, that not only points to the object but manages the reference-count of the object. Operator overloading allows a programmer to use these pointers very much like ordinary pointers and to have all the reference counting managed automatically, including the deletion of reference counted objects when the reference-count goes to 0.

The following is a very simple version of reference counted objects with smart pointers. There are many packages online that do a more complete implementation; the point of reviewing this is to understand the underpinnings of how these packages are built.

We start by defining the reference counted class. This is an abstract class that concrete classes inherit from to make the concrete class "reference countable."

```
1   class Ref_counted {
2   private:
3     int ref_count;
4   protected:
5     Ref_counted();
6     ~Ref_counted();
7   public:
8     void add_ref();
9     void rem_ref();
10    int get_ref();
11  };
```

Line 1 Any class that wants to be reference counted should be a subclass of Ref_counted.

Line 3 Here is the ref-count. It is private with public accessors. The choice to make public accessors available will be discussed below.

Line 4 The constructor and destructor are protected so they are accessible by subclasses but cannot be called independently, i.e., there should be no instances of a Ref_counted object, only subclasses of Ref_counted. Creating a pure virtual destructor would also facilitate this at the cost of a vtable pointer in the object (another 8 bytes). There are ways around the extraneous vtable but they can lead to somewhat obscure code (Coplien, 1995).

Lines 8–10 These are the functions we introduced above and are available publicly. They return the reference-count immediately after the increment or decrement. Unlike the previous example, the object is *not* automatically freed when the reference-count is decremented to 0. That operation will now be handled by the smart pointer.

A class becomes ref-counted simply by inheriting from Ref_counted:

```
class My_object: public Ref_counted…
```

This is already an improvement from the C approach since we don't have to treat pointers to reference counted objects as void pointers in add_ref, etc. Add_ref will know that it is being performed on an object that has a reference-count and doesn't need an awkward cast assuming the first field is the reference-count.

Another useful abstraction we can build is a smart pointer. This allows us to work with pointers to objects and automatically have the reference counts be managed. The deletion of a reference counted object is moved to this class.

```
template <class T>
class Smart_ptr {
private:
  T *the_pointer;
public:
  Smart_ptr<T>(): the_pointer(NULL) {};
  Smart_ptr<T>(T *ptr): the_pointer(ptr) { ptr->add_ref(); };
  ~Smart_ptr<T>() {
        if (the_pointer != NULL) {
          if ((the_pointer->rem_ref()) == 0) {
            delete the_pointer;
          }
        };
  Smart_ptr<T> &operator=(Smart_ptr<T>&rhs) {
      if (rhs.the_pointer != NULL) {
        rhs.the_pointer->add_ref();
      }
      if (the_pointer != NULL) {
        if (the_pointer->rem_ref() == 0) {
          delete the_pointer;
          the_pointer = NULL;
        }
      }
      the_pointer = rhs.the_pointer;
      return *this;
  }

  Smart_ptr<T> &operator=(T *rhs) {
      if (rhs != NULL) {
        rhs->add_ref();
      }
      if (the_pointer != NULL) {
        if (the_pointer->rem_ref() == 0) {
          delete the_pointer;
          the_pointer = NULL;
        }
      }
      the_pointer = rhs;
      return *this;
    }


    T & operator*() {
      return *the_pointer;
    }

    T * operator->() {
      return the_pointer;
    }

    T * get_ptr() {
      return the_pointer;
    }
  };
```

Lines 1–2 The smart pointer is templated with the class of the object it is pointing to. This must be a subclass of Ref_counted. If it is not a subclass, the template instantiation will fail at compile-time so there is much more protection against passing the wrong kind of object to add_ref and rem_ref functions (unlike the C implementation which blindly casted a void pointer to a Ref_counted struct).

Line 4 The smart pointer wraps an ordinary pointer to the object specified by the template parameter.

Lines 8–13 If a smart pointer is destroyed (for example, by going out of scope), it will no longer reference the object it points to and so that ref-count should be reduced. If the reference-count goes to 0, then the object should be deleted. This is a primary difference with the approach given in C. Invoking delete this in a base class is problematic (you can try it for yourself). Moving the delete to the smart pointer is not bulletproof either. For example, consider the initialization of a smart pointer with an automatic (stack allocated) object:

```
My_object obj;
{
  Smart_ptr p<My_object> = &obj;
}
```

When the `Smart_ptr p` goes out of scope, the destructor will be called and delete will be issued on the pointer to `obj`. `Obj` is stack allocated so freeing it would not be appropriate. Smart pointers must only be initialized with dynamically allocated objects. The smart pointer object itself may be stack allocated (as in the example).

Lines 14–26 Assignment of the smart pointer is where most of the action happens. In this case we are assigning a smart pointer (`rhs`) to another smart pointer (this). The object pointed to by `rhs` will therefore need to increase its references count (line 16). Likewise, the current reference of this smart pointer object will need to decrease its reference-count and if it is 0, be deleted.

Lines 28–40 This is another assignment. It allows a "naked" pointer to be assigned to a smart pointer and it functions very much like the previous assignment.

Lines 43–54 The underlying pointer can be accessed. For example, p → x will dereference the smart pointer, and return the x field in the corresponding object. (*p) → x is equivalent. `Get_ptr` is a more explicit form of `(*)`.

With smart pointers in place, the following code can be written:

```
1  My_object::~My_object() {
2     printf("Deleting %p\n";
3  }
4  Smart_ptr<My_object> p = new My_object(1);
5  printf("1: P is %p with value %d\n", p.get_ptr(), p->x);
6  p = new My_object(2);
7  printf("2: P is %p with value %d\n", p.get_ptr(), p->x);
```

Lines 1–3 Print a message when we are deleting objects.
Line 4 p is a smart pointer referencing class `My_object` with an x field initialized to 1. The reference-count of this object is 1.
Line 5 The underlying pointer of p (the reference to `My_object`) will be printed out.
Line 6 The smart pointerp is assigned a new value. Since it was the only referent to the object created on line 1, that object will be deleted. P now points to the new object with x initialized to 2.
Line 7 The new pointer is printed out as well as the value of x in that object (2).

The result is:

```
1  1: P is 0x5617080b8eb0 with value 1
2  Deleting 0x5617080b8eb0
3  2: P is 0x5617080b92e0 with value 2
4  Deleting 0x5617080b92e0
```

Line 1 P points to a dynamically allocated My_object with field x is 1.
Line 2 When p is reassigned with `new My_object (2)`, the sole reference to the original object is removed and so that object is deleted.
Line 3 P now points to the new object with field x equal to 2.
Line 4 When the program ends, the destructor on the smart pointer is called. It removes its reference to the object pointed to by p, which now has a reference-count of 0, so the referenced object must also be deleted.

Smart pointers can be extremely useful when programming in a language that supports the overloaded of operators. Code is fundamentally safer from accessing freed memory and from leaving memory orphaned.

Memory Checking Tools

Since memory leaks and using memory after freeing it are such common problems there are tools available to help diagnose these problems. Popular ones are valgrind (for Linux), Asan (on Windows and Linux), and Purify (Windows, Linux, and other UNIX platforms). These can be extremely useful for basic faults. Here is an example of how valgrind works.

Consider this program called `memory-errors`:

```
1  int main(int argc, char *argv[]) {
2    int *p1 = (int *) malloc(100);
3    p1[10] = 10;
4    free(p1);
5    printf("p1[10] = %d\n", p1[10]);
6    int *p2 = (int *) malloc(100);
7  }
```

If you run this program it will most like complete and print out:

```
p1[10] = 10
```

But this is actually wrong. On line 4, we freed the memory that line 5 is accessing. It will work most of the time in this case because nothing has come along and overwritten the freed memory. Later, as the program becomes more complex, the error will rear its head and you will be left wondering why p1[10] doesn't have the value you thought it should.

We can check the memory with:

```
valgrind --leak-check=full memory-errors
```

It will report:

```
==9601== Memcheck, a memory error detector
==9601== Copyright (C) 2002-2024, GNU GPL'd, by Julian Seward et al.
==9601== Using Valgrind-3.25.0 and LibVEX; rerun with -h for copy-
right
==9601== Command: ./memory-errors
==9601==
==9601== Invalid read of size 4
==9601==    at 0x40011CC: main (memory-errors.c:5)
==9601== Address 0x4a9f068 is 40 bytes inside a block of size 100
free'd
==9601==    at 0x4850B2C: free (vg_replace_malloc.c:989)
==9601==    by 0x40011C3: main (memory-errors.c:4)
==9601== Block was alloc'd at
==9601==    at 0x484D80F: malloc (vg_replace_malloc.c:446)
==9601==    by 0x40011A5: main (memory-errors.c:2)
==9601==
p1[10] =  10 (from printf)
==9601==
==9601== HEAP SUMMARY:
==9601==      in use at exit: 100 bytes in 1 blocks
==9601==   total heap usage: 3 allocs, 2 frees, 1,224 bytes allocated
==9601==
==9601== 100 bytes in 1 blocks are definitely lost
==9601==    at 0x484D80F: malloc (vg_replace_malloc.c:446)
==9601==    by 0x40011ED: main (memory-errors.c:6)
```

The report is indicating that referencing p1[10] on line 5 is accessing memory that was freed on line 4 and originally allocated on line 2. The report is also indicating that the memory allocated on line 6 (p2) was never deallocated and so is effectively a memory leak.

Tools like valgrind are invaluable for diagnosing memory errors. Unfortunately, they suffer from two fundamental shortcomings:

1. The program runs much, much slower than when run without the tools.
2. In the case of valgrind, threading behavior changes dramatically with threads often serialized when they would not otherwise be. This can often mask problems and memory errors can remain hidden.

While the first line of defense should always be careful use of techniques like reference counting and structuring allocations and deallocations judiciously, sometimes using a tool like valgrind can reveal bugs that are otherwise very difficult to hunt down.

Exercises

1. Create an object pool for objects that are 64 bytes long. Allocate and deallocate 2^{20} objects. Compare your solution's performance with allocating and deallocating one million objects with malloc.
2. Repeat exercise 1 but make sure the object pool is either thread-safe (i.e., accesses are serialized) or multithreaded (multiple threads may allocate simultaneously). Compare the performance for 2, 8, and 16 threads with each thread allocating/ deallocating $2^{20}/n$ objects where n is the number of threads.
3. Repeat exercise 2 but use a reference-count on the objects. Create objects and increment their reference-count. Then deallocate objects by decrement their reference-count to 0. Again, use multiple threads for access and allocation.

    a. Compare the performance of this exercise with exercise 2.

Chapter 10
Monitoring and Error Handling

One of the most common questions that engineers ask when observing their programs is "Why did it do that?" If the engineer is lucky, she is running the program in the lab. Unfortunately, it is often the case that the program is misbehaving at a customer site. This chapter will briefly outline some ways a program can anticipate questions like "Why did it do that?" or, maybe even more common, "What is it doing?".

In the second half of this chapter, we will examine detecting and handling errors which often answers another common question: Why did it break and what happens now?

Space Probes

Here are two examples illustrate how, when errors are planned for, infrastructure can be put in place that allows the system to recover from the errors.

Galileo

The Galileo space probe was launched in 1989 with the goal of investigating Jupiter. It was controlled with a total of eight 8-bit CPUs with approximately 176 K of memory split among them. Magnetic tape was used to store data before it was beamed back to Earth at a raw rate of 8–16 bits/second (compression increased this to nearly 1000 bits per second). By the time the signal reached Earth, it had a total power of 10^{-20} watts (your FM radio is typically receiving microwatts of radio signal, 100 trillion times stronger) (Galileo Wikipedia 2026).

In the case of Galileo, it experienced high radiation as it approached Jupiter and automatically shut down all of its instruments. Ten days later, it restarted them

M. Kilian, *Ten Software Patterns Every Student Should Know*,
https://doi.org/10.1007/978-981-92-0260-7_10

(Knight 2002; Swift et al. 2022). Unfortunately, the tape device failed to restart and engineers managed to trace this to an LED used within the tape player's motor control. It was suspected that radiation had damaged the lattice of the semiconductor in the LED. The engineers on the Galileo project were able to direct the probe to run electrical current through the diode for an hour at a time. This ultimately corrected the semiconductor lattice, the LED functioned again, and the mission continued.

Voyager 1

The Voyager 1 space probe preceded Galileo, launching in 1977. It has been in nearly continual service since the launch and, as of August 2024, is over 15 billion miles from Earth. Sending a radio signal to Voyager 1 takes nearly a full day to reach it traveling at the speed of light.

In November of 2023, 46 years after launch, the signals from the probe became garbled. The engineers determined that a memory bank had been damaged. That bank contained instructions, and it was decided to relocate the code to other memory banks. However, because there was no spare memory on the system (which was only just under 70 kilobytes), obsolete code used for the Jupiter flyby was deleted, and the rest rearranged to enable the system to restart smoothly. By June 13, 2024, the probe was returned to full service (Nasa JPL 2026).

Not only could engineers diagnose the errors on primitive hardware, but they could repair deep problems like relocating a piece of code on a system while it is only partially running 15 billion miles away. The flexibility afforded by these space systems is perhaps extreme. This chapter looks at how a programmer can incorporate more modest techniques to diagnose and analyze bugs and performance issues in systems under development as well as in production.

Timing Information

One of the most prevalent mysteries a programmer faces is determining why a program is taking so long to run on some given workload. Sometimes it is as simple as a routine designed to work fine with five items is handed one hundred items. Multi-threaded programs can be harder with threads delayed due to resource contention. In a distributed program (such as those developed in Chap. 8), the problem is compounded because there are now queuing effects, communication delays and failures, and a variety of synchronization issues that can impact the performance of a system.

A common approach to investigating performance issues is to use a *profiler*. Examples of profilers are oprofile and perf on Unix and Oracle's Developer Studio Performance Analyzer available on multiple systems. These tools use hardware registers to capture what is going on with the program, write this information to files, and then use other tools to visualize what is happening in the program. Here is sample output

Fig. 10.1 Output from perf. Each function is performing more work than the one below it, i.e., f2 doubles the amount of work that f1 does, f3 does three times as much as f1, and f4 does four times as much

```
main
|--39.10%--f4
|           |--29.97%--random_work
|
|--29.37%--f3
|           |--22.71%--random_work
|
|--19.61%--f2
|           |--15.15%--random_work
|
|--9.79%--f1
|           |--7.59%--random_work
```

from perf which shows that function f4 is taking up 39.10% of the runtime of main and that the bulk of the time is in the function random_work. We can quickly see the relative contribution of each of the functions to the overall runtime Fig. 10.1.

In almost all cases, these tools cannot be run on a production system since their impact on performance is non-negligible and since most production systems do not allow profiling systems to be installed or enabled on them. This is not to say these systems are not valuable. They are tremendously helpful in determining basic performance problems in systems under development. They help determine basic errors (e.g., a function is taking much longer than expected because it is an $O(n^2)$ algorithm with an unexpectedly large n). But even with these tools, it requires careful testing to ensure that the boundaries of performance are reached. For example, an $O(n^2)$ algorithm might run fine if n is never more than 10, but if n can be larger than 10, it is critical that the system is tested with such an input.

Including explicit timing metrics in the program can be extremely useful. For example, many of our examples in Chaps. 5, 7, and 8 loop waiting for an event and then processing the event (the *event-loop*). Two typical questions asked about this are: How much time elapses before an event arrives, and how long did it take to process the event? This leads to questions such as, "What are the averages of these times?" and "What are the minimum and maximum of these times?".

A simple implementation of this could be:

```
for (;;) {
 uint64_t start_wait = get_time();
 int n = Event_wait_for_events(event_system, events, 1000);
 uint64_t end_wait = get_time();
 uint64_t wait_time = end_wait - start_wait;
     ...Now do something with wait_time like store it, print it, check if it is too long
 for (int i=0; i<n; i++) {
  uint64_t start_processing = get_time();
  struct Event *ev = events[i];
      ...process the event...
  uint64_t end_processing = get_time();
  uint64_t processing_time = end_processing - start_processing;
     ... Now do something with processing_time...
```

Capturing the time spent is relatively simple. What to do with that timing information is more complex.

Getting Timestamps

How the get_time call above is implemented depends on the operating system where the code is running. On Windows, it might use QueryPerformanceCounter. On Linux, it might be clock_gettime. Timers should have the following characteristics:

1. They need to be high resolution. Microsecond resolution is sufficient but not any coarser. Hardware timers are often tied to instruction speed and will be measured in nanoseconds.
2. Timers should be consistent across cores on a processor. These days the processor hierarchy includes a core, multiple cores on the same processor chip, and multiple processor chips in a server. Ideally we want timers to be consistent across processor chips (i.e., a timing X at absolute time t_1 and a timing Y at absolute time t_2 will always have $Y > X$ if $t_2 > t_1$ even if timing X is on one chip and timing Y is on another chip).
3. The cost of taking a timestamp needs to be very cheap. As we'll see, this can be as low as single-digit nanoseconds.

Time Stamp Counter

It is possible to access hardware registers containing timing information. For example, Intel processors contain a register called the Time Stamp Counter (TSC). Historically this was incremented every clock cycle. As processors became more sophisticated, especially with respect to power management, the clock cycle could change making it very hard to get an accurate measurement. As of 2008, timing clocks no longer change and the TSC is stable regardless of the state of the processor (this is the *invariant* TSC).

The following discusses how to use the TSC to measure performance. Unfortunately this is not a universally applicable approach. What follows is specifically for Intel 86 processors and the Linux operating system. There are equivalents for other processors (e.g., ARM, AMD, etc.) and other operating systems (e.g., Windows).

The TSC is measured in ticks, not a given quantity like nanoseconds. For most cases ticks are fine since most judgments about execution time are relative, i.e., this operation is faster than that one, or this takes 20% of that. Converting ticks to a time unit like nanoseconds is possible (on modern machines) but tricky. See section Converting __rdtsc Output to Nanoseconds below for an approach to doing this. On machines that do not feature an invariant TSC (i.e., a machine where clock ticks can vary depending on whether the processor is in low power mode or turbo mode), TSC is almost impossible to use to get intelligible timings.

How you access the TSC and its accuracy will depend on what platform (e.g., Intel, AMD, Apple M3, etc.) you are using, what language and compiler you are using, and what operating system (e.g., Linux or Windows). For the C GNU compiler on Intel platform, the timestamp can be fetched with:

```
#include <x86intrin.h>
...
uint64_t start_timestamp = __rdtsc();
... do something
uint64_t end_timestamp = __rdtsc();
uint64_t duration = end_timestamp - start_timestamp;
```

On modern Intel platforms, the timestamps will be consistent across all cores within a given multicore chip. The __rdtsc call is very fast, a handful of nanoseconds. It is therefore consistent with the three characteristics required of timers listed above.

TSC is not necessarily accurate across chipsets. A chipset is a chip that contains one or more cores. For example, as of 2024, Supermicro offers servers with 8 sockets (Supermicro 2023). Each socket can hold a CPU with 60 cores for a total of 480 cores in a single server. TSC will be accurate for a given 60 cores in a single chipset (a socket) but is not guaranteed to be accurate across chipsets. Operating systems may try to synchronize the counters across chips. For example, on Linux when a computer is reset, it attempts to simultaneously set all the Time Stamp Counters to 0. Given the resolution of a Time Stamp Counter is typically less than a nanosecond, getting these precisely synchronized can be challenging (and typically out of scope for even an experienced programmer).

There is one way to assist in extremely fine-grained timing across chipsets (also called *NUMA nodes* or *socket numbers*). There is a variant of the __rdtsc function: __rdtscp. This returns not only the timestamp, but an identifier corresponding to the core and chipset that is being used to retrieve the TSC. A process running on core 2 of chipset 3 will have id 0 × 003002, i.e., the lower 12 bits identify the core on a chip, and the next 12 bits will identify the chipset:

```
uint32_t cpu;
uint64_t timestamp = rdtscp(&cpu);
uint32_t core_id = cpu & 0xFFF;
uint32_t chip_id = (cpu & 0xFFF000) >> 12;
```

Using this information, it is possible to at least determine when timings might be skewed. If a start timing is recorded on chipset ID 0, and the end timing is recorded on chipset ID 1, then the calculated interval (end–start) should be taken with a grain of salt.

A More Standard Timer

Using the RDTSC or equivalent instruction is very fast, a handful of machine cycles. The problem is that it is platform specific. There is a POSIX API that performs nearly the same function:

```
struct timespec ts;
clock_gettime(CLOCK_MONOTONIC, &ts);
```

The timespec has two fields (different operating systems are free to change the type of tv_sec, the following is typical):

```
struct timespec {
  int64_t tv_sec;
  int64_t tv_nsec;
};
```

The result of calling clock_gettime in this way is to return a timestamp, similar to what __rdtsc returns except it is always expressed in nanosecond units and the value returned in the timespec structure is the number of seconds and nanoseconds from some fixed point in time (usually when the system was booted which is the same as that used by __rdtsc).

The first parameter of clock_gettime specifies what timer to fetch. In the example above, we are fetching a clock that is simply ticking away, i.e., almost identical to the TSC clock. Other possibilities are CLOCK_REALTIME, which is the time of day (as measured in seconds and nanoseconds from the Epoch which is defined as midnight, midnight, January 1, 1970, UTC time).

The primary advantages of clock_gettime are that it is more portable and will be implemented according the platform and operating system using it. It is expressed in nanoseconds (as opposed to some arbitrary unit). The disadvantage is that it is doing some work that __rdtsc is not doing (though in fact, clock_gettime for CLOCK_MONOTONIC is typically implemented in terms of __rdtsc). Clock_gettime will run about twice as slow as __rdtsc, but this is still measured at around ten nanoseconds. It is not more accurate than __rdtsc since it is typically built from it and lacks the ability to discern on which chipset the measurement is taking place (as provided by __rdtscp).

Converting _rdtsc Output to Nanoseconds

With most modern processors (modern as of 2024), the processor's Time Stamp Counter is ticking at a given rate that is unvarying and consistent across cores of a chip and the __rdtsc value is measured in *ticks*. Most of the time ticks can be used without modification. However, the frequency of that ticking is not obvious. It is non-trivial to report a timestamp range in, for example, nanoseconds rather than ticks. Here is a naïve approach to converting ticks to nanoseconds.

```
struct timespec clock_start;
struct timespec clock_end;
uint64_t rdtsc_start;
uint64_t tdtsc_end;

clock_gettime(CLOCK_MONOTONIC, &clock_start);
rdtsc_start = __rdtsc();
```

```
8 usleep(1000000);
9 rdtsc_end = __rdtsc();
10 clock_gettime(CLOCK_MONOTONIC, &clock_end);
11
12 uint64_t timestamp_start_ns = clock_start.tv_sec * 1000000000 +
13 clock_start.tv_nsec;
14 uint64_t timestamp_end_ns = clock_end.tv_sec * 1000000000 +
15 clock_end.tv_nsec;
16
17 uint64_t duration_ns = timestamp_end_ns - timestamp_start_ns;
18 uint64_t tsc_duration_ticks = rdtsc_end - rdtsc_start;
19
20 double ticks_per_nanosecond = (double) tsc_duration_ticks /
21 (double) duration_ns;
```

Line 6	Start a timer measured in nanoseconds.
Line 7	Start a separate timer measuring the ticks of rdtsc.
Line 8	Sleep for some amount of time. Here we are sleeping for 1 s. It may be any time but it should be long enough to "wash away" some irregularities.
Line 9	Get the end of the ticks.
Line 10	And get the length of the interval in nanoseconds. Note that whether this is exactly the sleep time is not terribly important. We are only trying to correlate the time between the timing mechanisms.
Line 12–15	Convert the timespec structures to nanoseconds.
Lines 17–18	Calculate the durations for each of the timers in their respective units.
Line 20–21	The ratio of ticks to the duration gives us ticks/nanosecond.

Calculating the ticks_per_nanosecond above is naïve for several reasons:

1. The clock_gettime measurement surrounds the __rdtsc, so it is almost certainly longer in measurement. This is not a serious problem however, since the difference is on the order of 10 s of nanoseconds or one part in 100,000,000 if our delay is 1 s. The calls could be staggered (clock_gettime followed by __rdtsc for both start time and end time) to gain a slightly more accurate reading.
2. A more serious problem is making sure that the thread running this code starts and finishes on the same chip. We can work this out by either pinning the thread running this program to a single core or by using __rdtscp. If the chip IDs returned by the beginning and ending __rdtscp don't match, then we can try again, repeating until the code runs successfully on the same chip set.
3. More than one run should be performed with the values averaged out to provide a more accurate conversion factor.

It is also important to understand that measuring very short time intervals (e.g., how long a single addition instruction takes) can impact overall performance if that timing occurs frequently. The time to execute __rdtsc is not 0. If the time being measured is on the order of 100 ns, adding the timing instructions will not insignificantly lengthen the time the code is running. If the code being measured is short and in a tight loop, timing the body of the loop may cause unacceptable application performance degradation. This is especially true if the goal is to use this facility in a production system.

Recording Timestamps

Calculating timestamps isn't terribly useful unless they can be observed. There are multiple approaches that can be taken. One simple approach is to log the information. For example, suppose we want to measure the time it takes to process a message once it is dequeued. One approach is to simply write out the timed interval to a file:

```
1 if (introspection_turned_on) {
2   start_time = get_timestamp();
3 }
4 ... process message
5 if (introspection_turned_on) {
6   end_time = get_timestamp()
7   fprintf(logfile, "%u: MessageProcessing: %lu\n",
8           thread_id, start_time, end_time);
9 }
```

Lines 1–3 We can toggle whether performance information is collected or not at runtime. Usually, this timing information will not be saved. When enabled, we save the timestamp when message processing begins.

Lines 5–9 When message processing is done, we collect the end time, and write the timing information to a logfile tagging it with the thread ID and what was being timed (in this case, MessageProcessing).

This can work though the impact of writing to the file on production performance is unpredictable: Sometimes the information will be written to the file buffer (very quickly), and sometimes the fprintf will need to wait for a buffer to be written to logfile before it can complete. Writing formatted strings is also unnecessary and expensive; simply writing the timestamps out as integers is much more efficient.

Recording every timestamp may generate a huge amount of information (processing one million messages/second is not out of the question). An alternative is to keep these in a buffer and keep only the last million. The buffer can be shared across some or all of the application threads using either a thread-safe buffer (locking it on write or using a lock-free implementation as described in Chap. 7). Another approach is to use two buffers. When one buffer is filled, the other can be used for new entries. The first buffer can then be asynchronously processed (e.g., written to disk by another thread). This is not foolproof and delays can still happen if one buffer fills faster than the other can be written out.

It may also be useful to not record the duration but instead capture the beginning and end points in the timing. The reason to record separate points is that they can be used to correlate events. For example, suppose we have the following events across two threads:

Thread 1: Wait for message start. Timestamp (TS): 0.
Thread 2: Wait for message start. TS: 0.
Thread 2: Receive message (wait ends). TS: 1.
Thread 2: Process message start. TS: 1.
Thread 1: Receive message (wait ends). Start Processing. TS: 2.
Thread 1: Process Message start. TS 2.
Thread 2: Wait for lock "HashTable Mutex" Start. TS 2.
Thread 1: Wait for lock "HashTable Mutex" Start. TS 3.
Thread 2: Wait for lock "HashTable Mutex" End. TS 4.
Thread 2: Hold lock "HashTable Mutex" Start. TS 4.
Thread 2: Hold lock "HashTable Mutex" End. TS 7.
Thread 1: Wait for lock "HashTable Mutex" End. TS 7.
Thread 1: Hold lock "HashTable Mutex" Start. TS 7.
Thread 1: Hold lock "HashTable Mutex" End. TS 9.
Thread 2: Process message end. TS: 10.
Thread 1: Process message end. TS: 11.

We can now represent these events in a chart (Fig. 10.2):

It becomes apparent that thread 1's execution is dependent on thread 2, and a large chunk of that is being taken up by waiting for "HashTable Mutex" to be released by thread 2. Thread 2 also is waiting for Hash Table Mutex and we can assume there is some contention on this lock (presumably we would see other threads with Hold HashTable Mutex intervals occupying the same space). For example, you might have further down (Fig. 10.3):

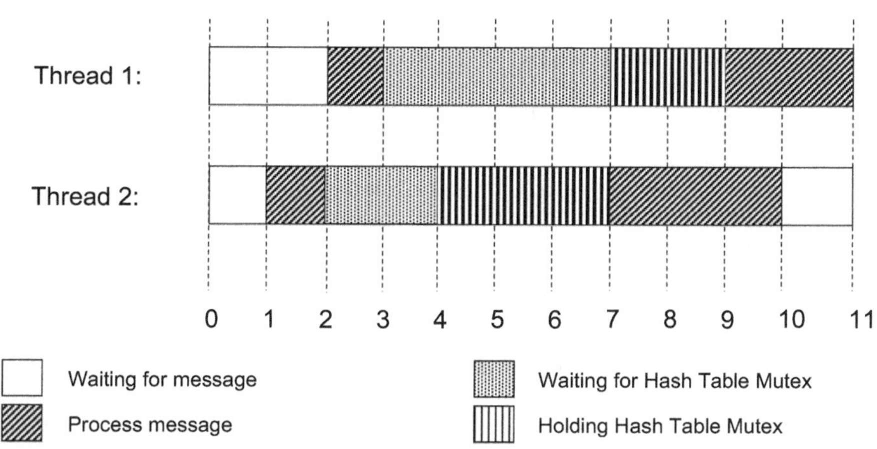

Fig. 10.2 Visualizing dependent thread performance

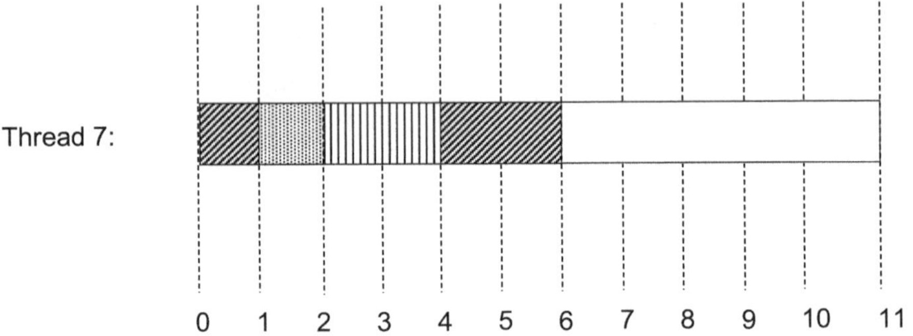

Fig. 10.3 Thread 7 grabbed the mutex before threads 1 and 2, preventing their progress

Looking at this combination we see that the Hash Table mutex seems to be the gating factor in our performance and that we may need to shard the table or take some other remediation to improve performance.

A good example of where to employ timestamping is mutexes. Understanding the behavior of mutexes is often key to understanding how threads interact, where contention significantly blocks execution, and indicating bottlenecks in the system. It makes sense to implement a wrapper around mutexes that includes timing information that can be interrogated in the course of waiting for a lock and holding a lock.

```
1 struct Timed_mutex {
2 struct Mutex mutex;
3 uint64_t wait_start_time;
4 uint64_t hold_start_time; // Implicitly marks the end of wait.
5 uint64_t hold_end_time; // How long the lock was held.
6 };
7
8 void Timed_mutex_lock(Timed_mutex *m) {
9 m->wait_start_time = __rdtsc();
10 Mutex_lock(&m->mutex);
11 m->hold_start = __rdtsc();
12 // Record the wait event...
13 }
14
15 void Timed_mutex_unlock(Timed_mutex *m) {
16 Mutex_unlock(&m->mutex);
17 m->hold_end_time = __rdtsc();
18 // Record the hold event...
19 }
```

Lines 9–11 Record how long it took to acquire the lock. If the lock is granted immediately (no wait), then the time will be a small number of nanoseconds.

Waiting for a lock will be considerably larger. Establishing the start time for holding the lock (line 11) implicitly marks the end time for the wait.

Line 17 Once we unlock, we establish the end time for holding the lock.

Timing Across the Network

It is tractable to get accurate timing within a single system, even with multiple chipsets as long as the intervals being measured are not too fine-grained (i.e., we are measuring microseconds and not nanoseconds). There is a greater problem with trying to record timestamps across systems connected by a network. Almost certainly they are not in sync. There are techniques to get some synchronization using the Network Time Protocol and synchronization techniques. This can probably at best get to around a microsecond resolution.

There is not a lot you can do about this. There is another protocol called Precision Time Protocol (PTP) that uses Ethernet hardware clocking to synchronize two or more systems sharing a network. With network interfaces that support PTP in hardware, PTP can synchronize to within nanoseconds. Setting up PTP is not for the faint of heart. It requires detailed knowledge of the devices on the network (including switches). While PTP can be implemented without hardware support in the Ethernet cards, its accuracy will suffer. Also the "master clock" used for PTP is often taken from the GPS signal which, again, is not a typical component in an "ordinary" data center. In some cases, very high-resolution stable clocks are combined with the GPS clock to create a highly accurate "master clock" that PTP uses to synchronize the other servers on the network.

It is a shame that timing across the network is so difficult since a question often asked is "How long did a message take to travel from A to B?" Often round-trip times for request/response where the measurements are taken on a single client server combined with how long the request took to be serviced by the server can provide a reasonable picture of the latency of the network traffic. Note that it is important in this case to be able to correlate such-and-such service time with a given request and response (i.e., the messages, even if one-way, must be able to be associated with one another).

This is at best an approximation and can provide a gross metric of the latency. Running these measurements on an uncongested, lightly loaded network will provide a reasonable guess at the minimal latency of the network exchange (Fig. 10.4).

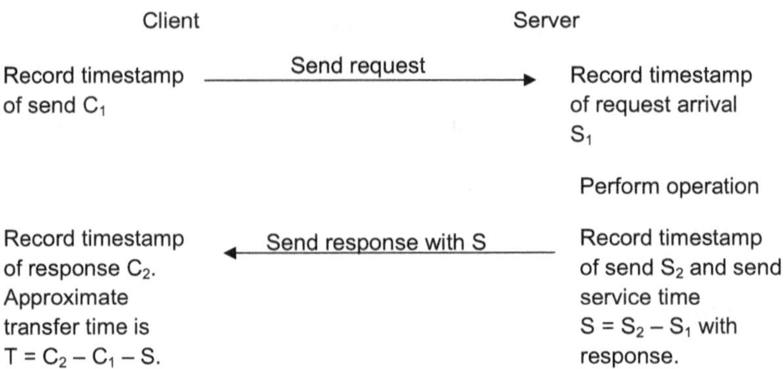

Fig. 10.4 Approximating network transport time from the client using service time at the server

Queues and Lists

Capturing timing is important especially when answering the question "What is this program doing?" There are some other key variables that make sense to monitor.

We have seen a number of examples of queues and lists. In the two concurrent programming patterns, messages are often queued to a thread that will process the message. A key metric is how many items are placed on a queue, not just instantaneously, but over time. The maximum queue size is extremely useful for determining when a system is falling behind on its work.

How long an entry waits on a queue is relatively easy to ascertain: Add timestamps to the Queue_entry struct to record the enqueue and dequeue times. The Queue struct can also keep total enqueued time and how many items have been queued so that average entry lifetime on the queue can be derived as well. The enqueue/dequeue times can sometimes indicate inconsistencies between when a work item is enqueued, dequeued, and processed and can provide insight into queuing problems that queue length alone can't.

As with Mutex, it is fairly simple to add a couple of fields to the Queue or List to keep track of these statistics. The length of the queue can be stored and incremented and decremented on the enqueue and dequeue operations. If the current length exceeds the max, then reset the max to the current length.

Acting on Introspection

Calculating timing and queue depth information without a way to inspect (and act on), the data is the proverbial tree falling in the forest with nobody there to hear. There is no common way of acting on this information and so we will stray from patterns that every student should know to patterns that students should ponder.

One common aspect in many event systems is to categorize the events that are being recorded. Regardless of whether individual events are being recorded or synopses of the events, it is useful to break down the events by category. For example, there might be events around locking, queuing, or message processing time. One or more of these can be enabled at a time. Each event should also be identified: Lock waiting time, lock hold time, main dispatch loop iteration time, etc.

A simple way of capturing this information is to have a relatively small set of categories and a larger range of event identifiers. The categories can be identified by individual bits in a category bit mask so that a 64-bit category bitmask can represent up to 64 categories of interest.

For example:

```
#define LOCK_CATEGORY 0x1
#define QUEUE_CATEGORY 0x2
#define PROCESSING_CATEGORY 0x4
...
uint64_t category = 0;
```

Up to 64 categories can be selected at once. To record events for the LOCK_CATEGORY and PROCESSING_CATEGORY means OR-ing the category bits together. For example:

```
category = LOCK_CATEGORY | PROCESSING_CATEGORY;
```

Code can then limit when events are recorded by comparing the categories of interest (in the category global variable) and a given combination of event categories. For example, to record events pertinent to the PROCESSING or MAIN_LOOP categories would look something like this:

```
if (category & (PROCESSING_CATEGORY | MAIN_LOOP_CATEGORY)) {
uint64_t processing_end = __rdtsc();
record_event(MAIN_LOOP_ITERATION_TIME,
processing_start, processing_end);
}
```

In this example, the code might be placed at the bottom of the worker loop in a message processing thread. If the category is either the PROCESSING_CATEGORY or MAIN_LOOP_CATEGORY, then the processing time is recorded with a specific event ID. By using a bit mask to represent the categories enabled, a single operation can match against multiple categories.

The record_event function has not been precisely defined yet. The important point in this statement is that the event is given an identifier. This can be as simple as an uint32_t.

```
#define MAIN_LOOP_ITERATION_TIME 10
#define PROCESS_KEY_INSERTION_TIME 11
#define MAIN_LOOP_QUEUE_LENGTH 12
...
```

We showed a very simplistic record_event above: writing the event to a file. The trouble with that is the cost of writing a file buffer to disk, even a solid-state disk, can become expensive relative to the code executing around it. If our goal is to allow introspection at runtime in a production system, it may be unacceptable to have these hiccups.

One approach is to write the event to memory. Using a lock-free circular buffer like the one discussed in Chap. 7 is one approach. The size of the buffer will determine how many events can be retained. A special message may be introduced that says, "I want to know what happened!" forcing the buffered events to be written to disk for later analysis. It may be the case that the system itself can identify anomalous events and trigger an action. For example, if a processing loop takes an excessive amount of time in a given iteration, the buffered events can be flushed, possibly with some annotation as to why they are being flushed out (the annotation itself can be an event). Other events might be that a queue length has exceeded some high-water mark indicating that the system is not processing fast enough to keep up with the incoming work items.

The decision on what to do with an event does not even need to occur statically. One or more routines for processing the events can be registered for a given category. For example, we might have one routine that captures the last million events and another routine that, if a queue length exceeds some maximum, dumps the events to a file for later analysis. Another routine might be used to trigger the termination of an action if its duration exceeds some limit.

The primary challenge with providing introspection in a system is ensuring that it is used in the most critical areas where problems are most likely to crop up. Furthermore, the event system needs to be tested under those problem scenarios. In short, the event system cannot be a second-class citizen and should be treated with as much attention as the code implementing the user-visible features. Unfortunately, when a system being developed is under a schedule constraint, instilling this discipline can be difficult to enforce.

Handling Errors

One of the greatest lessons most students learn when they take a professional position developing software is that it is entirely likely that as much code will be dedicated to error handling as to doing the "real work" of the program. In some estimates, the amount of error handling code is much greater than the main thread of code ((McConnel 2024) quotes a figure as high as 90%).

The real challenge is to become aware of how many ways a program can go south. Take this simple code that reads blocks of 1000 bytes from a file and reports the average number of bytes read per I/O:

```
count = 0;
total = 0;
amount = 0;
while ((amount = read(f, buffer, 1000)) > 0) {
  total += amount;
  count++;
}
printf("Average I/O is %d\n", total/count);
```

What happens if the file is empty? Total will be 0, but so will count, so total/count will cause a divide by 0. That's easy to fix (in general, always ensure your divisor is nonzero). What if an error occurs in the middle of the loop? For example, an interrupt has occurred that interrupted the I/O. What should happen? That will depend on the application and the error, but in most cases, an error should be handled. For example, in the case of an interrupt, the read might be retried. Note that even the printf can fail. If the output stream is redirected to a file and the file system fills up, the printf will return a -1 to indicate that the operation did not succeed. There are other reasons as well such as running out of memory.[1] Not all errors need to be handled since sometimes there is no recourse except to give up the ghost (running out of memory being one example).

Returning Errors

User-defined functions must also be able to indicate errors. There are several approaches to communicating errors from a function. One is to return error status as the return value of the function, sometimes augmented by putting more detail in a special variable. The C standard library typically works this way:

```
int f = open("somefile", O_RDRW);
if (f < 0) {
printf("Error…error code is %d\n", errno);
}
```

If the file descriptor returned from open is negative, an error has occurred and the integer errno (a thread-local variable, i.e., its value is specific to the thread asking for its value) will express a reason for the error. For example, if the file does not exist, then f will be -1 and errno will be set to 2 (ENOENT[2]).

When building your own error return in functions, this mechanism is cumbersome. To make it thread-safe, you must have the equivalent of a per-thread errno of your own. That is possible and there are different mechanisms depending on the language

[1] Despite this, almost no one actually checks the return status of a printf since it is unlikely that a printf failure will cause significant damage or, in the case of running out of memory, is going to be the only indication of a failure.

[2] ENOENT is the POSIX mnemonic for "No such file or directory." POSIX defines approximately 150 such error codes.

you are using (for example, C has POSIX pthread_key_create, pthread_setspecific, pthread_getspecific, Python uses the threading.local function). Ultimately using thread-local variables is clumsy.

A better solution is to simply pass a pointer to a local, stack-allocated error status variable (which can be, like errno, a simple integer) that is filled in by the called function. This has the advantage that multiple threads using the function can each get independent error codes without having to use a per-thread global variable like errno. Here is an example:

```
int open_file(char *filename, int open_mode, int *status) {
... Can't find file.
*status = ENOENT;
return -1;
...normal exit
*status = ENOERR;
return file_descriptor;
}
```

In this example, the open_file function returns -1 if there is a failure When a failure occurs, the status will carry information defining the error. The status may or may not be relevant if the function returns other than -1 (i.e., if open_file succeeds, the value in status may be undefined). A common construct is therefore:

```
int status = ENOERR;
if ((f = open_file("some_file", O_RDWR, &status)) < 0) {
...look at status for the reason of the failure.
}
```

There are disadvantages to this model for reporting and handling errors. One complaint is that the code will be "littered" with error processing along with the normal control flow. The ultimate purpose of the code can be obscured by the error handling. Exception handling was invented to try to avoid this by segregating error handling from the main control flow.

Exception Handling

Exception handling is a language-specific feature and will vary from programming language to programming language. C++ and Java will handle exceptions differently while C does not natively provide exception handling though there are libraries that can provide exception-like processing. This section is a high-level, general discussion of exception handling. Before using exception handling, please look at what features your programming language provides.

An alternate model for managing errors is to use *exception handling*. Not all programming languages provide facilities for exception handling (C, Go, and Rust do not). Simplistically, a function *throws* an exception indicating some event has occurred (for example, file not found). The calling function *catches* the exception. The syntax for this will vary. Here is a generic form that follows C++:

```
try {
int f = open_file("some_file", O_RDWR);
...read/write to file in f
}
catch (File_exception e) {
The open_file failed and raised an exception ...do something!
}
```

In this error-handling model, the open_file function is assumed to succeed and we process it. If the function fails, then it will *throw* the File_exception which will be caught by the exception *handler* indicated by the catch with a matching exception type. This handler can figure out how to process the error such as issuing an error message to the user. The exception value caught (e in the example above) can provide more details about what caused the exception.

The theory behind exceptions is that they move the code for handling exceptional events out of the main control path of the code, making that main control path easier to understand. The difficulty with exceptions is that when an error occurs, it can be difficult to figure out what led to the exception and what state the program is in. It can lead to unanticipated problems. Consider the code that opens a file and populates a File_info structure:

```
1 try {
2   struct File_info *finfo = (struct File_info *)
3   malloc (sizeof(struct File_info));
4
5   int f = open_file("some_file", O_RDWR);
6   finfo->filedes = f;
7   return finfo;
8}
9 catch (File_exception e) {
10  throw e;
11 }
```

Line 1	Establish a block of code where we may catch an exception.
Lines 2–3	This function's goal is to return a File_info structure after filling in the open file descriptor.
Lines 5–7	Open the file, add the descriptor to the File_info structure, and return the allocated structure.
Lines 9–11	If the file open fails, propagate the exception up to the caller.

There is a problem here. In the case of an exception, the File_info allocated at lines 2–3 will be abandoned but not freed, creating a memory leak (see Chap. 9 for more information about this). It is certainly possible to free the allocated File_info in the catch block if the allocation is moved outside of the try block (the catch block does not have visibility to variables declared in the try block). This begins to dilute the goal of exceptions to not distribute error-checking code in the middle of "normal" code.

Similarly, consider this code:

```
try {
  struct File_info *finfo = (struct File_info *)
  malloc (sizeof(struct File_info));

  int f = open_file("some_file", O_RDWR);
  finfo->filedes = f;
  seek_in_file(f, 0, SEEK_END);
  return finfo;
}
catch (File_exception e) {
  throw e;
}
```

In this case the seek_in_file could also raise a File_exception (some file descriptors map to non-seekable devices). Now the catch needs to distinguish between the exceptions. It may be the case that the finfo is still valid in the seek case and should not be cleaned up. The if-statements that were being removed from the main control path are now consolidated in the exception, and it can be argued that context for the errors is more opaque. Alternatively the try-catch could be placed around each operation that can raise an exception but that fails to streamline the main control path. An ordinary error-checking if-statement would probably be a better choice.

The use of exceptions therefore has to be carefully considered and the code properly organized. It requires that testing includes checking for memory leaks and other problems with abandoned or incompletely initialized structures (which arguably should be tested regardless but since the likelihood is higher with exceptions, testing is more pressing).

Of course, languages without explicit allocation (i.e., featuring garbage collection) like Java and Python are immune from memory leaks.

Cleaning up other items still requires careful consideration. For example, if a function must close a file after opening it, care must be taken to close the file in spite of an error. Exception handling often includes another clause that will be executed regardless of how a block of code is exited (either normally or through an exception). For example:

```
try {
    // open file for some processing for the life of this try block.
  File f = open_file("this_file");
  // work with f.
  return;
}
catch (File_Exception e) {
  // handle file error
}
finally {
  close_file(f);
```

```
12 }
```

In this case, whether the block returns normally (line 5) or deals with an exception (line 8), the code in the finally block (lines 10–12) will run, making sure that the file is closed. Note that finally can be used without the catch, providing a useful way to guarantee that certain cleanup code is executed regardless of how the function is being exited.

Most exception systems also allow exceptions to propagate not just to the routine that called the function raising the exception but, if not caught, to functions higher in the call stack. If f calls g calls h calls k and k raises an exception, it may be that if h and g do not handle the exception, they will be unceremoniously unwound and f may be the function that handles the exception. There are multiple thoughts on propagating exceptions. Some programmers prefer to let an unhandled exception simply unwind the chain of called functions until it is handled (or it spools off the end of the call chain which is itself an error). Others believe that if an exception can be raised, it probably should be handled by each function in the call chain until it is resolved if for no other reason to indicate explicitly that nothing must happen with that exception. The argument for this second approach is that without some documentation of the flow of exceptions, it can be very difficult to determine how an exception reaches a given handler, making the code harder to reason about.

Exception handling's goal is to allow "normal" code to appear as contiguous as possible in the program with exceptional events put to a more segregated area. It also allows exceptions to be better classified, i.e., we know when a file handling exception has occurred instead of an arithmetic exception. Unfortunately, given that so much of a program needs to be dedicated to error handling, whether it is by looking at a return value or by looking at an exception, having the exception handling spaced away from what might be raising the exception is not necessarily any clearer for understanding the program. Since understanding the flow of exceptions can be difficult, it may be that exceptions lower the ultimate readability and reasoning about code rather than enhancing it.

Exceptions are somewhat controversial. Many believe exceptions excessively complicate the control flow. I tend to fall in this camp. Note that the Mars rover, the first NASA extraterrestrial vehicle to use C++ in its programming, explicitly forbade exceptions in the code in particular because it made it more difficult to validate all possible control paths (Maimone 2014).

The Use of Assertions

Another mechanism to help ensure correctness is the *assert* statement. Assertions are statements in the code that assert something is true. For example, if a count should always be greater than 0, this can be asserted:

```
assert(count > 0);
```

If count is equal or less than 0, the program will abort, hopefully with a memory dump to allow a programmer to figure out why count did not meet the assertion.

Unfortunately, assertions are often used improperly. For example, suppose we add an assertion preceding the printf in the previous example where we had a divide by 0:

```
assert(count > 0);
```

The assertion is not stating a point of fact, but a hope that count is greater than 0. It has simply moved the division-by-zero failure to an assertion failure. That is not an appropriate use of assertions. Instead, the possible failure should be anticipated and corrected. For example:

```
printf("Average I/O is %d\n", count == 0 ? 0: total/count);
```

In assessing the appropriateness of an assertion, a simple question should be answered:

Is this condition so iron-clad that its failure means the entire program has become corrupted?

Or

Is this condition's failure indicative of a fundamental flaw in the algorithm being implemented?

The first statement should rarely be invoked. In almost all cases where an assertion of this type has failed, something unrelated to the assertion (like running out of memory or a file becoming inaccessible) has occurred and the failure will most likely be detected in short order and perhaps with more illuminating evidence.

The second statement is a better way of judging the appropriateness of an assertion. For example, consider a quicksort program. In one stage of the algorithm, an array of *n* items is divided into items that sort less than a middle item, the middle item, and the items that sort greater than the middle item (see (Hoare 1962) for the original Quicksort paper). The index of the middle item must be greater or equal to 0 and less than *n* assuming a 0-based indexing scheme for the array. A reasonable assertion is therefore:

```
assert(middle_index >= 0 && middle_index < n);
```

Obvious, right? But that is the point of an assertion: The statement is true, and if it isn't, then something is very wrong. Assume that items in the quicksort array are pointers to objects. Consider the assertion:

```
assert(array[middle_index] != NULL);
```

This is different than the previous assertion since instead of asserting a fundamental aspect of the algorithm, it is asserting an assumption about the contents of the array. Without some further qualifications, this assertion cannot be guaranteed to be true. One way to make the assertion more realistic is if we only allow the array to be updated with this function:

```
void array_push(void *a[], void *i) {
if (i == NULL) {
// signal an error....
return;
}
a[index++] = i;
}
```

Now we've ensured that any item stored in the array is non-null and the assertion above is more appropriate.

Assertions are useful for documenting fundamental assumptions of an algorithm. They should not be used as a way of flagging inconsistent data, for example, which is simply a basic error and should be checked and handled.

Remarks Monitoring and error handling has differed from the previous patterns. It has stressed the need to include mechanisms to allow the behavior of the program to be monitored without being prescriptive about how to achieve it. The goal is to instill a greater interest in providing ways of non-intrusively providing information about the execution of a program, even in a production system. As software becomes more mission critical, this type of introspection becomes more necessary.

The discussion of error handling was designed to similarly encourage thoughtfulness about the different mechanisms for handling errors. It has posed a potentially controversial point of view that exception handling can create more difficulties in understanding control flow in a program and that assertions are not an excuse for proper defensive programming (such as checking that values are non-NULL).

Exercises

1. Create a program that loops, reading words from a file, one word per line, until all the words are read. Keep track of the count of each word using a hash table. Measure how long each iteration of the loop takes once the word is read from the file (i.e., don't include the file read) and report the average. Also record the total time for the program. Repeat the measurement of the total time of the program without recording the loop iteration cost and compare the two.
2. Build an event recording system that can be turned on or off with a global variable. Each event should capture start and end times for events, a thread identifier, and in this case a message identifier. Write a program where a client thread queues messages, and a server thread dequeues the messages, performs some action, and then queues a response message back. The client thread should only allow 10 messages to be outstanding, i.e., if it has queued 10 messages and not

received a response message back, it must not enqueue another until it does receive a response. Record times to enqueue request and response messages, dequeue messages, to process messages, how long the client has to wait for a response, and how long it must wait to enqueue because the queue is full. Visualize this information to appear as:

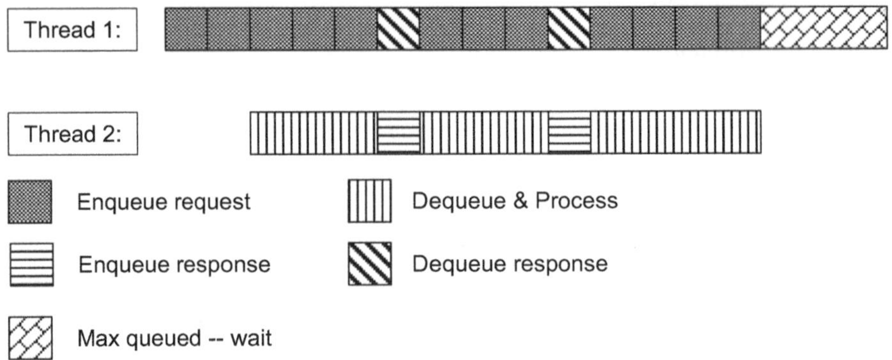

Acknowledgements Many people have helped with this book, and I would like to call out a few. First is my wife Valerie who copy-edited the book. She has been responsible for straightening out much of my tortuous prose. I would also like to thank my brother Joe who went over the text with a fine-tooth comb and challenged some of the reasoning, especially in the cryptographic discussions. Jan van Riel, a colleague from my days at EMC and a truly forward-thinking engineer, pointed out numerous details that needed correction as well as substantial gaps in explanations. Finally, I would like to acknowledge the many coworkers I've had the pleasure of learning from over the past forty years.

Bibliography

Agha, Gul. *Actors: A model of Concurrent Computation in Distributed Systems.* MIT Press, 1986.

Aho, Alfred and Ullman, Jeffrey. *Principles of Compiler Design.* Addison Wesley, 1978.

Almeida, Paulo Sergio, Baquero, Carlos, Preguica, Nuno, and Hutchison, David. "Scalable Bloom Filters". Information Processing Letters 101(6) 31 March 2007: 255–261.

API Park Blog. *Understanding Murmur Hash 2: An Overview of its Algorithmic Power*, Dec. 21, 2024, Web page https://apipark.com/techblog/en/understanding-murmur-hash-2-an-overview-of-its-algorithmic-power/.

Arpaci-Dusseau, Remzi H. and Arpaci-Dusseau, Andrea C. "Operating Systems: Three Easy Pieces". https://pages.cs.wisc.edu/~remzi/OSTEP/, 2013.

BBN Laboratories, "Butterfly® Parallel Processor Overview," BBN Report #6148, Version I, Cambridge, MA, 6 March 1986.

Bernat, Vincent. "Coping with the TCP TIME-WAIT state on busy Linux servers." Web page at https://vincent.bernat.ch/en/blog/2014-tcp-time-wait-state-linux. February, 2014.

Bishop, P.B. "Computer Systems with a Very Large Address Space and Garbage Collection." PhD thesis, Laboratory for Computer Science, Massachusetts Institute of Technology, May 1977. MIT/LCS/TR-178.

BISON. "Bison 3.8.1 Reference Manual." Web page at https://gnu.org/software/bison/manual/bison.html, Sept. 10, 2021.

Bloom, Burton H. (1970), "Space/Time Trade-offs in Hash Coding with Allowable Errors", Communications of the ACM, 13 (7): 422–426.

Bronson, Nathan, and Shi, Xiao. *Open-sourcing F14 for faster, more memory-efficient hash tables*, https://engineering.fb.com/2019/04/25/developer-tools/f14.

Cafriero, Nicholas and Gelertner, David. "Linda in Context" in *Communications of the ACM*, 32(4), April, 1989 pp 444–458.

CBR Staff Writer. "FRENCH MATISSE OBJECT DATABASE FOR KENDALL SQUARE." *Tech Monitor*, 5 May 1993, https://techmonitor.ai/technology/french_matisse_object_database_for_kendall_square.

CIO Applications. "VidScale | Top CDN Solutions Transforming Business 2017–2017." *CIO Applications*, https://www.cioapplications.com/vendor/vidscale-delivering-seamless-multimedia-experience-cid-124-mid-15.html. Accessed 18 September 2023.

Confluent documentation for Kafka: https://www.confluent.io/resources/ebook/kafka-the-definitive-guide/. Last accessed 2026.

Coplien, James O. "Curiously Recurring Template Patterns" in *C++ Report*. Feburary, 1995.

Corbato, F.G. "The Compatible Time-Sharing System A Programmer's Guide." MIT Press. 1963.

M. Kilian, *Ten Software Patterns Every Student Should Know*,
https://doi.org/10.1007/978-981-92-0260-7

cURL Documentation. “Documentation Overview”. Webpage https://curl.se/docs/. Last accessed 2026.

eG Innovations. “What is EMC Centera Storage.” *eG Innovations*, https://www.eginnovations.com/documentation/EMC-Centera/What-is-EMC-Centera.htm. Accessed 18 September 2023.

Fielding, Roy Thomas. “Architectural Styles and the Design of Network-based Software Architectures.” Ph.D. Dissertation, University of California, Irvine. 2000.

Friedman, Daniel, Haynes, Christopher, Kohlbecker, Eugene. “Programming with Continuations.” NATO ASI Series, Vol F8, *Program Transformation and Programming Environments.* Ed P. Pepper. Springer-Verlag, 1984.

Galileo Wikipedia. “Galileo (spacecraft)”. Webpage https://en.wikipedia.org/wiki/Galileo_(spacecraft) last accessed 2026.

Goldman, William. “Screenplay for the Princess Bride.” 1986. P. 92.

Gourley, David, Totty, Brian, Sayer, Marjorie, Aggarwal Anshu, Reddy, Sailu. “HTTP: The Definitive Guide.” O’Reilly Media, 2002.

Harris, Timothy. “A Pragmatic Implementation of Non-blocking Linked-Lists.” In DISC ’01: Proceedings of the 15 International Conference on Distributed Computing, October 2001, pp 300–314.

Hennesey, John; Patterson, David. *Computer Architecture: A Quantitative Approach.* Morgan Kaufman Publishers, Inc. 1990.

Hoare, C.A.R. *The Computer Journal*, Volume 5, Issue 1, 1962, Pages 10–16.

Karp, Richard M.; Rabin, Michael O. “Efficient randomized pattern-matching algorithms”. IBM Journal of Research and Development. 31 (2): 249–260. March 1987.

Kernighan, Brian W., and Dennis M. Ritchie. *The C Programming Language.* Prentice Hall, 1988.

Kilian, Michael. “Parallel Sets: An Object-Oriented Methodology for Massively Parallel Programming.” Ph.D. Thesis, Harvard University, May, 1992.

Knight, Will. “Galileo Spacecraft’s Last Testament Recovered”, New Scientist, December 18, 2002.

Knuth, Donald Vol 3. *The Art of Computer Programming*, 2 ed., vol. 3, Addison-Wesley, 1998, pp. 406–419.

Knuth, Donald. *Art of Computer Programming, The, Volumes 1-4B, Boxed Set.* Pearson, 2022.

Lewis II, Phil, Rosencrantz, Daniel and Stearns, Richard. *Compiler Design Theory.* Addison Wesley, 1976.

Litwin, Witold. “Linear Hashing: A New Tool for File and Table Addressing”, Sixth International Conference on Very Large Data Bases. October, 1980.

Maimone, Mark. “C++ on Mars”, CppCon, September 2014.

Manacher, Glenn (1975), “A new linear-time “on-line” algorithm or finding the smallest initial palindrome of a string”, Journal of the ACM, 22 (3): 346–351.

McConnell, Steve. *Code Complete, 2nd Edition.* Microsoft Press, 2004.

McNaughton, Robert. *Elementary Computability, Formal Languages, and Automata.* Prentice Hall, 1982.

Merkle, Ralph C. “One Way Hash Functions and DES.” Advances in Cryptology — CRYPTO ‘89, Lecture Notes in Computer Science, vol. 435, pp. 428–446. Springer, 1990.

Miklenic, Marina Svetec; Svetec, Ivan Kresimir. “Palindromes in DNA – A Risk for Genome Stability and Implications in Cancer,” International Journal of Molecular Science, March 2021.

Mitzenmacher, Michael. “Beyond Bloom Filters: Approximate Concurrent State Machines”, presentation summarizing SIGCOMM 2006.

Meyer, Bertrand. “Eiffel: The Language.” Prentice-Hall, 1991.

NASA JPL. “Voyager 1”. Webpage https://www.jpl.nasa.gov/missions/voyager-1/. Last accessed 2026.

NVIDIA. “ConnectX Nics.” Webpage https://www.nvidia.com/en-us/networking/ethernet-adapters/, 2026.

Ongaro, D., and Ousterhout, J. “In search of an understandable consensus algorithm.” In Proc ATC’14, USENIX Annual Technical Conference. 2014.

OpenMPI. "Open MPI: Open Source High Performance Computing", https://www.open-mpi.org/. Last accessed 2026.

OpenSSL. "OpenSSL Documentation". Webpage https://docs.openssl.org/master/. Last accessed 2026.

Paxson, Vern; Estes, Will; Millaway, John. *Lexical Analysis with Flex*. The Flex Project. November 2015.

Pease, Marshall; Shostak, Robert; Lamport, Leslie. "Reaching Agreement in the Presence of Faults". Journal of the Association for Computing Machinery. 27 (2): 228–234. April 1980.

Peterson, W. W.; Brown, D. T. "Cyclic Codes for Error Detection". Proceedings of the IRE. 49 (1): 228–235. January 1961.

Perlman, Radia. "An Algorithm for Distributed Computation of a Spanning Tree in an Extended LAN". ACM SIGCOMM Computer Communication Review. 15 (4): 44–53, 1985.

Press, Gil. "A Very Short History Of EMC Corporation", Forbes Magazine, September 6, 2016.

POSIX, "The Open Group Technical Standard Base Specifications", https:pubs.opengroup.org, 2001–2018.

Protobuf, "Protocol Buffers Documentation", https:protobuf.dev.

RabbitMQ documentation. Website https://www.rabbitmq.com/docs. Last accessed 2026.

RocksDB. Website https://rocksdb.org. Last accessed 2026.

Rothnie, James. "Kendall Square Research Introduction to the KSR1", Supercomputer, 1992. Pp 104–115.

Schaffert, Craig, et al. "An Introduction to Trellis/Owl." *OOPSLA '86 Conference Proceedings on Object-Oriented Programming Systems, Languages and Applications*, vol. 1, no. 1, 1986, pp. 9–16.

Schroeder, Bianca; Pinheiro, Eduardo; Weber, Wolf-Dietrich "DRAMErrors in the Wild: A Large-Scale Field Study", SIGMETRICS/Performance'09, June 15–19, 2009, Seattle, WA.

Schorr, H.; Waite, W.M. "An Efficient Machine-Independent Procedure for Garbage Collection in Various List Structures." *Communications of the ACM, Vol 10. Bumber 8*. August, 1967.

Sheldon, Robert. "What is content-addressed storage (CAS)?" TechTarget, December, 2021.

Sipser, Michael. *Introduction to the Theory of Computation*. Cengage Learning, 2013.

Stevens, W. Richard. *Unix Network Programming: The Sockets Networking API*. Addison-Wesley, 2003.

Stonebraker, Michael. "The Case for Shared Nothing Architecture." Database Engineering 9(1), 1986.

Supermicro. "Supermicro Leads the Industry with the First Eight-Socket and Four-Socket Servers for the Most Demanding Enterprise, Database, and Mission-Critical Workloads, Based On Intel CPUs". Press release. May 9, 2023.

Susnjara, Stephanie and Smalley, Ian. "What is blockchain?" IBM webpage https://www.ibm.com/think/topics/blockchain. Last accessed 2026.

Swift, Gary, Levanas, Gregory, Johnston, Allan. "In-flight Annealing of Displacement Damage in GaAs LEDS: A Galileo Story". NASA Electronic Parts and Packaging, August, 2022.

Tridgell, Andrew. "Efficient Algorithms for Sorting and Synchronization". Ph.D. Thesis, Australian National University, February, 1999.

Valois, J. D. "Implementing Lock-Free Queues". In Seventh International Conference on Parallel and Distributed Computing Systems, Las Vegas, NV, October 1994.

Wright, Gary R; Stevens, W. Richard. *TCP/IP Illustrated, Volume 2: The Implementation*. Addison-Wesley Publishing Company, Inc. 1995.

Index

M. Kilian, *Ten Software Patterns Every Student Should Know*,
https://doi.org/10.1007/978-981-92-0260-7

Zeitfracht Medien GmbH
Ferdinand-Jühlke-Straße 7
99095 Erfurt, Deutschland
produktsicherheit@kolibri360.de